The BOOK *of* MORMON FAMILY READER

The BOOK *of* MORMON FAMILY READER

EDITED BY

Tyler McKellar

ILLUSTRATED BY

Dan Burr

DESERET BOOK

SALT LAKE CITY, UTAH

Visit us at DeseretBook.com

Library of Congress Cataloging-in-Publication Data

(CIP on file)
ISBN 978-1-62972-334-1

Printed in China
RR Donnelley, Shenzhen, China

10 9 8 7 6 5 4 3 2 1

THIS BOOK BELONGS TO

DATE

Editor's Introduction

The *Book of Mormon Family Reader* was created to help children, youth, and families discover and discuss the most doctrinally significant passages in the Book of Mormon.

From my own experience, I know that reading the scriptures as a family can be challenging—for parents and children alike. Time is often short. Attention spans are even shorter. And the language and length of the Book of Mormon text can be bewildering to young readers in particular. This book is an effort to help families spend what limited study time they have on the Book of Mormon's most essential passages.

I am not a scholar or professional teacher. And it is not my intention to diminish in any way the portions of the Book of Mormon that are not included in this book; nor do I assume to know which passages of the Book of Mormon are ideal for every family. In deciding which passages to include, I considered three factors: my six children, ages six to eighteen, and the doctrines I want them to understand; my own impressions from reading the Book of Mormon throughout my life; and the doctrines currently emphasized by latter-day prophets. With these factors in mind and through prayerful consideration, I made my best effort to organize this book. Even so, I acknowledge my own limitations and the subjectivity of this undertaking.

The *Book of Mormon Family Reader* divides the content of the Book of Mormon into 245 sections, presented sequentially from the book of 1 Nephi to the book of Moroni. Each section is designed to be read and discussed in about five minutes, allowing families a simple, consistent method for discovering and exploring the doctrines taught in the Book of Mormon. Each section contains the following:

- A **title** that identifies who is speaking or writing and the doctrine or event being discussed.
- An **introduction** that reminds readers what is going on in the overall narrative of the Book of Mormon record. A great deal of content found in the Book of Mormon concerning travel, politics, war, and other non-doctrinal subjects are condensed into brief summaries in these introductions. Readers can thus follow the overarching narrative of the Book of Mormon while focusing their greatest time and effort on doctrinally rich passages of scriptures.
- **Selected scriptural verses from the Book of Mormon**. Portions of the actual scriptural text are then presented verbatim, helping retain the power and feeling of the inspired translation and language. While many verses are omitted (again, less doctrinal verses), the verses that are included are unaltered. The sequential order, language, and even the appearance are just as they are found in the Book of Mormon.
- A few **follow-up questions** at the end of each section that offer suggestions for contemplating and discussing the teachings of that section. Some questions focus on understanding the doctrines of a specific section, while others focus on how to apply those doctrines to our own lives. These questions are, of course, merely suggestions. Guided by experience and the Spirit, parents will know the questions that best encourage discussion and understanding tailored to the unique needs of their families.

- **150 original illustrations** featured throughout the book that bring the people, events, and doctrinal topics of the Book of Mormon to life. After an exhaustive search for an artist with the requisite skills for such a daunting task, the ideal artist turned out to be my neighbor here in Teton Valley, Idaho. Your experiences with this book will be made more vivid and memorable through the artistry of my friend, Dan Burr.

While designed for daily use by families, this book might also benefit personal study, family home evening lessons, and Primary and youth lessons. However it is used, it is my hope that the pivotal doctrines taught in the Book of Mormon will be more clearly understood and easily discussed.

I believe the Book of Mormon to be true—that the events it describes actually occurred and the doctrines it teaches are real and eternal. I have found peace, guidance, and understanding by trying to understand and apply its doctrines—especially the doctrines concerning Jesus Christ and His mercy, grace, and eternal sacrifice. Today there are more books available to read than ever before in the history of the world. I believe the Book of Mormon is the single most important book in humanity's search for eternal knowledge, peace, and salvation. It is my hope that the *Book of Mormon Family Reader* will help in this pursuit. In the midst of their hectic schedules, families can approach scripture study knowing it will be a rewarding endeavor. Children and parents can more easily focus their time on reading and discussing doctrinal topics of eternal significance. And by utilizing the familiar layout of the Book of Mormon, people of all ages will be better prepared to embark on a reading of the full scriptural text.

Tyler McKellar
Tetonia, Idaho, 2017

The First Book of Nephi

LEHI SEES A VISION OF THE SAVIOR

Lehi lived in Jerusalem with his family 600 years before Jesus Christ was born. Lehi saw a vision of God. Later, Lehi's son Nephi recorded the details of his father's vision.

1 Nephi 1:8–12, 14

And being thus overcome with the Spirit,
he was carried away in a vision, even
that he saw the heavens open, and he thought he
saw God sitting upon his throne, surrounded with
numberless concourses of angels in the attitude of
singing and praising their God.
9 And it came to pass that he saw One descend-
ing out of the midst of heaven, and he beheld that
his luster was above that of the sun at noon-day.
10 And he also saw twelve others following him,
and their brightness did exceed that of the stars in
the firmament.
11 And they came down and went forth upon
the face of the earth; and the first came and stood
before my father, and gave unto him a book, and
bade him that he should read.
12 And it came to pass that as he read, he was
filled with the Spirit of the Lord.
14 And it came to pass that when my father had
read and seen many great and marvelous things,
he did exclaim many things unto the Lord; such
as: Great and marvelous are thy works, O Lord
God Almighty! Thy throne is high in the heavens,
and thy power, and goodness, and mercy are over
all the inhabitants of the earth; and, because thou
art merciful, thou wilt not suffer those who come
unto thee that they shall perish!

What did Lehi learn about God from his vision? When have you felt God's goodness and mercy? How can you learn about God?

THE LORD SOFTENS NEPHI'S HEART AND HE IS OBEDIENT

Lehi proclaimed his vision to the wicked people of Jerusalem, calling them to repentance, and they sought to kill him. God told Lehi to take his family into the wilderness for protection. Lehi's two oldest sons, Laman and Lemuel, were resistant. Nephi prayed for guidance and shared what he learned with his brother Sam.

1 Nephi 2:16–20

And it came to pass that I, Nephi, being exceedingly young, nevertheless being large in stature, and also having great desires to know of the mysteries of God, wherefore, I did cry unto the Lord; and behold he did visit me, and did soften my heart that I did believe all the words which had been spoken by my father; wherefore, I did not rebel against him like unto my brothers.

17 And I spake unto Sam, making known unto him the things which the Lord had manifested unto me by his Holy Spirit. And it came to pass that he believed in my words.

18 But, behold, Laman and Lemuel would not hearken unto my words; and being grieved because of the hardness of their hearts I cried unto the Lord for them.

19 And it came to pass that the Lord spake unto me, saying: Blessed art thou, Nephi, because of thy faith, for thou hast sought me diligently, with lowliness of heart.

20 And inasmuch as ye shall keep my commandments, ye shall prosper, and shall be led to a land of promise; yea, even a land which I have prepared for you; yea, a land which is choice above all other lands.

How were Nephi's actions different from his brothers' actions? What happened as a result of his prayer? Share any experiences you have had asking God for a witness.

NEPHI IS DETERMINED TO OBEY THE COMMANDMENT TO OBTAIN THE BRASS PLATES

While in the wilderness, Lehi received a commandment from God to return to Jerusalem for something very important: the brass plates. These plates contained a collection of scriptures that included the genealogy of Lehi's family and the commandments of God. A powerful and wicked man named Laban had the brass plates in his possession in Jerusalem. God commanded Lehi to tell his sons to go back to the city and obtain the plates. Knowing it would be very difficult, Laman and Lemuel complained. Nephi said he knew the Lord would prepare a way for them to succeed.

1 Nephi 3:5–8

And now, behold thy brothers murmur, saying it is a hard thing which I have required of them; but behold I have not required it of them, but it is a commandment of the Lord.
6 Therefore go, my son, and thou shalt be favored of the Lord, because thou hast not murmured.
7 And it came to pass that I, Nephi, said unto my father: I will go and do the things which the Lord hath commanded, for I know that the Lord giveth no commandments unto the children of men, save he shall prepare a way for them that they may accomplish the thing which he commandeth them.
8 And it came to pass that when my father had heard these words he was exceedingly glad, for he knew that I had been blessed of the Lord.

How did Laman and Lemuel react to the command to go and get the plates? How did Nephi react to the same commandment? How has God helped "prepare a way" for you to obey His commandments?

NEPHI SLAYS LABAN AND OBTAINS THE BRASS PLATES

When Lehi's sons arrived at the house of Laban, they asked him for the brass plates, even offering to buy them. Laban refused and sent his guards to kill them. The four brothers escaped and hid outside the city. Laman and Lemuel wanted to give up. Nephi convinced his brothers to remain outside the city while he journeyed to the house of Laban at night. As he did so, Nephi followed the guidance of the Spirit.

1 Nephi 4:5–12, 18–20, 24

And it was by night; and I caused that
they should hide themselves without
the walls. And after they had hid themselves, I,
Nephi, crept into the city and went forth towards
the house of Laban.
6 And I was led by the Spirit, not knowing be-
forehand the things which I should do.
7 Nevertheless I went forth, and as I came near
unto the house of Laban I beheld a man, and
he had fallen to the earth before me, for he was
drunken with wine.
8 And when I came to him I found that it was
Laban.
9 And I beheld his sword, and I drew it forth
from the sheath thereof; and the hilt thereof was
of pure gold, and the workmanship thereof was
exceedingly fine, and I saw that the blade thereof
was of the most precious steel.
10 And it came to pass that I was constrained by
the Spirit that I should kill Laban; but I said in
my heart: Never at any time have I shed the blood
of man. And I shrunk and would that I might not
slay him.
11 And the Spirit said unto me again: Behold the
Lord hath delivered him into thy hands. Yea, and
I also knew that he had sought to take away mine
own life; yea, and he would not hearken unto
the commandments of the Lord; and he also had
taken away our property.
12 And it came to pass that the Spirit said unto
me again: Slay him, for the Lord hath delivered
him into thy hands;
18 Therefore I did obey the voice of the Spirit,
and took Laban by the hair of the head, and I
smote off his head with his own sword.
19 And after I had smitten off his head with his
own sword, I took the garments of Laban and put
them upon mine own body; yea, even every whit;
and I did gird on his armor about my loins.
20 And after I had done this, I went forth unto
the treasury of Laban. And as I went forth towards
the treasury of Laban, behold, I saw the servant of
Laban who had the keys of the treasury. And I
commanded him in the voice of Laban, that he
should go with me into the treasury.
24 And I also spake unto him that I should carry
the engravings, which were upon the plates of
brass, to my elder brethren, who were without the
walls.

Nephi said he was led by the Spirit—without knowing exactly what he would do next. When have you felt the Spirit guiding you? What blessings did you receive from following the Spirit's guidance? How does it feel to know the Lord will guide you as you follow the Spirit?

NEPHI FORGIVES HIS BROTHERS FOR ATTEMPTING TO KILL HIM

After Nephi and his brothers returned to the wilderness with the brass plates, the Lord commanded them to return once again to Jerusalem—this time to invite another family to journey with them. Lehi's sons obeyed and soon returned with a man named Ishmael, his wife, and his sons and daughters. But while returning from Jerusalem, Laman, Lemuel, and some of Ishmael's family became angry with Nephi and the others. They wanted to return to Jerusalem. Nephi invited them to have faith and to obey the commandments. Laman and Lemuel became even angrier.

1 Nephi 7:16–21

And it came to pass that when I, Nephi,
had spoken these words unto my breth-
ren, they were angry with me. And it came to pass
that they did lay their hands upon me, for behold,
they were exceedingly wroth, and they did bind
me with cords, for they sought to take away my
life, that they might leave me in the wilderness to
be devoured by wild beasts.
17 But it came to pass that I prayed unto the
Lord, saying: O Lord, according to my faith which
is in thee, wilt thou deliver me from the hands
of my brethren; yea, even give me strength that
I may burst these bands with which I am bound.
18 And it came to pass that when I had said these
words, behold, the bands were loosed from off my
hands and feet, and I stood before my brethren,
and I spake unto them again.
19 And it came to pass that they were angry with
me again, and sought to lay hands upon me; but
behold, one of the daughters of Ishmael, yea, and
also her mother, and one of the sons of Ishmael,
did plead with my brethren, insomuch that they
did soften their hearts; and they did cease striving
to take away my life.
20 And it came to pass that they were sorrowful,
because of their wickedness, insomuch that they
did bow down before me, and did plead with me
that I would forgive them of the thing that they
had done against me.
21 And it came to pass that I did frankly for-
give them all that they had done, and I did exhort
them that they would pray unto the Lord their
God for forgiveness. And it came to pass that they
did so. And after they had done praying unto the
Lord we did again travel on our journey towards
the tent of our father.

Imagine how Nephi might have felt when his brothers tried to kill him. Why do you think he was able to forgive them so quickly? How can you find a way to forgive others—especially those in your own family?

LEHI SHARES HIS VISION OF THE TREE OF LIFE

After Lehi led his family further into the wilderness, he told them of a vision he'd had that made him both excited and worried for his family.

1 Nephi 8:5–12

And it came to pass that I saw a man, and
he was dressed in a white robe; and he
came and stood before me.
6 And it came to pass that he spake unto me, and
bade me follow him.
7 And it came to pass that as I followed him I be-
held myself that I was in a dark and dreary waste.
8 And after I had traveled for the space of many
hours in darkness, I began to pray unto the Lord
that he would have mercy on me, according to the
multitude of his tender mercies.
9 And it came to pass after I had prayed unto the
Lord I beheld a large and spacious field.
10 And it came to pass that I beheld a tree, whose
fruit was desirable to make one happy.
11 And it came to pass that I did go forth and
partake of the fruit thereof; and I beheld that it
was most sweet, above all that I ever before tasted.
Yea, and I beheld that the fruit thereof was white,
to exceed all the whiteness that I had ever seen.
12 And as I partook of the fruit thereof it filled
my soul with exceedingly great joy; wherefore, I
began to be desirous that my family should par-
take of it also; for I knew that it was desirable
above all other fruit.

How is the fruit of the tree of life like God's love? How can you choose to partake of that fruit? When has feeling God's love for you filled you with joy?

LEHI SEES THE GREAT AND SPACIOUS BUILDING IN THE VISION OF THE TREE OF LIFE

Lehi's vision of the tree of life continued. He saw that his wife, Sariah, and his sons Nephi and Sam came to the tree and partook of the fruit. But Laman and Lemuel would not come to the tree. As you read this passage, look for different groups of people and what they do after partaking of the fruit of the tree of life.

1 Nephi 8:19–28, 30

And I beheld a rod of iron, and it extended along the bank of the river, and led to the tree by which I stood.

20 And I also beheld a strait and narrow path, which came along by the rod of iron, even to the tree by which I stood; and it also led by the head of the fountain, unto a large and spacious field, as if it had been a world.

21 And I saw numberless concourses of people, many of whom were pressing forward, that they might obtain the path which led unto the tree by which I stood.

22 And it came to pass that they did come forth, and commence in the path which led to the tree.

23 And it came to pass that there arose a mist of darkness; yea, even an exceedingly great mist of darkness, insomuch that they who had commenced in the path did lose their way, that they wandered off and were lost.

24 And it came to pass that I beheld others pressing forward, and they came forth and caught hold of the end of the rod of iron; and they did press forward through the mist of darkness, clinging to the rod of iron, even until they did come forth and partake of the fruit of the tree.

25 And after they had partaken of the fruit of the tree they did cast their eyes about as if they were ashamed.

26 And I also cast my eyes round about, and beheld, on the other side of the river of water, a great and spacious building; and it stood as it were in the air, high above the earth.

27 And it was filled with people, both old and young, both male and female; and their manner of dress was exceedingly fine; and they were in the attitude of mocking and pointing their fingers towards those who had come at and were partaking of the fruit.

28 And after they had tasted of the fruit they were ashamed, because of those that were scoffing at them; and they fell away into forbidden paths and were lost.

30 But to be short in writing, behold, he saw other multitudes pressing forward; and they came and caught hold of the end of the rod of iron; and they did press their way forward, continually holding fast to the rod of iron, until they came forth and fell down and partook of the fruit of the tree.

How do different groups of people react after partaking of the fruit of the tree of life? Has anyone ever made fun of you for trying to obey God? What can you do when other people mock you for trying to do the right thing?

LEHI PROPHESIES OF THE BAPTISM OF JESUS CHRIST

After Lehi shared his vision of the tree of life, he prophesied of future events that would soon occur in Jerusalem, including the coming of Jesus Christ and His baptism by a special prophet prepared for that purpose.

1 NEPHI 10:4–10

Yea, even six hundred years from the time that my father left Jerusalem, a prophet would the Lord God raise up among the Jews—even a Messiah, or, in other words, a Savior of the world.
5 And he also spake concerning the prophets, how great a number had testified of these things, concerning this Messiah, of whom he had spoken, or this Redeemer of the world.
6 Wherefore, all mankind were in a lost and in a fallen state, and ever would be save they should rely on this Redeemer.
7 And he spake also concerning a prophet who should come before the Messiah, to prepare the way of the Lord—
8 Yea, even he should go forth and cry in the wilderness: Prepare ye the way of the Lord, and make his paths straight; for there standeth one among you whom ye know not; and he is mightier than I, whose shoe's latchet I am not worthy to unloose. And much spake my father concerning this thing.
9 And my father said he should baptize in Bethabara, beyond Jordan; and he also said he should baptize with water; even that he should baptize the Messiah with water.
10 And after he had baptized the Messiah with water, he should behold and bear record that he had baptized the Lamb of God, who should take away the sins of the world.

Who was the prophet that prepared the way for Christ? What did this prophet tell the people about Jesus Christ (see Matthew 1:1–11)? How are we all "in a lost and in a fallen state" today?

NEPHI SEEKS FOR AN UNDERSTANDING OF HIS FATHER'S PROPHECIES

Nephi listened carefully to what his father taught—and he believed him. But Nephi also wanted to see and learn these same truths for himself. And he knew that he could.

1 Nephi 10:17–19

And it came to pass after I, Nephi, having
heard all the words of my father, con-
cerning the things which he saw in a vision, and
also the things which he spake by the power of
the Holy Ghost, which power he received by faith
on the Son of God—and the Son of God was the
Messiah who should come—I, Nephi, was de-
sirous also that I might see, and hear, and know
of these things, by the power of the Holy Ghost,
which is the gift of God unto all those who dili-
gently seek him, as well in times of old as in the
time that he should manifest himself unto the
children of men.
18 For he is the same yesterday, today, and for-
ever; and the way is prepared for all men from
the foundation of the world, if it so be that they
repent and come unto him.
19 For he that diligently seeketh shall find; and
the mysteries of God shall be unfolded unto
them, by the power of the Holy Ghost, as well in
these times as in times of old, and as well in times
of old as in times to come; wherefore, the course
of the Lord is one eternal round.

What did Nephi define as the "gift of God" to all who diligently seek Him? How can you learn the "mysteries of God"? What have you learned through the power of the Holy Ghost?

NEPHI SEES A VISION OF THE BIRTH OF JESUS CHRIST

One day while pondering his father's vision, Nephi had a vision of his own. Look for the word *condescension* in this passage—this word refers to Jesus Christ leaving His high position in heaven and coming to earth to fulfill His atoning sacrifice.

1 Nephi 11:13–23

And it came to pass that I looked and beheld the great city of Jerusalem, and also other cities. And I beheld the city of Nazareth; and in the city of Nazareth I beheld a virgin, and she was exceedingly fair and white.

14 And it came to pass that I saw the heavens open; and an angel came down and stood before me; and he said unto me: Nephi, what beholdest thou?

15 And I said unto him: A virgin, most beautiful and fair above all other virgins.

16 And he said unto me: Knowest thou the condescension of God?

17 And I said unto him: I know that he loveth his children; nevertheless, I do not know the meaning of all things.

18 And he said unto me: Behold, the virgin whom thou seest is the mother of the Son of God, after the manner of the flesh.

19 And it came to pass that I beheld that she was carried away in the Spirit; and after she had been carried away in the Spirit for the space of a time the angel spake unto me, saying: Look!

20 And I looked and beheld the virgin again, bearing a child in her arms.

21 And the angel said unto me: Behold the Lamb of God, yea, even the Son of the Eternal Father! Knowest thou the meaning of the tree which thy father saw?

22 And I answered him, saying: Yea, it is the love of God, which sheddeth itself abroad in the hearts of the children of men; wherefore, it is the most desirable above all things.

23 And he spake unto me, saying: Yea, and the most joyous to the soul.

What can you learn about the nature of Christ from this passage? How does His condescension show that He and our Father in Heaven love us? What does Nephi say is "desirable above all things"?

NEPHI SEES A VISION OF CHRIST'S MINISTRY AND DEATH ON THE CROSS

Nephi's vision continued. He saw Jesus Christ—who is also called the Lamb of God—healing the sick and dying for our sins.

1 Nephi 11:31–33

And he spake unto me again, saying: Look! And I looked, and I beheld the Lamb of God going forth among the children of men. And I beheld multitudes of people who were sick, and who were afflicted with all manner of diseases, and with devils and unclean spirits; and the angel spake and showed all these things unto me. And they were healed by the power of the Lamb of God; and the devils and the unclean spirits were cast out.

32 And it came to pass that the angel spake unto me again, saying: Look! And I looked and beheld the Lamb of God, that he was taken by the people; yea, the Son of the everlasting God was judged of the world; and I saw and bear record.
33 And I, Nephi, saw that he was lifted up upon the cross and slain for the sins of the world.

Picture yourself living at the time Christ was here on earth. How do you think it felt to be healed by the Savior? How can you come unto the Savior to be cleansed and healed by Him now?

NEPHI SPEAKS OF THE PURITY OF GOD AND THE CONSEQUENCES OF SIN

After witnessing many other things in his vision, Nephi told his family what he had seen. He taught them about a filthy river of water that separated people who were trying to reach the fruit of the tree of life and those who had turned away from the tree. Nephi explained the meaning of the filthy river and the consequences of sin.

1 Nephi 15:26–27, 32–36

And they said unto me: What meaneth the
river of water which our father saw?
27 And I said unto them that the water which
my father saw was filthiness; and so much was his
mind swallowed up in other things that he beheld
not the filthiness of the water.
32 And it came to pass that I said unto them
that it was a representation of things both tem-
poral and spiritual; for the day should come that
they must be judged of their works, yea, even the
works which were done by the temporal body in
their days of probation.
33 Wherefore, if they should die in their wick-
edness they must be cast off also, as to the things
which are spiritual, which are pertaining to righ-
teousness; wherefore, they must be brought to
stand before God, to be judged of their works;
and if their works have been filthiness they must
needs be filthy; and if they be filthy it must needs
be that they cannot dwell in the kingdom of God;
if so, the kingdom of God must be filthy also.
34 But behold, I say unto you, the kingdom of
God is not filthy, and there cannot any unclean
thing enter into the kingdom of God; wherefore
there must needs be a place of filthiness prepared
for that which is filthy.
35 And there is a place prepared, yea, even that
awful hell of which I have spoken, and the devil
is the preparator of it; wherefore the final state of
the souls of men is to dwell in the kingdom of
God, or to be cast out because of that justice of
which I have spoken.
36 Wherefore, the wicked are rejected from the
righteous, and also from that tree of life, whose
fruit is most precious and most desirable above
all other fruits; yea, and it is the greatest of all the
gifts of God. And thus I spake unto my brethren.
Amen.

What are the consequences for those who "die in their wickedness"? Since we all commit sin, how can we become clean and worthy to enter God's presence?

NEPHI CONDEMNS WICKEDNESS AND PLEADS WITH HIS BROTHERS TO BE RIGHTEOUS

After Nephi told his family about his vision, his brothers complained about the high standard of righteousness that the Lord requires.

1 Nephi 16:1–5

And now it came to pass that after I, Nephi, had made an end of speaking to my brethren, behold they said unto me: Thou hast declared unto us hard things, more than we are able to bear.

2 And it came to pass that I said unto them that I knew that I had spoken hard things against the wicked, according to the truth; and the righteous have I justified, and testified that they should be lifted up at the last day; wherefore, the guilty taketh the truth to be hard, for it cutteth them to the very center.

3 And now my brethren, if ye were righteous and were willing to hearken to the truth, and give heed unto it, that ye might walk uprightly before God, then ye would not murmur because of the truth, and say: Thou speakest hard things against us.

4 And it came to pass that I, Nephi, did exhort my brethren, with all diligence, to keep the commandments of the Lord.

5 And it came to pass that they did humble themselves before the Lord; insomuch that I had joy and great hopes of them, that they would walk in the paths of righteousness.

Why was it hard for Laman and Lemuel to accept the things Nephi learned in his vision? What can you do to show your desire to accept the word of the Lord?

THE LORD BLESSES LEHI'S FAMILY WITH THE LIAHONA

As Lehi continued his journey into the wilderness with his family, he arose one morning to find an unexpected gift outside his tent.

1 Nephi 16:10–16

And it came to pass that as my father arose in the morning, and went forth to the tent door, to his great astonishment he beheld upon the ground a round ball of curious workmanship; and it was of fine brass. And within the ball were two spindles; and the one pointed the way whither we should go into the wilderness.

11 And it came to pass that we did gather together whatsoever things we should carry into the wilderness, and all the remainder of our provisions which the Lord had given unto us; and we did take seed of every kind that we might carry into the wilderness.

12 And it came to pass that we did take our tents and depart into the wilderness, across the river Laman.

13 And it came to pass that we traveled for the space of four days, nearly a south-southeast direction, and we did pitch our tents again; and we did call the name of the place Shazer.

14 And it came to pass that we did take our bows and our arrows, and go forth into the wilderness to slay food for our families; and after we had slain food for our families we did return again to our families in the wilderness, to the place of Shazer. And we did go forth again in the wilderness, following the same direction, keeping in the most fertile parts of the wilderness, which were in the borders near the Red Sea.

15 And it came to pass that we did travel for the space of many days, slaying food by the way, with our bows and our arrows and our stones and our slings.

16 And we did follow the directions of the ball, which led us in the more fertile parts of the wilderness.

The "round ball of curious workmanship" is later referred to as the "Liahona." How was Lehi's family blessed by following the directions given through the Liahona? How does God give us direction now? How have you and your family been blessed by trying to follow God's directions?

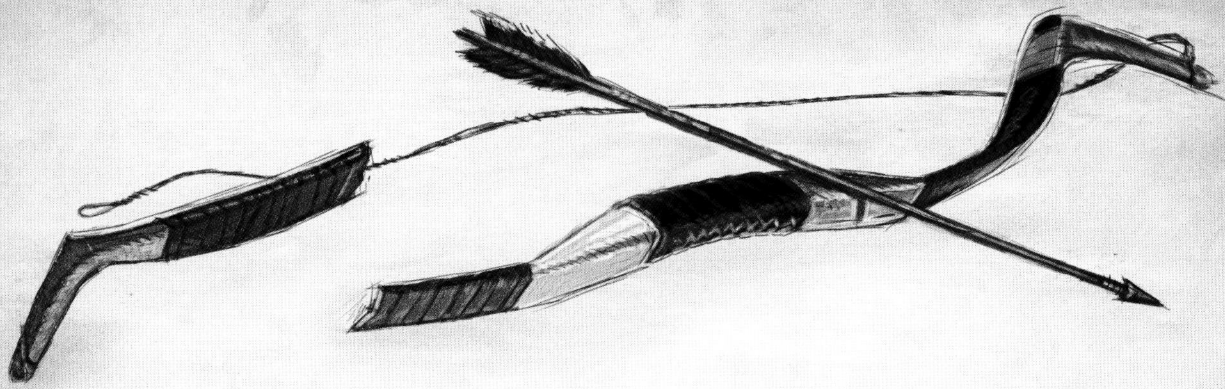

NEPHI'S STEEL BOW BREAKS AND HE IS GUIDED BY THE LIAHONA

Nephi had a hunting bow made of steel. One day while he was traveling in the wilderness, his bow broke, leaving his family with no way to hunt for food. Without Nephi's bow, they were suffering. Nephi's brothers and father complained to the Lord. Nephi took action.

1 Nephi 16:23–32

And it came to pass that I, Nephi, did
make out of wood a bow, and out of a
straight stick, an arrow; wherefore, I did arm my-
self with a bow and an arrow, with a sling and
with stones. And I said unto my father: Whither
shall I go to obtain food?
24 And it came to pass that he did inquire of the
Lord, for they had humbled themselves because of
my words; for I did say many things unto them in
the energy of my soul.
25 And it came to pass that the voice of the Lord
came unto my father; and he was truly chastened
because of his murmuring against the Lord, inso-
much that he was brought down into the depths
of sorrow.
26 And it came to pass that the voice of the Lord
said unto him: Look upon the ball, and behold
the things which are written.
27 And it came to pass that when my father be-
held the things which were written upon the ball,
he did fear and tremble exceedingly, and also my
brethren and the sons of Ishmael and our wives.
28 And it came to pass that I, Nephi, beheld
the pointers which were in the ball, that they did
work according to the faith and diligence and
heed which we did give unto them.
29 And there was also written upon them a new
writing, which was plain to be read, which did
give us understanding concerning the ways of the
Lord; and it was written and changed from time
to time, according to the faith and diligence which
we gave unto it. And thus we see that by small
means the Lord can bring about great things.
30 And it came to pass that I, Nephi, did go
forth up into the top of the mountain, according
to the directions which were given upon the ball.
31 And it came to pass that I did slay wild beasts,
insomuch that I did obtain food for our families.
32 And it came to pass that I did return to our
tents, bearing the beasts which I had slain; and
now when they beheld that I had obtained food,
how great was their joy! And it came to pass that
they did humble themselves before the Lord, and
did give thanks unto him.

How did Nephi react to the trial before him? What made the Liahona work? How can you be like Nephi when you face challenges or trials?

NEPHI IS COMMANDED TO BUILD A BOAT

After eight years of traveling in the wilderness, Lehi's family arrived at the shore of the sea. They named the area "Bountiful" because of the abundance of food, which the Lord had provided for them. Here the Lord gave Nephi another commandment that would require great effort and would lead the family of Lehi to happiness.

1 Nephi 17:7–16

And it came to pass that after I, Nephi, had been in the land of Bountiful for the space of many days, the voice of the Lord came unto me, saying: Arise, and get thee into the mountain. And it came to pass that I arose and went up into the mountain, and cried unto the Lord.
8 And it came to pass that the Lord spake unto me, saying: Thou shalt construct a ship, after the manner which I shall show thee, that I may carry thy people across these waters.
9 And I said: Lord, whither shall I go that I may find ore to molten, that I may make tools to construct the ship after the manner which thou hast shown unto me?
10 And it came to pass that the Lord told me whither I should go to find ore, that I might make tools.
11 And it came to pass that I, Nephi, did make a bellows wherewith to blow the fire, of the skins of beasts; and after I had made a bellows, that I might have wherewith to blow the fire, I did smite two stones together that I might make fire.
12 For the Lord had not hitherto suffered that we should make much fire, as we journeyed in the wilderness; for he said: I will make thy food become sweet, that ye cook it not;
13 And I will also be your light in the wilderness; and I will prepare the way before you, if it so be that ye shall keep my commandments; wherefore, inasmuch as ye shall keep my commandments ye shall be led towards the promised land; and ye shall know that it is by me that ye are led.
14 Yea, and the Lord said also that: After ye have arrived in the promised land, ye shall know that I, the Lord, am God; and that I, the Lord, did deliver you from destruction; yea, that I did bring you out of the land of Jerusalem.
15 Wherefore, I, Nephi, did strive to keep the commandments of the Lord, and I did exhort my brethren to faithfulness and diligence.
16 And it came to pass that I did make tools of the ore which I did molten out of the rock.

When the Lord told Nephi to build a boat, what did Nephi do first? How did the Lord help Nephi? What did Nephi have to do for himself? What does this teach us about how we should respond when we are called upon to do something difficult?

NEPHI TEACHES ABOUT COVENANTS AND GOD'S DESIRE TO LEAD HIS CHILDREN TO HAPPINESS

Nephi began making tools to build the ship, but his brothers complained about having to work and doubted Nephi's ability to succeed. They felt they had been misled into leaving Jerusalem. Nephi reminded his brothers that God was leading their family away from Jerusalem so they would not be destroyed and that if God's children reject His commandments, they will not receive all of His blessings. In teaching his brothers, Nephi used the example of Moses leading the children of Israel to the promised land.

1 Nephi 17:26, 30–31, 35–38, 40

Now ye know that Moses was commanded of the Lord to do that great work; and ye know that by his word the waters of the Red Sea were divided hither and thither, and they passed through on dry ground.

30 And notwithstanding they being led, the Lord their God, their Redeemer, going before them, leading them by day and giving light unto them by night, and doing all things for them which were expedient for man to receive, they hardened their hearts and blinded their minds, and reviled against Moses and against the true and living God.

31 And it came to pass that according to his word he did destroy them; and according to his word he did lead them; and according to his word he did do all things for them; and there was not any thing done save it were by his word.

35 Behold, the Lord esteemeth all flesh in one; he that is righteous is favored of God. But behold, this people had rejected every word of God, and they were ripe in iniquity; and the fulness of the wrath of God was upon them; and the Lord did curse the land against them, and bless it unto our fathers; yea, he did curse it against them unto their destruction, and he did bless it unto our fathers unto their obtaining power over it.

36 Behold, the Lord hath created the earth that it should be inhabited; and he hath created his children that they should possess it.

37 And he raiseth up a righteous nation, and destroyeth the nations of the wicked.

38 And he leadeth away the righteous into precious lands, and the wicked he destroyeth, and curseth the land unto them for their sakes.

40 And he loveth those who will have him to be their God. Behold, he loved our fathers, and he covenanted with them, yea, even Abraham, Isaac, and Jacob; and he remembered the covenants which he had made; wherefore, he did bring them out of the land of Egypt.

How did the Lord respond to the children of Israel's actions and attitudes? What does the Lord do when we are righteous? What is a covenant? What covenants will you make with God?

NEPHI SPEAKS OF GOD'S ABILITY TO HELP HIS CHILDREN OBEY ALL HIS COMMANDMENTS

Nephi continued to teach his brothers about obedience and chastised them for not following the promptings of the Spirit, the voice of the Lord, or even the angel that had appeared to them. Nephi was frustrated with his brother's actions but spoke boldly to them in the hope that they would repent and be obedient.

1 Nephi 17:47–52

Behold, my soul is rent with anguish be-
cause of you, and my heart is pained; I
fear lest ye shall be cast off forever. Behold, I am
full of the Spirit of God, insomuch that my frame
has no strength.
48 And now it came to pass that when I had
spoken these words they were angry with me,
and were desirous to throw me into the depths of
the sea; and as they came forth to lay their hands
upon me I spake unto them, saying: In the name
of the Almighty God, I command you that ye
touch me not, for I am filled with the power of
God, even unto the consuming of my flesh; and
whoso shall lay his hands upon me shall wither
even as a dried reed; and he shall be as naught
before the power of God, for God shall smite
him.
49 And it came to pass that I, Nephi, said unto
them that they should murmur no more against
their father; neither should they withhold their
labor from me, for God had commanded me that
I should build a ship.
50 And I said unto them: If God had com-
manded me to do all things I could do them. If he
should command me that I should say unto this
water, be thou earth, it should be earth; and if I
should say it, it would be done.
51 And now, if the Lord has such great power,
and has wrought so many miracles among the
children of men, how is it that he cannot instruct
me, that I should build a ship?
52 And it came to pass that I, Nephi, said many
things unto my brethren, insomuch that they
were confounded and could not contend against
me; neither durst they lay their hands upon me
nor touch me with their fingers, even for the
space of many days. Now they durst not do this
lest they should wither before me, so powerful
was the Spirit of God; and thus it had wrought
upon them.

What gave Nephi the strength to stand up to his brothers? What are some challenging things the Lord has commanded you to do? How have you felt God's help as you've tried to obey?

NEPHI IS BOUND BY HIS BROTHERS AND HIS FAMILY LOSES THEIR WAY AT SEA

The Lord continued to show Nephi how to build the ship. When it was completed, the families of Lehi and Ishmael began sailing toward the promised land. Soon, Nephi's brothers and the sons of Ishmael began to act "with much rudeness."

1 Nephi 18:9–16, 21–23

And after we had been driven forth before the wind for the space of many days, behold, my brethren and the sons of Ishmael and also their wives began to make themselves merry, insomuch that they began to dance, and to sing, and to speak with much rudeness, yea, even that they did forget by what power they had been brought thither; yea, they were lifted up unto exceeding rudeness.

10 And I, Nephi, began to fear exceedingly lest the Lord should be angry with us, and smite us because of our iniquity, that we should be swallowed up in the depths of the sea; wherefore, I, Nephi, began to speak to them with much soberness; but behold they were angry with me, saying: We will not that our younger brother shall be a ruler over us.

11 And it came to pass that Laman and Lemuel did take me and bind me with cords, and they did treat me with much harshness; nevertheless, the Lord did suffer it that he might show forth his power, unto the fulfilling of his word which he had spoken concerning the wicked.

12 And it came to pass that after they had bound me insomuch that I could not move, the compass, which had been prepared of the Lord, did cease to work.

13 Wherefore, they knew not whither they should steer the ship, insomuch that there arose a great storm, yea, a great and terrible tempest, and we were driven back upon the waters for the space of three days; and they began to be frightened exceedingly lest they should be drowned in the sea; nevertheless they did not loose me.

14 And on the fourth day, which we had been driven back, the tempest began to be exceedingly sore.

15 And it came to pass that we were about to be swallowed up in the depths of the sea. And after we had been driven back upon the waters for the space of four days, my brethren began to see that the judgments of God were upon them, and that they must perish save that they should repent of their iniquities; wherefore, they came unto me, and loosed the bands which were upon my wrists, and behold they had swollen exceedingly; and also mine ankles were much swollen, and great was the soreness thereof.

16 Nevertheless, I did look unto my God, and I did praise him all the day long; and I did not murmur against the Lord because of mine afflictions.

21 And it came to pass after they had loosed me, behold, I took the compass, and it did work whither I desired it. And it came to pass that I prayed unto the Lord; and after I had prayed the winds did cease, and the storm did cease, and there was a great calm.

22 And it came to pass that I, Nephi, did guide the ship, that we sailed again towards the promised land.

23 And it came to pass that after we had sailed for the space of many days we did arrive at the promised land; and we went forth upon the land, and did pitch our tents; and we did call it the promised land.

Throughout Nephi's youth, his brothers persecuted him, beat him, and even attempted to kill him. How do you think Nephi was able to feel gratitude for his blessings—and even love for his brothers—during such trials? How has looking to God during difficult times helped you?

NEPHI SPEAKS OF THE PATIENT SUFFERING OF THE SAVIOR AT THE HANDS OF WICKED MEN

After arriving in the promised land, Nephi was commanded to make a record of his family's journey from Jerusalem and the prophecies he and Lehi had received. Nephi considered his record to be sacred and of great worth to those who would come after him. He also knew that much of the world would reject the scriptural record, just as many would eventually reject Jesus Christ. As you read, look for specific references to the numerous ways Jesus Christ would patiently suffer as He fulfilled His atoning sacrifice.

1 Nephi 19:6–10, 12

Nevertheless, I do not write anything upon plates save it be that I think it be sacred. And now, if I do err, even did they err of old; not that I would excuse myself because of other men, but because of the weakness which is in me, according to the flesh, I would excuse myself.
7 For the things which some men esteem to be of great worth, both to the body and soul, others set at naught and trample under their feet. Yea, even the very God of Israel do men trample under their feet; I say, trample under their feet but I would speak in other words—they set him at naught, and hearken not to the voice of his counsels.
8 And behold he cometh, according to the words of the angel, in six hundred years from the time my father left Jerusalem.
9 And the world, because of their iniquity, shall judge him to be a thing of naught; wherefore they scourge him, and he suffereth it; and they smite him, and he suffereth it. Yea, they spit upon him, and he suffereth it, because of his loving kindness and his long-suffering towards the children of men.
10 And the God of our fathers, who were led out of Egypt, out of bondage, and also were preserved in the wilderness by him, yea, the God of Abraham, and of Isaac, and the God of Jacob, yieldeth himself, according to the words of the angel, as a man, into the hands of wicked men, to be lifted up, according to the words of Zenock, and to be crucified, according to the words of Neum, and to be buried in a sepulchre, according to the words of Zenos, which he spake concerning the three days of darkness, which should be a sign given of his death unto those who should inhabit the isles of the sea, more especially given unto those who are of the house of Israel.
12 And all these things must surely come, saith the prophet Zenos. And the rocks of the earth must rend; and because of the groanings of the earth, many of the kings of the isles of the sea shall be wrought upon by the Spirit of God, to exclaim: The God of nature suffers.

Nephi said he wrote on the plates only things that were sacred. What sacred teachings do you find in this passage of scripture? What are the many ways Nephi said that Jesus Christ would patiently suffer? According to Nephi, why did Christ willingly suffer in such ways?

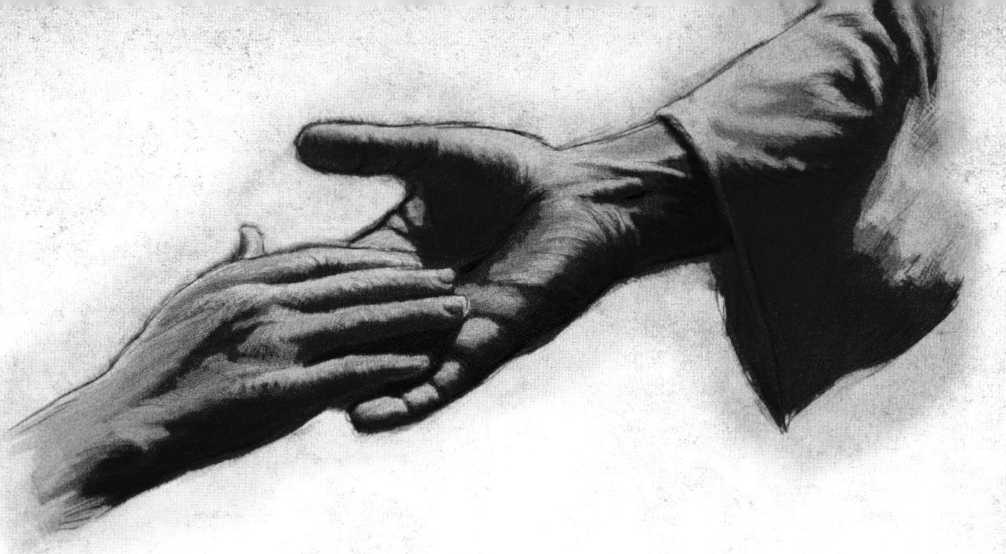

NEPHI QUOTES ISAIAH'S PROPHECY OF THE SAVIOR'S COMMITMENT TO HIS PEOPLE

Nephi wanted his family—and the future readers of the Book of Mormon—to understand the role of Jesus Christ in the plan of salvation. To teach this, Nephi quoted the words of a prophet named Isaiah, who lived in Jerusalem about 150 years before Lehi and his family. Isaiah's prophecies, which used symbolism and poetry, were recorded on the brass plates.

1 NEPHI 19:22–24; 21:13–16

Now it came to pass that I, Nephi, did
teach my brethren these things; and it
came to pass that I did read many things to them,
which were engraven upon the plates of brass,
that they might know concerning the doings of
the Lord in other lands, among people of old.
23 And I did read many things unto them which
were written in the books of Moses; but that I
might more fully persuade them to believe in the
Lord their Redeemer I did read unto them that
which was written by the prophet Isaiah; for I did
liken all scriptures unto us, that it might be for
our profit and learning.
24 Wherefore I spake unto them, saying: Hear ye
the words of the prophet, ye who are a remnant of
the house of Israel, a branch who have been broken
off; hear ye the words of the prophet, which were
written unto all the house of Israel, and liken them
unto yourselves, that ye may have hope as well as
your brethren from whom ye have been broken off;
for after this manner has the prophet written.

1 NEPHI 21

13 Sing, O heavens; and be joyful, O earth; for
the feet of those who are in the east shall be es-
tablished; and break forth into singing, O moun-
tains; for they shall be smitten no more; for the
Lord hath comforted his people, and will have
mercy upon his afflicted.
14 But, behold, Zion hath said: The Lord hath
forsaken me, and my Lord hath forgotten me—
but he will show that he hath not.
15 For can a woman forget her sucking child,
that she should not have compassion on the son
of her womb? Yea, they may forget, yet will I not
forget thee, O house of Israel.
16 Behold, I have graven thee upon the palms
of my hands; thy walls are continually before me.

What words and ideas does Isaiah use to illustrate the Savior's enduring love for His people? How have you felt Christ's love for you? In return, how can you show your love for Him?

NEPHI INTERPRETS ISAIAH'S PROPHECY OF THE SCATTERING AND GATHERING OF ISRAEL

After Nephi read Isaiah's prophecies to his family, he explained some prophetic events that had already occurred and others that would yet occur with the house of Israel.

"The house of Israel" refers to all descendants of Abraham, who were scattered throughout the world but given a promise that the Lord would gather them together again in the last days through the covenant He originally made with Abraham, Isaac, and Jacob.

1 NEPHI 22:3–9, 11–12

Wherefore, the things of which I have read are things pertaining to things both temporal and spiritual; for it appears that the house of Israel, sooner or later, will be scattered upon all the face of the earth, and also among all nations.

4 And behold, there are many who are already lost from the knowledge of those who are at Jerusalem. Yea, the more part of all the tribes have been led away; and they are scattered to and fro upon the isles of the sea; and whither they are none of us knoweth, save that we know that they have been led away.

5 And since they have been led away, these things have been prophesied concerning them, and also concerning all those who shall hereafter be scattered and be confounded, because of the Holy One of Israel; for against him will they harden their hearts; wherefore, they shall be scattered among all nations and shall be hated of all men.

6 Nevertheless, after they shall be nursed by the Gentiles, and the Lord has lifted up his hand upon the Gentiles and set them up for a standard, and their children have been carried in their arms, and their daughters have been carried upon their shoulders, behold these things of which are spoken are temporal; for thus are the covenants of the Lord with our fathers; and it meaneth us in the days to come, and also all our brethren who are of the house of Israel.

7 And it meaneth that the time cometh that after all the house of Israel have been scattered and confounded, that the Lord God will raise up a mighty nation among the Gentiles, yea, even upon the face of this land; and by them shall our seed be scattered.

8 And after our seed is scattered the Lord God will proceed to do a marvelous work among the Gentiles, which shall be of great worth unto our seed; wherefore, it is likened unto their being nourished by the Gentiles and being carried in their arms and upon their shoulders.

9 And it shall also be of worth unto the Gentiles; and not only unto the Gentiles but unto all the house of Israel, unto the making known of the covenants of the Father of heaven unto Abraham, saying: In thy seed shall all the kindreds of the earth be blessed.

11 Wherefore, the Lord God will proceed to make bare his arm in the eyes of all the nations, in bringing about his covenants and his gospel unto those who are of the house of Israel.

12 Wherefore, he will bring them again out of captivity, and they shall be gathered together to the lands of their inheritance; and they shall be brought out of obscurity and out of darkness; and they shall know that the Lord is their Savior and their Redeemer, the Mighty One of Israel.

What does Nephi say will happen with the house of Israel in the latter days? What opportunities and responsibilities do you have in the "marvelous work" that Nephi describes?

The Second Book of Nephi

LEHI PLEADS WITH HIS SONS TO ARISE AND BE RIGHTEOUS MEN

Soon after arriving in the promised land, Lehi had a vision showing that the city of Jerusalem had been destroyed. He told his family of the vision and of a covenant the Lord had made with him that the promised land would remain a land of liberty for his descendants as long as they were obedient. Lehi pleaded with his sons to be righteous in order to receive that blessing. As you read, look for the specific things Lehi asked his sons to do.

2 NEPHI 1:13–17, 19–23

O that ye would awake; awake from a deep
sleep, yea, even from the sleep of hell, and
shake off the awful chains by which ye are bound,
which are the chains which bind the children of
men, that they are carried away captive down to
the eternal gulf of misery and woe.
14 Awake! and arise from the dust, and hear the
words of a trembling parent, whose limbs ye must
soon lay down in the cold and silent grave, from
whence no traveler can return; a few more days
and I go the way of all the earth.
15 But behold, the Lord hath redeemed my soul
from hell; I have beheld his glory, and I am encir-
cled about eternally in the arms of his love.
16 And I desire that ye should remember to ob-
serve the statutes and the judgments of the Lord;
behold, this hath been the anxiety of my soul
from the beginning.
17 My heart hath been weighed down with sor-
row from time to time, for I have feared, lest for
the hardness of your hearts the Lord your God
should come out in the fulness of his wrath upon
you, that ye be cut off and destroyed forever;
19 O my sons, that these things might not come
upon you, but that ye might be a choice and a fa-
vored people of the Lord. But behold, his will be
done; for his ways are righteousness forever.
20 And he hath said that: Inasmuch as ye shall
keep my commandments ye shall prosper in the
land; but inasmuch as ye will not keep my com-
mandments ye shall be cut off from my presence.
21 And now that my soul might have joy in you,
and that my heart might leave this world with glad-
ness because of you, that I might not be brought
down with grief and sorrow to the grave, arise from
the dust, my sons, and be men, and be determined
in one mind and in one heart, united in all things,
that ye may not come down into captivity;
22 That ye may not be cursed with a sore cursing;
and also, that ye may not incur the displeasure of
a just God upon you, unto the destruction, yea,
the eternal destruction of both soul and body.
23 Awake, my sons; put on the armor of righ-
teousness. Shake off the chains with which ye are
bound, and come forth out of obscurity, and arise
from the dust.

What specific things did Lehi ask his sons to do? How can you "put on the armor of righteousness"?

LEHI TEACHES OF THE REDEMPTION MADE AVAILABLE THROUGH THE HOLY MESSIAH

Near the end of his life, Lehi gave counsel to each of his sons. As he spoke to Jacob, he recounted the hardships of Jacob's youth, told of future blessings that awaited him, and taught that redemption through Jesus Christ is made available to all.

2 Nephi 2:2–8

Nevertheless, Jacob, my firstborn in the
wilderness, thou knowest the greatness
of God; and he shall consecrate thine afflictions
for thy gain.
3 Wherefore, thy soul shall be blessed, and thou
shalt dwell safely with thy brother, Nephi; and
thy days shall be spent in the service of thy God.
Wherefore, I know that thou art redeemed, be-
cause of the righteousness of thy Redeemer; for
thou hast beheld that in the fulness of time he
cometh to bring salvation unto men.
4 And thou hast beheld in thy youth his glory;
wherefore, thou art blessed even as they unto
whom he shall minister in the flesh; for the Spirit
is the same, yesterday, today, and forever. And the
way is prepared from the fall of man, and salva-
tion is free.
5 And men are instructed sufficiently that they
know good from evil. And the law is given unto
men. And by the law no flesh is justified; or, by
the law men are cut off. Yea, by the temporal law
they were cut off; and also, by the spiritual law
they perish from that which is good, and become
miserable forever.
6 Wherefore, redemption cometh in and through
the Holy Messiah; for he is full of grace and truth.
7 Behold, he offereth himself a sacrifice for sin,
to answer the ends of the law, unto all those who
have a broken heart and a contrite spirit; and unto
none else can the ends of the law be answered.
8 Wherefore, how great the importance to make
these things known unto the inhabitants of the
earth, that they may know that there is no flesh
that can dwell in the presence of God, save it be
through the merits, and mercy, and grace of the
Holy Messiah, who layeth down his life according
to the flesh, and taketh it again by the power of
the Spirit, that he may bring to pass the resurrec-
tion of the dead, being the first that should rise.

What would happen to us if Jesus Christ had not offered Himself as a sacrifice for our sins? What does it mean to have a broken heart and a contrite spirit? How can you help others know that repentance is available through the sacrifice of Jesus Christ?

LEHI TEACHES OF AN OPPOSITION IN ALL THINGS AND MAN'S ABILITY TO ACT FOR HIMSELF

As Lehi continued to give counsel to his sons, he spoke of righteousness, sin, and agency.

2 Nephi 2:11, 13–16

For it must needs be, that there is an opposition in all things. If not so, my first-born in the wilderness, righteousness could not be brought to pass, neither wickedness, neither holiness nor misery, neither good nor bad. Wherefore, all things must needs be a compound in one; wherefore, if it should be one body it must needs remain as dead, having no life neither death, nor corruption nor incorruption, happiness nor misery, neither sense nor insensibility.

13 And if ye shall say there is no law, ye shall also say there is no sin. If ye shall say there is no sin, ye shall also say there is no righteousness. And if there be no righteousness there be no happiness. And if there be no righteousness nor happiness there be no punishment nor misery. And if these things are not there is no God. And if there is no God we are not, neither the earth; for there could have been no creation of things, neither to act nor to be acted upon; wherefore, all things must have vanished away.

14 And now, my sons, I speak unto you these things for your profit and learning; for there is a God, and he hath created all things, both the heavens and the earth, and all things that in them are, both things to act and things to be acted upon.

15 And to bring about his eternal purposes in the end of man, after he had created our first parents, and the beasts of the field and the fowls of the air, and in fine, all things which are created, it must needs be that there was an opposition; even the forbidden fruit in opposition to the tree of life; the one being sweet and the other bitter.

16 Wherefore, the Lord God gave unto man that he should act for himself. Wherefore, man could not act for himself save it should be that he was enticed by the one or the other.

According to Lehi, why does there need to be opposition in all things? What are some examples of opposition in your life? How does opposition allow you to exercise your agency?

LEHI TEACHES OF THE BLESSINGS THAT CAME FROM THE FALL OF ADAM

As Lehi continued to teach his sons, he spoke of mortal life made possible through the Fall of Adam and of the opportunity to repent and find joy.

2 Nephi 2:19–25

And after Adam and Eve had partaken of the forbidden fruit they were driven out of the garden of Eden, to till the earth.

20 And they have brought forth children; yea, even the family of all the earth.

21 And the days of the children of men were prolonged, according to the will of God, that they might repent while in the flesh; wherefore, their state became a state of probation, and their time was lengthened, according to the commandments which the Lord God gave unto the children of men. For he gave commandment that all men must repent; for he showed unto all men that they were lost, because of the transgression of their parents.

22 And now, behold, if Adam had not transgressed he would not have fallen, but he would have remained in the garden of Eden. And all things which were created must have remained in the same state in which they were after they were created; and they must have remained forever, and had no end.

23 And they would have had no children; wherefore they would have remained in a state of innocence, having no joy, for they knew no misery; doing no good, for they knew no sin.

24 But behold, all things have been done in the wisdom of him who knoweth all things.

25 Adam fell that men might be; and men are, that they might have joy.

What blessings have come to the world because of the Fall of Adam? When have you felt joy in following God's plan for you? How can you share that joy with others?

LEHI INVITES HIS SONS TO LOOK TO JESUS CHRIST AND CHOOSE ETERNAL LIFE

As Lehi concluded his teachings about the Fall of Adam, he spoke of redemption from the Fall, which would be made possible by Jesus Christ.

2 Nephi 2:26–30

And the Messiah cometh in the fulness of
time, that he may redeem the children
of men from the fall. And because that they are
redeemed from the fall they have become free for-
ever, knowing good from evil; to act for themselves
and not to be acted upon, save it be by the punish-
ment of the law at the great and last day, according
to the commandments which God hath given.
27 Wherefore, men are free according to the
flesh; and all things are given them which
are expedient unto man. And they are free to
choose liberty and eternal life, through the great
Mediator of all men, or to choose captivity and
death, according to the captivity and power of the
devil; for he seeketh that all men might be miser-
able like unto himself.
28 And now, my sons, I would that ye should
look to the great Mediator, and hearken unto his
great commandments; and be faithful unto his
words, and choose eternal life, according to the
will of his Holy Spirit;
29 And not choose eternal death, according to
the will of the flesh and the evil which is therein,
which giveth the spirit of the devil power to capti-
vate, to bring you down to hell, that he may reign
over you in his own kingdom.
30 I have spoken these few words unto you all,
my sons, in the last days of my probation; and I
have chosen the good part, according to the words
of the prophet. And I have none other object save
it be the everlasting welfare of your souls. Amen.

What does it mean to be "redeemed"? What do we have to do to access the redemption made possible by Jesus Christ? How can you "choose eternal life" through your daily actions?

LEHI SPEAKS OF JOSEPH SMITH'S ROLE IN BRINGING FORTH THE BOOK OF MORMON

As Lehi gave counsel to his youngest son, named Joseph, he quoted a prophecy given by Joseph of Egypt, an ancestor of Lehi. In the prophecy, Joseph of Egypt made reference to Lehi's posterity receiving the latter-day blessings of the Bible (written by the "fruit of the loins of Judah") and the Book of Mormon (written by the "fruit of [the] loins" of Joseph). The Book of Mormon would be brought about by a "seer" also named Joseph, who would be named after his father. Joseph Smith Jr. was that seer, and, like Lehi, he was a descendent of Joseph of Egypt.

2 Nephi 3:7, 12–15

Yea, Joseph truly said: Thus saith the Lord unto me: A choice seer will I raise up out of the fruit of thy loins; and he shall be esteemed highly among the fruit of thy loins. And unto him will I give commandment that he shall do a work for the fruit of thy loins, his brethren, which shall be of great worth unto them, even to the bringing of them to the knowledge of the covenants which I have made with thy fathers.

12 Wherefore, the fruit of thy loins shall write; and the fruit of the loins of Judah shall write; and that which shall be written by the fruit of thy loins, and also that which shall be written by the fruit of the loins of Judah, shall grow together, unto the confounding of false doctrines and laying down of contentions, and establishing peace among the fruit of thy loins, and bringing them to the knowledge of their fathers in the latter days, and also to the knowledge of my covenants, saith the Lord.

13 And out of weakness he shall be made strong, in that day when my work shall commence among all my people, unto the restoring thee, O house of Israel, saith the Lord.

14 And thus prophesied Joseph, saying: Behold, that seer will the Lord bless; and they that seek to destroy him shall be confounded; for this promise, which I have obtained of the Lord, of the fruit of my loins, shall be fulfilled. Behold, I am sure of the fulfilling of this promise;

15 And his name shall be called after me; and it shall be after the name of his father. And he shall be like unto me; for the thing, which the Lord shall bring forth by his hand, by the power of the Lord shall bring my people unto salvation.

What does this passage teach you about Joseph Smith and his role as a prophet? How is his translation of the Book of Mormon of "great worth" in the latter days? How do the Bible and Book of Mormon work together to confound false doctrine, lay down contention, and establish peace?

NEPHI LAMENTS HIS WEAKNESSES AND REJOICES IN THE LORD'S MERCY

After leaving a final blessing upon his children, Lehi died. Laman and Lemuel soon became angry with Nephi over the counsel and commandments of the Lord. Nephi expressed his feelings for God's work, his frustration at his own weaknesses, and his dependency on the Lord. As you read, consider the relationship Nephi had with the Lord and the specific blessings Nephi desired.

2 Nephi 4:16–21, 26–27, 30–31, 34–35

Behold, my soul delighteth in the things
of the Lord; and my heart pondereth
continually upon the things which I have seen
and heard.
17 Nevertheless, notwithstanding the great
goodness of the Lord, in showing me his great
and marvelous works, my heart exclaimeth: O
wretched man that I am! Yea, my heart sorroweth
because of my flesh; my soul grieveth because of
mine iniquities.
18 I am encompassed about, because of the temp-
tations and the sins which do so easily beset me.
19 And when I desire to rejoice, my heart
groaneth because of my sins; nevertheless, I know
in whom I have trusted.
20 My God hath been my support; he hath led
me through mine afflictions in the wilderness;
and he hath preserved me upon the waters of the
great deep.
21 He hath filled me with his love, even unto the
consuming of my flesh.
26 O then, if I have seen so great things, if the
Lord in his condescension unto the children of
men hath visited men in so much mercy, why
should my heart weep and my soul linger in the
valley of sorrow, and my flesh waste away, and my
strength slacken, because of mine afflictions?
27 And why should I yield to sin, because of my
flesh? Yea, why should I give way to temptations,
that the evil one have place in my heart to destroy
my peace and afflict my soul? Why am I angry
because of mine enemy?
30 Rejoice, O my heart, and cry unto the Lord,
and say: O Lord, I will praise thee forever; yea,
my soul will rejoice in thee, my God, and the rock
of my salvation.
31 O Lord, wilt thou redeem my soul? Wilt thou
deliver me out of the hands of mine enemies?
Wilt thou make me that I may shake at the ap-
pearance of sin?
34 O Lord, I have trusted in thee, and I will trust
in thee forever. I will not put my trust in the arm
of flesh; for I know that cursed is he that putteth
his trust in the arm of flesh. Yea, cursed is he that
putteth his trust in man or maketh flesh his arm.
35 Yea, I know that God will give liberally to him
that asketh. Yea, my God will give me, if I ask not
amiss; therefore I will lift up my voice unto thee;
yea, I will cry unto thee, my God, the rock of my
righteousness. Behold, my voice shall forever as-
cend up unto thee, my rock and mine everlasting
God. Amen.

What lessons can you learn from Nephi's relationship with the Lord? How can you develop a closer relationship with Jesus Christ?

JACOB QUOTES ISAIAH'S PROPHECIES OF THE LORD'S POWER TO SAVE HIS PEOPLE

Laman and Lemuel became increasingly hostile toward Nephi and were determined to kill him. Being commanded by the Lord, Nephi separated himself from his older brothers and departed into the wilderness with those who would follow him. There they established a righteous and industrious civilization and became known as Nephites. The followers of Laman and Lemuel, who became known as Lamanites, remained in their own land and became idle and mischievous. In the land of the Nephites, Nephi's brother Jacob read to the people the prophecies of Isaiah, which spoke of the Lord's commitment to the house of Israel and His power to comfort them.

2 NEPHI 7:1–2, 6; 8:11–12, 15

Yea, for thus saith the Lord: Have I put thee away, or have I cast thee off forever? For thus saith the Lord: Where is the bill of your mother's divorcement? To whom have I put thee away, or to which of my creditors have I sold you? Yea, to whom have I sold you? Behold, for your iniquities have ye sold yourselves, and for your transgressions is your mother put away.

2 Wherefore, when I came, there was no man; when I called, yea, there was none to answer. O house of Israel, is my hand shortened at all that it cannot redeem, or have I no power to deliver? Behold, at my rebuke I dry up the sea, I make their rivers a wilderness and their fish to stink because the waters are dried up, and they die because of thirst.

6 I gave my back to the smiter, and my cheeks to them that plucked off the hair. I hid not my face from shame and spitting.

2 NEPHI 8

11 Therefore, the redeemed of the Lord shall return, and come with singing unto Zion; and everlasting joy and holiness shall be upon their heads; and they shall obtain gladness and joy; sorrow and mourning shall flee away.

12 I am he; yea, I am he that comforteth you. Behold, who art thou, that thou shouldst be afraid of man, who shall die, and of the son of man, who shall be made like unto grass?

15 But I am the Lord thy God, whose waves roared; the Lord of Hosts is my name.

Isaiah spoke of the Lord's powerful ability to comfort and redeem His people. What evidence have you seen of this in your own life? What can you do to receive all of the blessings and comfort the Lord is prepared to give you? What comparison does the Lord make between His power and the power of man?

JACOB TEACHES OF JESUS CHRIST'S INFINITE ATONEMENT

After reading the words of Isaiah to the Nephites, Jacob spoke of Jesus Christ's mortal ministry among the people at Jerusalem and of His infinite Atonement—the only way we can escape sin and death. As you read, look for how Jacob describes our Heavenly Father and His plan for us.

2 NEPHI 9:5–10

Yea, I know that ye know that in the
body he shall show himself unto those at
Jerusalem, from whence we came; for it is expe-
dient that it should be among them; for it be-
hooveth the great Creator that he suffereth him-
self to become subject unto man in the flesh, and
die for all men, that all men might become sub-
ject unto him.
6 For as death hath passed upon all men, to fulfil
the merciful plan of the great Creator, there must
needs be a power of resurrection, and the resurrec-
tion must needs come unto man by reason of the
fall; and the fall came by reason of transgression;
and because man became fallen they were cut off
from the presence of the Lord.
7 Wherefore, it must needs be an infinite
atonement—save it should be an infinite atone-
ment this corruption could not put on incorrup-
tion. Wherefore, the first judgment which came
upon man must needs have remained to an end-
less duration. And if so, this flesh must have laid
down to rot and to crumble to its mother earth,
to rise no more.
8 O the wisdom of God, his mercy and grace!
For behold, if the flesh should rise no more our
spirits must become subject to that angel who fell
from before the presence of the Eternal God, and
became the devil, to rise no more.
9 And our spirits must have become like unto
him, and we become devils, angels to a devil, to
be shut out from the presence of our God, and
to remain with the father of lies, in misery, like
unto himself; yea, to that being who beguiled our
first parents, who transformeth himself nigh unto
an angel of light, and stirreth up the children of
men unto secret combinations of murder and all
manner of secret works of darkness.
10 O how great the goodness of our God, who
prepareth a way for our escape from the grasp of
this awful monster; yea, that monster, death and
hell, which I call the death of the body, and also
the death of the spirit.

What words does Jacob use to describe our Heavenly Father and His plan for us? What would happen to us if we didn't have the Savior's infinite Atonement? When have you seen God's goodness?

JACOB REJOICES IN GOD'S PLAN AND THE JOY OF THE RIGHTEOUS

Jacob continued to teach the people about the plan of salvation and the blessings brought about by Christ's Atonement.

2 Nephi 9:13–15, 18

O how great the plan of our God! For on the
other hand, the paradise of God must de-
liver up the spirits of the righteous, and the grave
deliver up the body of the righteous; and the
spirit and the body is restored to itself again, and
all men become incorruptible, and immortal, and
they are living souls, having a perfect knowledge
like unto us in the flesh, save it be that our knowl-
edge shall be perfect.
14 Wherefore, we shall have a perfect knowledge
of all our guilt, and our uncleanness, and our na-
kedness; and the righteous shall have a perfect
knowledge of their enjoyment, and their righ-
teousness, being clothed with purity, yea, even
with the robe of righteousness.
15 And it shall come to pass that when all men
shall have passed from this first death unto life,
insomuch as they have become immortal, they
must appear before the judgment-seat of the Holy
One of Israel; and then cometh the judgment,
and then must they be judged according to the
holy judgment of God.
18 But, behold, the righteous, the saints of the
Holy One of Israel, they who have believed in the
Holy One of Israel, they who have endured the
crosses of the world, and despised the shame of
it, they shall inherit the kingdom of God, which
was prepared for them from the foundation of the
world, and their joy shall be full forever.

According to Jacob's teachings, who will inherit the kingdom of God? How can you prepare to be among those who inherit the kingdom of God?

JACOB TEACHES OF JESUS CHRIST SUFFERING THE PAINS OF ALL MEN

Jacob continued to teach the people the plan of salvation, emphasizing that Jesus Christ's Atonement would satisfy the demands of justice.

2 Nephi 9:20–26

O how great the holiness of our God! For he
knoweth all things, and there is not any-
thing save he knows it.
21 And he cometh into the world that he may
save all men if they will hearken unto his voice;
for behold, he suffereth the pains of all men,
yea, the pains of every living creature, both men,
women, and children, who belong to the family
of Adam.
22 And he suffereth this that the resurrection
might pass upon all men, that all might stand be-
fore him at the great and judgment day.
23 And he commandeth all men that they must
repent, and be baptized in his name, having per-
fect faith in the Holy One of Israel, or they can-
not be saved in the kingdom of God.
24 And if they will not repent and believe in his
name, and be baptized in his name, and endure to
the end, they must be damned; for the Lord God,
the Holy One of Israel, has spoken it.
25 Wherefore, he has given a law; and where
there is no law given there is no punishment; and
where there is no punishment there is no con-
demnation; and where there is no condemnation
the mercies of the Holy One of Israel have claim
upon them, because of the atonement; for they
are delivered by the power of him.
26 For the atonement satisfieth the demands of
his justice upon all those who have not the law
given to them, that they are delivered from that
awful monster, death and hell, and the devil, and
the lake of fire and brimstone, which is endless
torment; and they are restored to that God who
gave them breath, which is the Holy One of
Israel.

According to Jacob, what was the purpose of Jesus Christ suffering "the pains of all men"? What must all people do in order to be saved in the kingdom of God (see verse 23)? How does it feel to know that Jesus Christ willingly suffered those pains for you? How does it make you want to act?

JACOB SPEAKS OF MAN'S VANITY AND THE NEED FOR HUMILITY TO RECEIVE GOD'S GIFTS

As Jacob continued his sermon on the plan of salvation, he warned people of the temptation for men to become proud of their riches and learning.

2 Nephi 9:28–30, 41–42

O that cunning plan of the evil one! O the vainness, and the frailties, and the foolishness of men! When they are learned they think they are wise, and they hearken not unto the counsel of God, for they set it aside, supposing they know of themselves, wherefore, their wisdom is foolishness and it profiteth them not. And they shall perish.
29 But to be learned is good if they hearken unto the counsels of God.
30 But wo unto the rich, who are rich as to the things of the world. For because they are rich they despise the poor, and they persecute the meek, and their hearts are upon their treasures; wherefore, their treasure is their god. And behold, their treasure shall perish with them also.
41 O then, my beloved brethren, come unto the Lord, the Holy One. Remember that his paths are righteous. Behold, the way for man is narrow, but it lieth in a straight course before him, and the keeper of the gate is the Holy One of Israel; and he employeth no servant there; and there is none other way save it be by the gate; for he cannot be deceived, for the Lord God is his name.
42 And whoso knocketh, to him will he open; and the wise, and the learned, and they that are rich, who are puffed up because of their learning, and their wisdom, and their riches—yea, they are they whom he despiseth; and save they shall cast these things away, and consider themselves fools before God, and come down in the depths of humility, he will not open unto them.

Why does pride lead people to disobey or ignore God's commandments? How can you set aside your own pride and humbly follow His commandments?

JACOB PROPHESIES OF CHRIST'S DEATH AND URGES PEOPLE TO BE RECONCILED TO GOD

Jacob was shown future events related to his posterity on the American continent and the life and death of Jesus Christ in Jerusalem. As he shared his knowledge with the people, he counseled them to act for themselves and be reconciled to God through His grace.

2 Nephi 10:3–7, 23–25

Wherefore, as I said unto you, it must needs
be expedient that Christ—for in the last
night the angel spake unto me that this should be
his name—should come among the Jews, among
those who are the more wicked part of the world;
and they shall crucify him—for thus it behooveth
our God, and there is none other nation on earth
that would crucify their God.
4 For should the mighty miracles be wrought
among other nations they would repent, and
know that he be their God.
5 But because of priestcrafts and iniquities, they
at Jerusalem will stiffen their necks against him,
that he be crucified.
6 Wherefore, because of their iniquities, destruc-
tions, famines, pestilences, and bloodshed shall
come upon them; and they who shall not be de-
stroyed shall be scattered among all nations.
7 But behold, thus saith the Lord God: When
the day cometh that they shall believe in me, that
I am Christ, then have I covenanted with their fa-
thers that they shall be restored in the flesh, upon
the earth, unto the lands of their inheritance.
23 Therefore, cheer up your hearts, and remem-
ber that ye are free to act for yourselves—to
choose the way of everlasting death or the way of
eternal life.
24 Wherefore, my beloved brethren, reconcile
yourselves to the will of God, and not to the will
of the devil and the flesh; and remember, after ye
are reconciled unto God, that it is only in and
through the grace of God that ye are saved.
25 Wherefore, may God raise you from death by
the power of the resurrection, and also from ever-
lasting death by the power of the atonement, that
ye may be received into the eternal kingdom of
God, that ye may praise him through grace di-
vine. Amen.

Jacob encourages us to "cheer up [our] hearts" and remember we are free to act for ourselves. Why does freedom to choose for ourselves bring joy? What choices have you made recently to choose "the way of eternal life"? What can you do this week to show God that you want to follow him?

NEPHI SPEAKS OF HIS DELIGHT IN THE GOSPEL

In addition to his own prophecies and teachings, Nephi recorded many of the prophecies and teachings of his brother Jacob and of Isaiah. All three men saw Jesus Christ and prophesied of Him. The act of understanding and teaching about Jesus Christ filled Nephi with joy. As you read these verses, notice how often Nephi uses the phrase "my soul delighteth."

2 Nephi 11:2–7

And now I, Nephi, write more of the
words of Isaiah, for my soul delighteth
in his words. For I will liken his words unto my
people, and I will send them forth unto all my
children, for he verily saw my Redeemer, even as
I have seen him.
3 And my brother, Jacob, also has seen him as I
have seen him; wherefore, I will send their words
forth unto my children to prove unto them that
my words are true. Wherefore, by the words of
three, God hath said, I will establish my word.
Nevertheless, God sendeth more witnesses, and
he proveth all his words.
4 Behold, my soul delighteth in proving unto my
people the truth of the coming of Christ; for, for
this end hath the law of Moses been given; and
all things which have been given of God from the
beginning of the world, unto man, are the typify-
ing of him.
5 And also my soul delighteth in the covenants of
the Lord which he hath made to our fathers; yea,
my soul delighteth in his grace, and in his justice,
and power, and mercy in the great and eternal
plan of deliverance from death.
6 And my soul delighteth in proving unto my
people that save Christ should come all men must
perish.
7 For if there be no Christ there be no God; and
if there be no God we are not, for there could
have been no creation. But there is a God, and
he is Christ, and he cometh in the fulness of his
own time.

What brought Nephi delight? Share a time when your knowledge of Christ has brought you delight. Think of people you know who have found delight in the gospel. How can you follow their examples?

NEPHI SPEAKS OF HIS DESIRE TO TEACH AND TESTIFY OF JESUS CHRIST

Nephi prophesied of future events that would take place in Jerusalem. After being gathered to the land of their inheritance, the descendants of the house of Israel would reject Jesus Christ as He ministered among them.

2 Nephi 25:13, 23–26, 29

Behold, they will crucify him; and after he is laid in a sepulchre for the space of three days he shall rise from the dead, with healing in his wings; and all those who shall believe on his name shall be saved in the kingdom of God. Wherefore, my soul delighteth to prophesy concerning him, for I have seen his day, and my heart doth magnify his holy name.

23 For we labor diligently to write, to persuade our children, and also our brethren, to believe in Christ, and to be reconciled to God; for we know that it is by grace that we are saved, after all we can do.

24 And, notwithstanding we believe in Christ, we keep the law of Moses, and look forward with steadfastness unto Christ, until the law shall be fulfilled.

25 For, for this end was the law given; wherefore the law hath become dead unto us, and we are made alive in Christ because of our faith; yet we keep the law because of the commandments.

26 And we talk of Christ, we rejoice in Christ, we preach of Christ, we prophesy of Christ, and we write according to our prophecies, that our children may know to what source they may look for a remission of their sins.

29 And now behold, I say unto you that the right way is to believe in Christ, and deny him not; and Christ is the Holy One of Israel; wherefore ye must bow down before him, and worship him with all your might, mind, and strength, and your whole soul; and if ye do this ye shall in nowise be cast out.

According to Nephi, how is mankind saved? How can we "talk of Christ" and "rejoice in Christ" more often?

NEPHI SPEAKS OF GOD'S UNIVERSAL INVITATION OF SALVATION

As Nephi continued to prophesy, he spoke of the coming forth of the Book of Mormon in the latter days and of God's offer of salvation to every inhabitant of the earth.

2 NEPHI 26:23–28, 32–33

For behold, my beloved brethren, I say
unto you that the Lord God worketh not
in darkness.
24 He doeth not anything save it be for the bene-
fit of the world; for he loveth the world, even that
he layeth down his own life that he may draw all
men unto him. Wherefore, he commandeth none
that they shall not partake of his salvation.
25 Behold, doth he cry unto any, saying: Depart
from me? Behold, I say unto you, Nay; but he
saith: Come unto me all ye ends of the earth,
buy milk and honey, without money and without
price.
26 Behold, hath he commanded any that they
should depart out of the synagogues, or out of
the houses of worship? Behold, I say unto you,
Nay.
27 Hath he commanded any that they should not
partake of his salvation? Behold I say unto you,
Nay; but he hath given it free for all men; and
he hath commanded his people that they should
persuade all men to repentance.
28 Behold, hath the Lord commanded any that
they should not partake of his goodness? Behold I
say unto you, Nay; but all men are privileged the
one like unto the other, and none are forbidden.
32 And again, the Lord God hath commanded
that men should not murder; that they should not
lie; that they should not steal; that they should not
take the name of the Lord their God in vain; that
they should not envy; that they should not have
malice; that they should not contend one with an-
other; that they should not commit whoredoms;
and that they should do none of these things; for
whoso doeth them shall perish.
33 For none of these iniquities come of the Lord;
for he doeth that which is good among the chil-
dren of men; and he doeth nothing save it be
plain unto the children of men; and he inviteth
them all to come unto him and partake of his
goodness; and he denieth none that come unto
him, black and white, bond and free, male and
female; and he remembereth the heathen; and all
are alike unto God, both Jew and Gentile.

In these verses, who is invited to partake of salvation? What do these verses teach us about God's love for His children? What can you do this week to treat all people with love and to show that they are valued by God?

NEPHI SPEAKS OF THREE LATTER-DAY WITNESSES OF THE BOOK OF MORMON

As Nephi continued to prophesy, he spoke of wickedness and destruction that would occur throughout the world in the latter days and of three witnesses who would testify to the truth of the Book of Mormon.

2 Nephi 27:6–7, 11–12, 14, 26

And it shall come to pass that the Lord
God shall bring forth unto you the
words of a book, and they shall be the words of
them which have slumbered.
7 And behold the book shall be sealed; and in
the book shall be a revelation from God, from the
beginning of the world to the ending thereof.
11 And the day cometh that the words of the
book which were sealed shall be read upon the
house tops; and they shall be read by the power
of Christ; and all things shall be revealed unto the
children of men which ever have been among the
children of men, and which ever will be even unto
the end of the earth.
12 Wherefore, at that day when the book shall be
delivered unto the man of whom I have spoken,
the book shall be hid from the eyes of the world,
that the eyes of none shall behold it save it be that
three witnesses shall behold it, by the power of
God, besides him to whom the book shall be de-
livered; and they shall testify to the truth of the
book and the things therein.
14 Wherefore, the Lord God will proceed to
bring forth the words of the book; and in the
mouth of as many witnesses as seemeth him good
will he establish his word; and wo be unto him
that rejecteth the word of God!
26 Therefore, I will proceed to do a marvelous
work among this people, yea, a marvelous work
and a wonder, for the wisdom of their wise and
learned shall perish, and the understanding of
their prudent shall be hid.

How was the coming forth of the Book of Mormon a "marvelous work and a wonder"? How do we benefit from there being three witnesses (in addition to Joseph Smith) who viewed the plates?

NEPHI WARNS OF FALSE DOCTRINES THAT WILL BE TAUGHT IN THE LATTER DAYS

As Nephi continued to prophesy, he spoke of dangerous falsehoods that would be taught in the latter days. He then taught the Lord's way of revealing truth to His people. As you read, look for the consequences of teaching false doctrines.

2 Nephi 28:3, 5, 7–9, 15, 30

For it shall come to pass in that day that
the churches which are built up, and not
unto the Lord, when the one shall say unto the
other: Behold, I, I am the Lord's; and the others
shall say: I, I am the Lord's; and thus shall every
one say that hath built up churches, and not unto
the Lord—
5 And they deny the power of God, the Holy
One of Israel; and they say unto the people:
Hearken unto us, and hear ye our precept; for be-
hold there is no God today, for the Lord and the
Redeemer hath done his work, and he hath given
his power unto men;
7 Yea, and there shall be many which shall say:
Eat, drink, and be merry, for tomorrow we die;
and it shall be well with us.
8 And there shall also be many which shall
say: Eat, drink, and be merry; nevertheless, fear
God—he will justify in committing a little sin;
yea, lie a little, take the advantage of one because
of his words, dig a pit for thy neighbor; there is no
harm in this; and do all these things, for tomor-
row we die; and if it so be that we are guilty, God
will beat us with a few stripes, and at last we shall
be saved in the kingdom of God.
9 Yea, and there shall be many which shall teach
after this manner, false and vain and foolish doc-
trines, and shall be puffed up in their hearts, and
shall seek deep to hide their counsels from the
Lord; and their works shall be in the dark.
15 O the wise, and the learned, and the rich, that
are puffed up in the pride of their hearts, and all
those who preach false doctrines, and all those
who commit whoredoms, and pervert the right
way of the Lord, wo, wo, wo be unto them, saith
the Lord God Almighty, for they shall be thrust
down to hell!
30 For behold, thus saith the Lord God: I will
give unto the children of men line upon line, pre-
cept upon precept, here a little and there a little;
and blessed are those who hearken unto my pre-
cepts, and lend an ear unto my counsel, for they
shall learn wisdom; for unto him that receiveth I
will give more; and from them that shall say, We
have enough, from them shall be taken away even
that which they have.

What "false and vain and foolish doctrines" did Nephi say would be taught in the latter days? What is the consequence of teaching false doctrines? What is something you've learned "line upon line, precept upon precept, here a little and there a little"?

NEPHI WARNS OF THOSE WHO WILL REJECT THE BOOK OF MORMON BECAUSE THEY ALREADY HAVE THE BIBLE

As Nephi continued to prophesy of the coming forth of the Book of Mormon, he spoke of foolish people who will reject that scriptural record and insist that God's words and covenants are found only in the Bible.

2 Nephi 29:3–4, 6–10

And because my words shall hiss forth—
many of the Gentiles shall say: A Bible!
A Bible! We have got a Bible, and there cannot be
any more Bible.
4 But thus saith the Lord God: O fools, they shall
have a Bible; and it shall proceed forth from the
Jews, mine ancient covenant people. And what
thank they the Jews for the Bible which they re-
ceive from them? Yea, what do the Gentiles mean?
Do they remember the travails, and the labors,
and the pains of the Jews, and their diligence unto
me, in bringing forth salvation unto the Gentiles?
6 Thou fool, that shall say: A Bible, we have got
a Bible, and we need no more Bible. Have ye ob-
tained a Bible save it were by the Jews?
7 Know ye not that there are more nations than
one? Know ye not that I, the Lord your God, have
created all men, and that I remember those who
are upon the isles of the sea; and that I rule in
the heavens above and in the earth beneath; and
I bring forth my word unto the children of men,
yea, even upon all the nations of the earth?
8 Wherefore murmur ye, because that ye shall
receive more of my word? Know ye not that the
testimony of two nations is a witness unto you
that I am God, that I remember one nation like
unto another? Wherefore, I speak the same words
unto one nation like unto another. And when the
two nations shall run together the testimony of
the two nations shall run together also.
9 And I do this that I may prove unto many that
I am the same yesterday, today, and forever; and
that I speak forth my words according to mine
own pleasure. And because that I have spoken
one word ye need not suppose that I cannot speak
another; for my work is not yet finished; neither
shall it be until the end of man, neither from that
time henceforth and forever.
10 Wherefore, because that ye have a Bible ye
need not suppose that it contains all my words;
neither need ye suppose that I have not caused
more to be written.

What is the purpose of scriptural records? How do these records prove that God is the same "yesterday, today, and forever"?

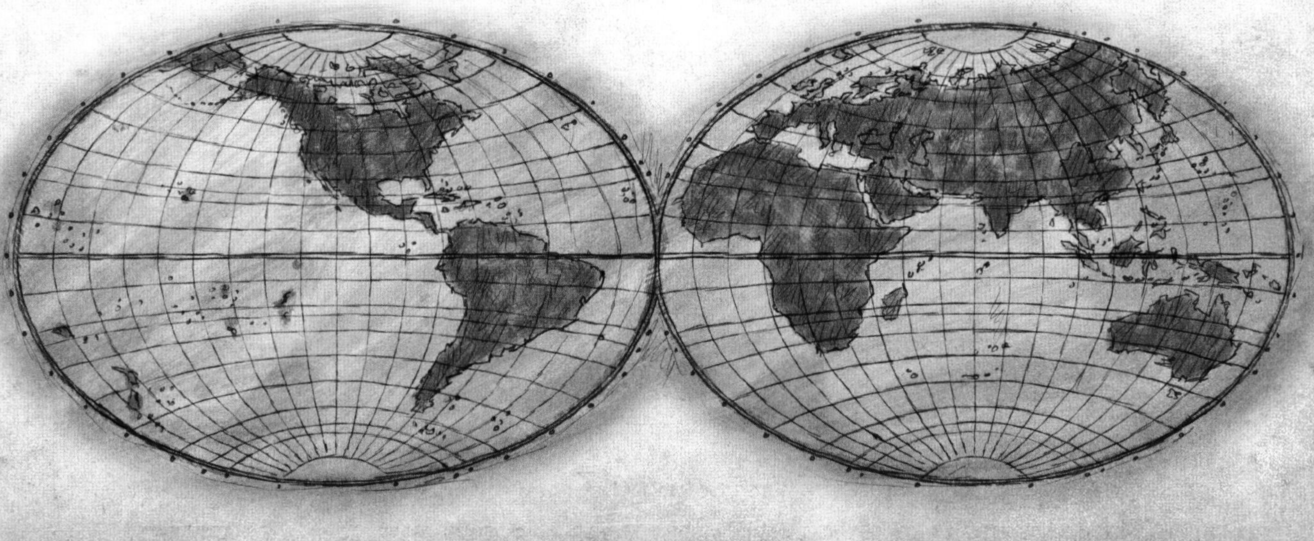

NEPHI EXPLAINS THE PURPOSE OF JESUS CHRIST'S BAPTISM

As Nephi continued to teach his people, he reminded them of the vision he saw of John the Baptist baptizing Jesus Christ. Nephi emphasized the specific reason Jesus Christ—who was perfect and often called "the Lamb of God"—was baptized.

2 NEPHI 31:4–7, 9–13, 17, 20–21

Wherefore, I would that ye should remember that I have spoken unto you concerning that prophet which the Lord showed unto me, that should baptize the Lamb of God, which should take away the sins of the world.

5 And now, if the Lamb of God, he being holy, should have need to be baptized by water, to fulfil all righteousness, O then, how much more need have we, being unholy, to be baptized, yea, even by water!

6 And now, I would ask of you, my beloved brethren, wherein the Lamb of God did fulfil all righteousness in being baptized by water?

7 Know ye not that he was holy? But notwithstanding he being holy, he showeth unto the children of men that, according to the flesh he humbleth himself before the Father, and witnesseth unto the Father that he would be obedient unto him in keeping his commandments.

9 And again, it showeth unto the children of men the straitness of the path, and the narrowness of the gate, by which they should enter, he having set the example before them.

10 And he said unto the children of men: Follow thou me. Wherefore, my beloved brethren, can we follow Jesus save we shall be willing to keep the commandments of the Father?

11 And the Father said: Repent ye, repent ye, and be baptized in the name of my Beloved Son.

12 And also, the voice of the Son came unto me, saying: He that is baptized in my name, to him will the Father give the Holy Ghost, like unto me; wherefore, follow me, and do the things which ye have seen me do.

13 Wherefore, my beloved brethren, I know that if ye shall follow the Son, with full purpose of heart, acting no hypocrisy and no deception before God, but with real intent, repenting of your sins, witnessing unto the Father that ye are willing to take upon you the name of Christ, by baptism—yea, by following your Lord and your Savior down into the water, according to his word, behold, then shall ye receive the Holy Ghost; yea, then cometh the baptism of fire and of the Holy Ghost; and then can ye speak with the tongue of angels, and shout praises unto the Holy One of Israel.

17 Wherefore, do the things which I have told you I have seen that your Lord and your Redeemer should do; for, for this cause have they been shown unto me, that ye might know the gate by which ye should enter. For the gate by which ye should enter is repentance and baptism by water; and then cometh a remission of your sins by fire and by the Holy Ghost.

20 Wherefore, ye must press forward with a steadfastness in Christ, having a perfect brightness of hope, and a love of God and of all men. Wherefore, if ye shall press forward, feasting upon the word of Christ, and endure to the end, behold, thus saith the Father: Ye shall have eternal life.

21 And now, behold, my beloved brethren, this is the way; and there is none other way nor name given under heaven whereby man can be saved in the kingdom of God. And now, behold, this is the doctrine of Christ, and the only and true doctrine of the Father, and of the Son, and of the Holy Ghost, which is one God, without end. Amen.

Why was Jesus Christ baptized? What did Nephi say would come to the righteous after their baptism by water? What else does Nephi instruct us to do in order to obtain eternal life?

NEPHI PLEADS WITH HIS PEOPLE TO FEAST UPON THE WORDS OF CHRIST

After Nephi taught his people the necessity of being baptized, he emphasized the importance of receiving the Holy Ghost.

2 Nephi 32:3–9

Angels speak by the power of the Holy Ghost; wherefore, they speak the words of Christ. Wherefore, I said unto you, feast upon the words of Christ; for behold, the words of Christ will tell you all things what ye should do.

4 Wherefore, now after I have spoken these words, if ye cannot understand them it will be because ye ask not, neither do ye knock; wherefore, ye are not brought into the light, but must perish in the dark.

5 For behold, again I say unto you that if ye will enter in by the way, and receive the Holy Ghost, it will show unto you all things what ye should do.

6 Behold, this is the doctrine of Christ, and there will be no more doctrine given until after he shall manifest himself unto you in the flesh. And when he shall manifest himself unto you in the flesh, the things which he shall say unto you shall ye observe to do.

7 And now I, Nephi, cannot say more; the Spirit stoppeth mine utterance, and I am left to mourn because of the unbelief, and the wickedness, and the ignorance, and the stiffneckedness of men; for they will not search knowledge, nor understand great knowledge, when it is given unto them in plainness, even as plain as word can be.

8 And now, my beloved brethren, I perceive that ye ponder still in your hearts; and it grieveth me that I must speak concerning this thing. For if ye would hearken unto the Spirit which teacheth a man to pray, ye would know that ye must pray; for the evil spirit teacheth not a man to pray, but teacheth him that he must not pray.

9 But behold, I say unto you that ye must pray always, and not faint; that ye must not perform any thing unto the Lord save in the first place ye shall pray unto the Father in the name of Christ, that he will consecrate thy performance unto thee, that thy performance may be for the welfare of thy soul.

According to Nephi, what are some specific blessings the Holy Ghost brings to people? What does it mean to "feast upon the words of Christ," and why should we do it?

NEPHI INVITES ALL TO BELIEVE HIS TESTIMONY OF JESUS CHRIST

In the concluding statement of his own record, Nephi invited latter-day readers of the Book of Mormon to carefully consider his words and believe in Jesus Christ.

2 Nephi 33:1–6, 10–13

And now I, Nephi, cannot write all the
things which were taught among my
people; neither am I mighty in writing, like unto
speaking; for when a man speaketh by the power
of the Holy Ghost the power of the Holy Ghost
carrieth it unto the hearts of the children of men.
2 But behold, there are many that harden their
hearts against the Holy Spirit, that it hath no
place in them; wherefore, they cast many things
away which are written and esteem them as things
of naught.
3 But I, Nephi, have written what I have written,
and I esteem it as of great worth, and especially
unto my people. For I pray continually for them
by day, and mine eyes water my pillow by night,
because of them; and I cry unto my God in faith,
and I know that he will hear my cry.
4 And I know that the Lord God will consecrate
my prayers for the gain of my people. And the
words which I have written in weakness will be
made strong unto them; for it persuadeth them
to do good; it maketh known unto them of their
fathers; and it speaketh of Jesus, and persuadeth
them to believe in him, and to endure to the end,
which is life eternal.
5 And it speaketh harshly against sin, according
to the plainness of the truth; wherefore, no man
will be angry at the words which I have written
save he shall be of the spirit of the devil.
6 I glory in plainness; I glory in truth; I glory in
my Jesus, for he hath redeemed my soul from hell.
10 And now, my beloved brethren, and also Jew,
and all ye ends of the earth, hearken unto these
words and believe in Christ; and if ye believe not
in these words believe in Christ. And if ye shall
believe in Christ ye will believe in these words, for
they are the words of Christ, and he hath given
them unto me; and they teach all men that they
should do good.
11 And if they are not the words of Christ, judge
ye—for Christ will show unto you, with power
and great glory, that they are his words, at the last
day; and you and I shall stand face to face before
his bar; and ye shall know that I have been com-
manded of him to write these things, notwith-
standing my weakness.
12 And I pray the Father in the name of Christ
that many of us, if not all, may be saved in his
kingdom at that great and last day.
13 And now, my beloved brethren, all those who
are of the house of Israel, and all ye ends of the
earth, I speak unto you as the voice of one crying
from the dust: Farewell until that great day shall
come.

Nephi spoke of the power of the Holy Ghost carrying truth "unto the hearts of the children of men." As you have read the words recorded by Nephi in the Book of Mormon, what truths have been carried to your heart? In Nephi's final words, what does he plead with us to do?

JACOB WARNS THE NEPHITES OF THE PRIDEFUL PURSUIT OF RICHES

Fifty-five years had passed from the time Lehi's family left Jerusalem. After anointing a man to rule as king over the Nephites and entrusting his brother Jacob with the scriptural record, Nephi died. The people began to be prideful, hard-hearted, and carnal. As part of his calling as a priest and teacher of the people, Jacob received direction from the Lord and taught the Nephites from the temple.

JACOB 2:2, 12–19

Now, my beloved brethren, I, Jacob, according to the responsibility which I am under to God, to magnify mine office with soberness, and that I might rid my garments of your sins, I come up into the temple this day that I might declare unto you the word of God.

12 And now behold, my brethren, this is the word which I declare unto you, that many of you have begun to search for gold, and for silver, and for all manner of precious ores, in the which this land, which is a land of promise unto you and to your seed, doth abound most plentifully.

13 And the hand of providence hath smiled upon you most pleasingly, that you have obtained many riches; and because some of you have obtained more abundantly than that of your brethren ye are lifted up in the pride of your hearts, and wear stiff necks and high heads because of the costliness of your apparel, and persecute your brethren because ye suppose that ye are better than they.

14 And now, my brethren, do ye suppose that God justifieth you in this thing? Behold, I say unto you, Nay. But he condemneth you, and if ye persist in these things his judgments must speedily come unto you.

15 O that he would show you that he can pierce you, and with one glance of his eye he can smite you to the dust!

16 O that he would rid you from this iniquity and abomination. And, O that ye would listen unto the word of his commands, and let not this pride of your hearts destroy your souls!

17 Think of your brethren like unto yourselves, and be familiar with all and free with your substance, that they may be rich like unto you.

18 But before ye seek for riches, seek ye for the kingdom of God.

19 And after ye have obtained a hope in Christ ye shall obtain riches, if ye seek them; and ye will seek them for the intent to do good—to clothe the naked, and to feed the hungry, and to liberate the captive, and administer relief to the sick and the afflicted.

What does it mean to "think of your brethren like unto yourselves"? Who can you serve today by sharing your possessions and talents?

JACOB CONDEMNS SEXUAL SIN AND TEACHES THE IMPORTANCE OF CHASTITY

As Jacob continued to teach the Nephites in the temple, he spoke directly to men who had committed sexual sin. As you read, consider the feelings of the Lord toward those who are pure in heart and those who are wicked.

Jacob 2:27–28, 31–33, 35; 3:1–2

Wherefore, my brethren, hear me, and hearken to the word of the Lord: For there shall not any man among you have save it be one wife; and concubines he shall have none;

28 For I, the Lord God, delight in the chastity of women. And whoredoms are an abomination before me; thus saith the Lord of Hosts.

31 For behold, I, the Lord, have seen the sorrow, and heard the mourning of the daughters of my people in the land of Jerusalem, yea, and in all the lands of my people, because of the wickedness and abominations of their husbands.

32 And I will not suffer, saith the Lord of Hosts, that the cries of the fair daughters of this people, which I have led out of the land of Jerusalem, shall come up unto me against the men of my people, saith the Lord of Hosts.

33 For they shall not lead away captive the daughters of my people because of their tenderness, save I shall visit them with a sore curse, even unto destruction; for they shall not commit whoredoms, like unto them of old, saith the Lord of Hosts.

35 Behold, ye have done greater iniquities than the Lamanites, our brethren. Ye have broken the hearts of your tender wives, and lost the confidence of your children, because of your bad examples before them; and the sobbings of their hearts ascend up to God against you. And because of the strictness of the word of God, which cometh down against you, many hearts died, pierced with deep wounds.

Jacob 3

1 But behold, I, Jacob, would speak unto you that are pure in heart. Look unto God with firmness of mind, and pray unto him with exceeding faith, and he will console you in your afflictions, and he will plead your cause, and send down justice upon those who seek your destruction.

2 O all ye that are pure in heart, lift up your heads and receive the pleasing word of God, and feast upon his love; for ye may, if your minds are firm, forever.

In these verses, what sin is the Lord condemning? What are the consequences of that sin? What counsel does Jacob give the "pure in heart," and what blessings will they receive?

JACOB EXPLAINS THE PURPOSE OF SCRIPTURES AND INVITES MEN TO BE RECONCILED TO GOD

As Jacob continued to teach the people, he explained the purpose for recording prophecies of Jesus Christ on metal plates—a task that was not easy. Jacob and other Nephite leaders wanted future generations to know what they knew.

JACOB 4:4–11

For, for this intent have we written these
things, that they may know that we knew
of Christ, and we had a hope of his glory many
hundred years before his coming; and not only we
ourselves had a hope of his glory, but also all the
holy prophets which were before us.
5 Behold, they believed in Christ and worshiped
the Father in his name, and also we worship
the Father in his name. And for this intent we
keep the law of Moses, it pointing our souls to
him; and for this cause it is sanctified unto us
for righteousness, even as it was accounted unto
Abraham in the wilderness to be obedient unto
the commands of God in offering up his son
Isaac, which is a similitude of God and his Only
Begotten Son.
6 Wherefore, we search the prophets, and we
have many revelations and the spirit of prophecy;
and having all these witnesses we obtain a hope,
and our faith becometh unshaken, insomuch that
we truly can command in the name of Jesus and
the very trees obey us, or the mountains, or the
waves of the sea.
7 Nevertheless, the Lord God showeth us our
weakness that we may know that it is by his grace,
and his great condescensions unto the children of
men, that we have power to do these things.
8 Behold, great and marvelous are the works of
the Lord. How unsearchable are the depths of the
mysteries of him; and it is impossible that man
should find out all his ways. And no man knoweth
of his ways save it be revealed unto him; where-
fore, brethren, despise not the revelations of God.
9 For behold, by the power of his word man
came upon the face of the earth, which earth was
created by the power of his word. Wherefore, if
God being able to speak and the world was, and
to speak and man was created, O then, why not
able to command the earth, or the workmanship
of his hands upon the face of it, according to his
will and pleasure?
10 Wherefore, brethren, seek not to counsel the
Lord, but to take counsel from his hand. For be-
hold, ye yourselves know that he counseleth in
wisdom, and in justice, and in great mercy, over
all his works.
11 Wherefore, beloved brethren, be reconciled
unto him through the atonement of Christ, his
Only Begotten Son, and ye may obtain a resur-
rection, according to the power of the resurrec-
tion which is in Christ, and be presented as the
first-fruits of Christ unto God, having faith, and
obtained a good hope of glory in him before he
manifesteth himself in the flesh.

What actions led Jacob and many others to the point that their "faith becometh unshaken"? What opportunities do you have to "search the prophets" to learn more of Jesus Christ? How can we "seek not to counsel the Lord, but to take counsel from his hand"?

JACOB INVITES MEN TO REPENT AND EMBRACE GOD'S MERCY

As he continued to teach the people, Jacob spoke of God's enduring commitment to the house of Israel and warned of rejecting the words of the prophets.

Jacob 6:4–13

And how merciful is our God unto us, for he remembereth the house of Israel, both roots and branches; and he stretches forth his hands unto them all the day long; and they are a stiffnecked and a gainsaying people; but as many as will not harden their hearts shall be saved in the kingdom of God.

5 Wherefore, my beloved brethren, I beseech of you in words of soberness that ye would repent, and come with full purpose of heart, and cleave unto God as he cleaveth unto you. And while his arm of mercy is extended towards you in the light of the day, harden not your hearts.

6 Yea, today, if ye will hear his voice, harden not your hearts; for why will ye die?

7 For behold, after ye have been nourished by the good word of God all the day long, will ye bring forth evil fruit, that ye must be hewn down and cast into the fire?

8 Behold, will ye reject these words? Will ye reject the words of the prophets; and will ye reject all the words which have been spoken concerning Christ, after so many have spoken concerning him; and deny the good word of Christ, and the power of God, and the gift of the Holy Ghost, and quench the Holy Spirit, and make a mock of the great plan of redemption, which hath been laid for you?

9 Know ye not that if ye will do these things, that the power of the redemption and the resurrection, which is in Christ, will bring you to stand with shame and awful guilt before the bar of God?

10 And according to the power of justice, for justice cannot be denied, ye must go away into that lake of fire and brimstone, whose flames are unquenchable, and whose smoke ascendeth up forever and ever, which lake of fire and brimstone is endless torment.

11 O then, my beloved brethren, repent ye, and enter in at the strait gate, and continue in the way which is narrow, until ye shall obtain eternal life.

12 O be wise; what can I say more?

13 Finally, I bid you farewell, until I shall meet you before the pleasing bar of God, which bar striketh the wicked with awful dread and fear. Amen.

Jacob pleaded with the people to come unto God with "full purpose of heart." What does that statement mean to you? How can you apply Jacob's teaching in your life?

JACOB REFUTES THE WICKED TEACHINGS OF SHEREM THE ANTICHRIST

After several years had passed away, a man named Sherem began to preach false doctrines among the Nephites. He was a powerful speaker who led many people astray as he taught that there would be no Christ and that no man could know of things to come in the future. Sherem confronted Jacob and attempted to shake his faith. Jacob responded.

JACOB 7:8–23

But behold, the Lord God poured in his
Spirit into my soul, insomuch that I did
confound him in all his words.
9 And I said unto him: Deniest thou the Christ
who shall come? And he said: If there should be
a Christ, I would not deny him; but I know that
there is no Christ, neither has been, nor ever will
be.
10 And I said unto him: Believest thou the scrip-
tures? And he said, Yea.
11 And I said unto him: Then ye do not un-
derstand them; for they truly testify of Christ.
Behold, I say unto you that none of the prophets
have written, nor prophesied, save they have spo-
ken concerning this Christ.
12 And this is not all—it has been made man-
ifest unto me, for I have heard and seen; and
it also has been made manifest unto me by the
power of the Holy Ghost; wherefore, I know if
there should be no atonement made all mankind
must be lost.
13 And it came to pass that he said unto me:
Show me a sign by this power of the Holy Ghost,
in the which ye know so much.
14 And I said unto him: What am I that I should
tempt God to show unto thee a sign in the thing
which thou knowest to be true? Yet thou wilt deny
it, because thou art of the devil. Nevertheless, not
my will be done; but if God shall smite thee, let
that be a sign unto thee that he has power, both

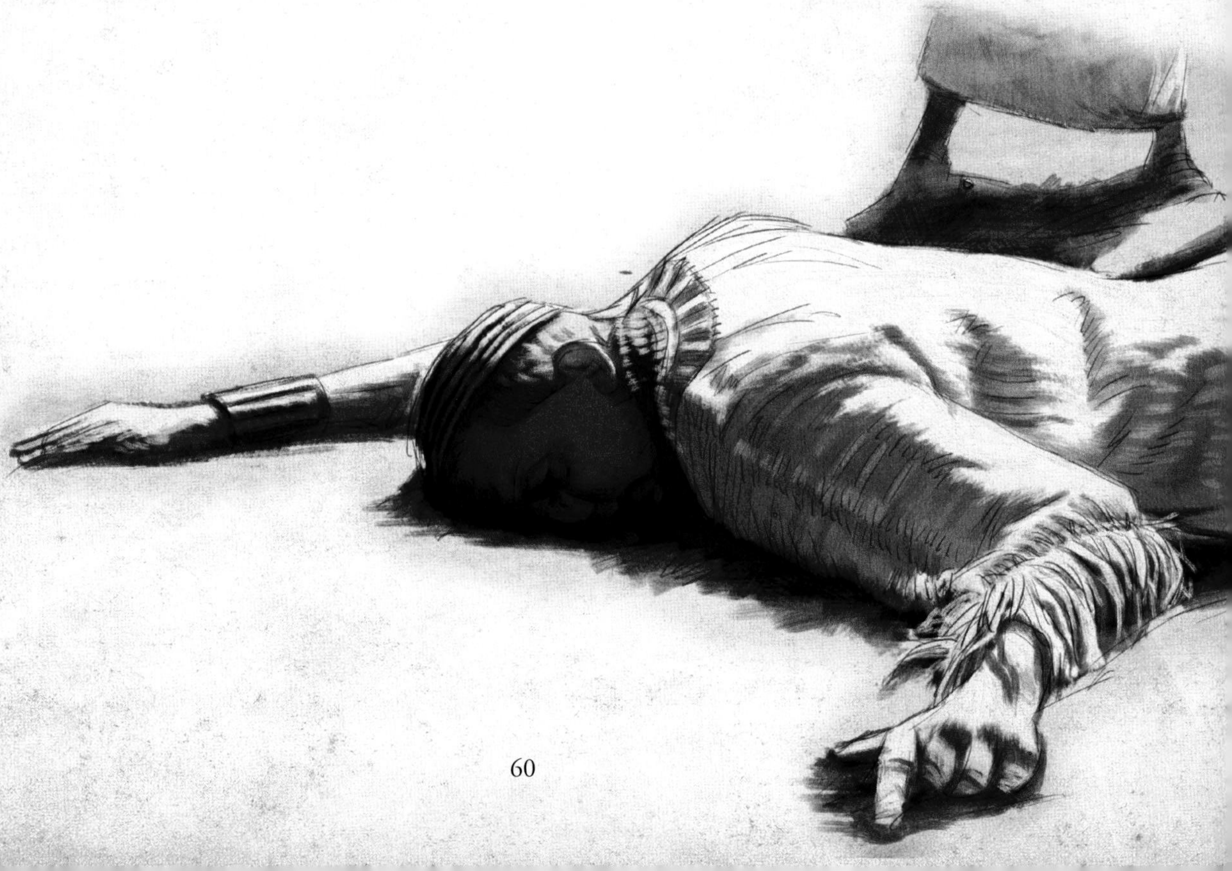

in heaven and in earth; and also, that Christ shall come. And thy will, O Lord, be done, and not mine.
15 And it came to pass that when I, Jacob, had spoken these words, the power of the Lord came upon him, insomuch that he fell to the earth. And it came to pass that he was nourished for the space of many days.
16 And it came to pass that he said unto the people: Gather together on the morrow, for I shall die; wherefore, I desire to speak unto the people before I shall die.
17 And it came to pass that on the morrow the multitude were gathered together; and he spake plainly unto them and denied the things which he had taught them, and confessed the Christ, and the power of the Holy Ghost, and the ministering of angels.
18 And he spake plainly unto them, that he had been deceived by the power of the devil. And he spake of hell, and of eternity, and of eternal punishment.
19 And he said: I fear lest I have committed the unpardonable sin, for I have lied unto God; for I denied the Christ, and said that I believed the scriptures; and they truly testify of him. And because I have thus lied unto God I greatly fear lest my case shall be awful; but I confess unto God.
20 And it came to pass that when he had said these words he could say no more, and he gave up the ghost.
21 And when the multitude had witnessed that he spake these things as he was about to give up the ghost, they were astonished exceedingly; insomuch that the power of God came down upon them, and they were overcome that they fell to the earth.
22 Now, this thing was pleasing unto me, Jacob, for I had requested it of my Father who was in heaven; for he had heard my cry and answered my prayer.
23 And it came to pass that peace and the love of God was restored again among the people; and they searched the scriptures, and hearkened no more to the words of this wicked man.

According to Jacob, what have all prophets always done? What can you do to prevent being deceived by the false teachings of wicked people?

ENOS PRAYS MIGHTILY AND RECEIVES FORGIVENESS OF HIS SINS

Before his death, Jacob conferred the scriptural record upon his son Enos, who recorded an experience he had with prayer.

Enos 1:3–8

Behold, I went to hunt beasts in the forests; and the words which I had often heard my father speak concerning eternal life, and the joy of the saints, sunk deep into my heart.
4 And my soul hungered; and I kneeled down before my Maker, and I cried unto him in mighty prayer and supplication for mine own soul; and all the day long did I cry unto him; yea, and when the night came I did still raise my voice high that it reached the heavens.
5 And there came a voice unto me, saying: Enos, thy sins are forgiven thee, and thou shalt be blessed.
6 And I, Enos, knew that God could not lie; wherefore, my guilt was swept away.
7 And I said: Lord, how is it done?
8 And he said unto me: Because of thy faith in Christ, whom thou hast never before heard nor seen. And many years pass away before he shall manifest himself in the flesh; wherefore, go to, thy faith hath made thee whole.

How would you describe Enos' prayer? What experiences have you had with personal prayer? According to this passage, how is it possible for our sins to be forgiven?

The Book of Mosiah

KING BENJAMIN TEACHES HIS SONS THE IMPORTANCE OF SCRIPTURAL RECORDS

About 470 years had passed since Lehi left Jerusalem. Over the course of several generations, many of the Nephites had become wicked, engaged in war with the Lamanites, and been killed. In about 175 BC, Mosiah, a righteous Nephite leader, was warned by the Lord to leave the land of Nephi and flee into the wilderness with those who would follow him. There they discovered the land of Zarahemla, occupied by the descendants of a man named Mulek, who was led by the Lord from Jerusalem to the American continent in about 590 BC. The people of Mosiah and Zarahemla joined together, called themselves Nephites, and appointed Mosiah to be their king. Upon Mosiah's death, his son Benjamin became king. He helped drive invading Lamanite forces out of the land of Zarahemla and reigned in righteousness.

MOSIAH 1:1–7

And now there was no more contention
in all the land of Zarahemla, among all
the people who belonged to king Benjamin, so
that king Benjamin had continual peace all the
remainder of his days.
2 And it came to pass that he had three sons;
and he called their names Mosiah, and Helorum,
and Helaman. And he caused that they should
be taught in all the language of his fathers, that
thereby they might become men of understand-
ing; and that they might know concerning the
prophecies which had been spoken by the mouths
of their fathers, which were delivered them by the
hand of the Lord.
3 And he also taught them concerning the re-
cords which were engraven on the plates of brass,
saying: My sons, I would that ye should remem-
ber that were it not for these plates, which contain
these records and these commandments, we must
have suffered in ignorance, even at this present
time, not knowing the mysteries of God.
4 For it were not possible that our father, Lehi,
could have remembered all these things, to have
taught them to his children, except it were for the
help of these plates; for he having been taught
in the language of the Egyptians therefore he
could read these engravings, and teach them to
his children, that thereby they could teach them
to their children, and so fulfilling the command-
ments of God, even down to this present time.
5 I say unto you, my sons, were it not for these
things, which have been kept and preserved by the
hand of God, that we might read and understand
of his mysteries, and have his commandments al-
ways before our eyes, that even our fathers would
have dwindled in unbelief, and we should have
been like unto our brethren, the Lamanites, who
know nothing concerning these things, or even do
not believe them when they are taught them, be-
cause of the traditions of their fathers, which are
not correct.
6 O my sons, I would that ye should remem-
ber that these sayings are true, and also that these
records are true. And behold, also the plates of
Nephi, which contain the records and the sayings
of our fathers from the time they left Jerusalem
until now, and they are true; and we can know of
their surety because we have them before our eyes.
7 And now, my sons, I would that ye should re-
member to search them diligently, that ye may
profit thereby; and I would that ye should keep
the commandments of God, that ye may prosper
in the land according to the promises which the
Lord made unto our fathers.

According to King Benjamin, what kept their Nephite ancestors from falling into a state of unbelief? What truths have you learned from the scriptures that you hope to always remember? How can you ensure you remember those truths?

KING BENJAMIN TEACHES THAT SERVICE TO YOUR FELLOW MAN IS SERVICE TO GOD

King Benjamin was aging and knew he would soon die. He told his son Mosiah to call the people of Nephi together to hear his departing words. The Nephites gathered as families around the temple. So great were the crowds that a tower was constructed for King Benjamin to stand upon and speak to the people. His words were also written down and presented to those who were too far away to hear his voice.

Mosiah 2:9–17

And these are the words which he spake and caused to be written, saying: My brethren, all ye that have assembled yourselves together, you that can hear my words which I shall speak unto you this day; for I have not commanded you to come up hither to trifle with the words which I shall speak, but that you should hearken unto me, and open your ears that ye may hear, and your hearts that ye may understand, and your minds that the mysteries of God may be unfolded to your view.

10 I have not commanded you to come up hither that ye should fear me, or that ye should think that I of myself am more than a mortal man.

11 But I am like as yourselves, subject to all manner of infirmities in body and mind; yet I have been chosen by this people, and consecrated by my father, and was suffered by the hand of the Lord that I should be a ruler and a king over this people; and have been kept and preserved by his matchless power, to serve you with all the might, mind and strength which the Lord hath granted unto me.

12 I say unto you that as I have been suffered to spend my days in your service, even up to this time, and have not sought gold nor silver nor any manner of riches of you;

13 Neither have I suffered that ye should be confined in dungeons, nor that ye should make slaves one of another, nor that ye should murder, or plunder, or steal, or commit adultery; nor even have I suffered that ye should commit any manner of wickedness, and have taught you that ye should keep the commandments of the Lord, in all things which he hath commanded you—

14 And even I, myself, have labored with mine own hands that I might serve you, and that ye should not be laden with taxes, and that there should nothing come upon you which was grievous to be borne—and of all these things which I have spoken, ye yourselves are witnesses this day.

15 Yet, my brethren, I have not done these things that I might boast, neither do I tell these things that thereby I might accuse you; but I tell you these things that ye may know that I can answer a clear conscience before God this day.

16 Behold, I say unto you that because I said unto you that I had spent my days in your service, I do not desire to boast, for I have only been in the service of God.

17 And behold, I tell you these things that ye may learn wisdom; that ye may learn that when ye are in the service of your fellow beings ye are only in the service of your God.

What can you learn from King Benjamin's example of service? According to King Benjamin, what are some reasons that we should serve? What opportunities do you presently have to provide service to someone in need?

KING BENJAMIN ADMONISHES THE PEOPLE TO HUMBLE THEMSELVES BEFORE GOD

King Benjamin continued teaching the Nephites from atop the tower at the temple.

Mosiah 2:18–26

Behold, ye have called me your king; and
if I, whom ye call your king, do labor to
serve you, then ought not ye to labor to serve one
another?
19 And behold also, if I, whom ye call your king,
who has spent his days in your service, and yet has
been in the service of God, do merit any thanks
from you, O how you ought to thank your heav-
enly King!
20 I say unto you, my brethren, that if you should
render all the thanks and praise which your whole
soul has power to possess, to that God who has
created you, and has kept and preserved you, and
has caused that ye should rejoice, and has granted
that ye should live in peace one with another—
21 I say unto you that if ye should serve him
who has created you from the beginning, and is
preserving you from day to day, by lending you
breath, that ye may live and move and do accord-
ing to your own will, and even supporting you
from one moment to another—I say, if ye should
serve him with all your whole souls yet ye would
be unprofitable servants.
22 And behold, all that he requires of you is to
keep his commandments; and he has promised
you that if ye would keep his commandments
ye should prosper in the land; and he never doth
vary from that which he hath said; therefore, if
ye do keep his commandments he doth bless you
and prosper you.
23 And now, in the first place, he hath created
you, and granted unto you your lives, for which
ye are indebted unto him.
24 And secondly, he doth require that ye should
do as he hath commanded you; for which if ye do,
he doth immediately bless you; and therefore he
hath paid you. And ye are still indebted unto him,
and are, and will be, forever and ever; therefore, of
what have ye to boast?
25 And now I ask, can ye say aught of yourselves?
I answer you, Nay. Ye cannot say that ye are even
as much as the dust of the earth; yet ye were cre-
ated of the dust of the earth; but behold, it belon-
geth to him who created you.
26 And I, even I, whom ye call your king, am no
better than ye yourselves are; for I am also of the
dust. And ye behold that I am old, and am about
to yield up this mortal frame to its mother earth.

According to King Benjamin, what does God promise to do for those who keep His commandments? When might you be tempted to boast in your own strength? Share examples of people who are truly humble and discuss things you can do to be more like them.

KING BENJAMIN WARNS THE PEOPLE OF THE SPIRIT OF CONTENTION

King Benjamin continued to address the Nephites from atop the tower. He said the Lord had commanded him to announce that his son Mosiah was now their king.

MOSIAH 2:31–33, 36–37, 40–41

And now, my brethren, I would that ye should do as ye have hitherto done. As ye have kept my commandments, and also the commandments of my father, and have prospered, and have been kept from falling into the hands of your enemies, even so if ye shall keep the commandments of my son, or the commandments of God which shall be delivered unto you by him, ye shall prosper in the land, and your enemies shall have no power over you.

32 But, O my people, beware lest there shall arise contentions among you, and ye list to obey the evil spirit, which was spoken of by my father Mosiah.

33 For behold, there is a wo pronounced upon him who listeth to obey that spirit; for if he listeth to obey him, and remaineth and dieth in his sins, the same drinketh damnation to his own soul; for he receiveth for his wages an everlasting punishment, having transgressed the law of God contrary to his own knowledge.

36 And now, I say unto you, my brethren, that after ye have known and have been taught all these things, if ye should transgress and go contrary to that which has been spoken, that ye do withdraw yourselves from the Spirit of the Lord, that it may have no place in you to guide you in wisdom's paths that ye may be blessed, prospered, and preserved—

37 I say unto you, that the man that doeth this, the same cometh out in open rebellion against God; therefore he listeth to obey the evil spirit, and becometh an enemy to all righteousness; therefore, the Lord has no place in him, for he dwelleth not in unholy temples.

40 O, all ye old men, and also ye young men, and you little children who can understand my words, for I have spoken plainly unto you that ye might understand, I pray that ye should awake to a remembrance of the awful situation of those that have fallen into transgression.

41 And moreover, I would desire that ye should consider on the blessed and happy state of those that keep the commandments of God. For behold, they are blessed in all things, both temporal and spiritual; and if they hold out faithful to the end they are received into heaven, that thereby they may dwell with God in a state of never-ending happiness. O remember, remember that these things are true; for the Lord God hath spoken it.

According to this passage, what is the consequence of contention? How can you keep contention out of your relationships with family and friends? King Benjamin spoke of the "blessed and happy state of those that keep the commandments." What blessings have you received from keeping the commandments?

KING BENJAMIN SHARES HIS VISION OF THE MINISTRY AND ATONING SACRIFICE OF JESUS CHRIST

As King Benjamin continued to teach the Nephites from the tower, he shared the words that an angel had spoken to him about the Savior. This was about 124 years before Jesus Christ was born.

MOSIAH 3:3–11

And he said unto me: Awake, and hear
the words which I shall tell thee; for
behold, I am come to declare unto you the glad
tidings of great joy.
4 For the Lord hath heard thy prayers, and hath
judged of thy righteousness, and hath sent me to
declare unto thee that thou mayest rejoice; and
that thou mayest declare unto thy people, that
they may also be filled with joy.
5 For behold, the time cometh, and is not far dis-
tant, that with power, the Lord Omnipotent who
reigneth, who was, and is from all eternity to all
eternity, shall come down from heaven among the
children of men, and shall dwell in a tabernacle
of clay, and shall go forth amongst men, working
mighty miracles, such as healing the sick, raising
the dead, causing the lame to walk, the blind to
receive their sight, and the deaf to hear, and cur-
ing all manner of diseases.
6 And he shall cast out devils, or the evil spirits
which dwell in the hearts of the children of men.
7 And lo, he shall suffer temptations, and pain
of body, hunger, thirst, and fatigue, even more
than man can suffer, except it be unto death; for
behold, blood cometh from every pore, so great
shall be his anguish for the wickedness and the
abominations of his people.
8 And he shall be called Jesus Christ, the Son of
God, the Father of heaven and earth, the Creator
of all things from the beginning; and his mother
shall be called Mary.
9 And lo, he cometh unto his own, that salva-
tion might come unto the children of men even
through faith on his name; and even after all this
they shall consider him a man, and say that he
hath a devil, and shall scourge him, and shall cru-
cify him.
10 And he shall rise the third day from the dead;
and behold, he standeth to judge the world; and
behold, all these things are done that a righteous
judgment might come upon the children of men.
11 For behold, and also his blood atoneth for the
sins of those who have fallen by the transgression
of Adam, who have died not knowing the will of
God concerning them, or who have ignorantly
sinned.

What are some of the ways that Jesus Christ served others when He was on earth? What did His service and sacrifice accomplish for you, living today? How can remembering Jesus and His sacrifice fill our souls with "great joy"?

KING BENJAMIN TEACHES THAT THE NATURAL MAN IS AN ENEMY TO GOD

As King Benjamin taught the Nephites from the tower, he continued to share his vision of the Atonement of Jesus Christ.

Mosiah 3:12–19

But wo, wo unto him who knoweth that
he rebelleth against God! For salvation
cometh to none such except it be through repen-
tance and faith on the Lord Jesus Christ.
13 And the Lord God hath sent his holy prophets
among all the children of men, to declare these
things to every kindred, nation, and tongue, that
thereby whosoever should believe that Christ
should come, the same might receive remission of
their sins, and rejoice with exceedingly great joy,
even as though he had already come among them.
14 Yet the Lord God saw that his people were a
stiffnecked people, and he appointed unto them a
law, even the law of Moses.
15 And many signs, and wonders, and types, and
shadows showed he unto them, concerning his
coming; and also holy prophets spake unto them
concerning his coming; and yet they hardened
their hearts, and understood not that the law of
Moses availeth nothing except it were through the
atonement of his blood.
16 And even if it were possible that little children
could sin they could not be saved; but I say unto
you they are blessed; for behold, as in Adam, or
by nature, they fall, even so the blood of Christ
atoneth for their sins.
17 And moreover, I say unto you, that there shall
be no other name given nor any other way nor
means whereby salvation can come unto the chil-
dren of men, only in and through the name of
Christ, the Lord Omnipotent.
18 For behold he judgeth, and his judgment is
just; and the infant perisheth not that dieth in his
infancy; but men drink damnation to their own
souls except they humble themselves and become
as little children, and believe that salvation was,
and is, and is to come, in and through the atoning
blood of Christ, the Lord Omnipotent.
19 For the natural man is an enemy to God, and
has been from the fall of Adam, and will be, for-
ever and ever, unless he yields to the enticings of
the Holy Spirit, and putteth off the natural man
and becometh a saint through the atonement of
Christ the Lord, and becometh as a child, submis-
sive, meek, humble, patient, full of love, willing
to submit to all things which the Lord seeth fit to
inflict upon him, even as a child doth submit to
his father.

According to these scriptures, what is the only way we can receive salvation? How do we "put off the natural man"? What personal qualities would you like to develop as you strive to follow the Holy Spirit?

KING BENJAMIN TEACHES THAT CHRIST'S ATONEMENT IS THE ONLY WAY TO SALVATION

As King Benjamin concluded the retelling of his vision from atop the tower, he looked upon the Nephites for their reaction. As you read, consider the specific blessings the Nephites asked for and what they were given.

Mosiah 4:1–8

And now, it came to pass that when king Benjamin had made an end of speaking the words which had been delivered unto him by the angel of the Lord, that he cast his eyes round about on the multitude, and behold they had fallen to the earth, for the fear of the Lord had come upon them.
2 And they had viewed themselves in their own carnal state, even less than the dust of the earth. And they all cried aloud with one voice, saying: O have mercy, and apply the atoning blood of Christ that we may receive forgiveness of our sins, and our hearts may be purified; for we believe in Jesus Christ, the Son of God, who created heaven and earth, and all things; who shall come down among the children of men.
3 And it came to pass that after they had spoken these words the Spirit of the Lord came upon them, and they were filled with joy, having received a remission of their sins, and having peace of conscience, because of the exceeding faith which they had in Jesus Christ who should come, according to the words which king Benjamin had spoken unto them.
4 And king Benjamin again opened his mouth and began to speak unto them, saying: My friends and my brethren, my kindred and my people, I would again call your attention, that ye may hear and understand the remainder of my words which I shall speak unto you.
5 For behold, if the knowledge of the goodness of God at this time has awakened you to a sense of your nothingness, and your worthless and fallen state—
6 I say unto you, if ye have come to a knowledge of the goodness of God, and his matchless power, and his wisdom, and his patience, and his long-suffering towards the children of men; and also, the atonement which has been prepared from the foundation of the world, that thereby salvation might come to him that should put his trust in the Lord, and should be diligent in keeping his commandments, and continue in the faith even unto the end of his life, I mean the life of the mortal body—
7 I say, that this is the man who receiveth salvation, through the atonement which was prepared from the foundation of the world for all mankind, which ever were since the fall of Adam, or who are, or who ever shall be, even unto the end of the world.
8 And this is the means whereby salvation cometh. And there is none other salvation save this which hath been spoken of; neither are there any conditions whereby man can be saved except the conditions which I have told you.

What specific blessings did the Nephites ask for? What was given in response to their request? According to King Benjamin, what kind of person "receiveth salvation"?

KING BENJAMIN INVITES PEOPLE TO BE FILLED WITH THE LOVE OF GOD AND LIVE PEACEABLEY WITH ONE ANOTHER

King Benjamin continued his counsel to the humbled Nephites gathered at the temple. As you read, consider the specific things King Benjamin invited the people to believe.

Mosiah 4:9–15

Believe in God; believe that he is, and that
he created all things, both in heaven and
in earth; believe that he has all wisdom, and all
power, both in heaven and in earth; believe that
man doth not comprehend all the things which
the Lord can comprehend.
10 And again, believe that ye must repent of your
sins and forsake them, and humble yourselves
before God; and ask in sincerity of heart that he
would forgive you; and now, if you believe all
these things see that ye do them.
11 And again I say unto you as I have said be-
fore, that as ye have come to the knowledge of the
glory of God, or if ye have known of his goodness
and have tasted of his love, and have received a
remission of your sins, which causeth such ex-
ceedingly great joy in your souls, even so I would
that ye should remember, and always retain in re-
membrance, the greatness of God, and your own
nothingness, and his goodness and long-suffering
towards you, unworthy creatures, and humble
yourselves even in the depths of humility, calling
on the name of the Lord daily, and standing
steadfastly in the faith of that which is to come,
which was spoken by the mouth of the angel.
12 And behold, I say unto you that if ye do this
ye shall always rejoice, and be filled with the love
of God, and always retain a remission of your sins;
and ye shall grow in the knowledge of the glory of
him that created you, or in the knowledge of that
which is just and true.
13 And ye will not have a mind to injure one an-
other, but to live peaceably, and to render to every
man according to that which is his due.
14 And ye will not suffer your children that they
go hungry, or naked; neither will ye suffer that
they transgress the laws of God, and fight and
quarrel one with another, and serve the devil, who
is the master of sin, or who is the evil spirit which
hath been spoken of by our fathers, he being an
enemy to all righteousness.
15 But ye will teach them to walk in the ways
of truth and soberness; ye will teach them to love
one another, and to serve one another.

What did King Benjamin invite the people to believe? How will we be blessed if we believe these things? What are we told to teach our children?

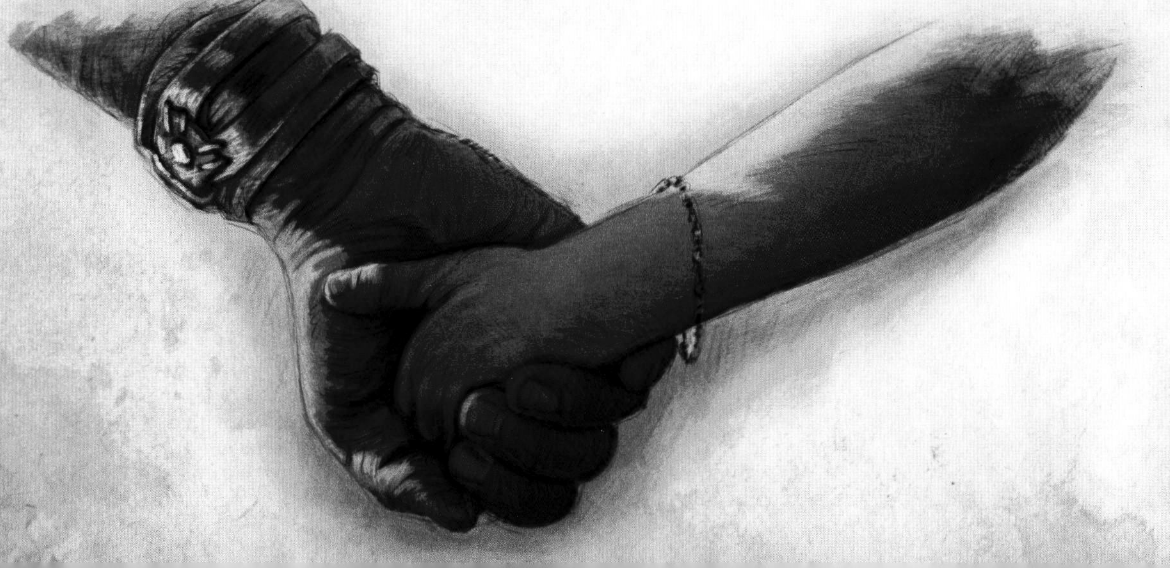

KING BENJAMIN TEACHES THAT WE ARE ALL BEGGARS BEFORE GOD

King Benjamin continued his counsel to the Nephites gathered at the temple.

Mosiah 4:16–23, 26–27

And also, ye yourselves will succor those
that stand in need of your succor; ye
will administer of your substance unto him that
standeth in need; and ye will not suffer that the
beggar putteth up his petition to you in vain, and
turn him out to perish.
17 Perhaps thou shalt say: The man has brought
upon himself his misery; therefore I will stay my
hand, and will not give unto him of my food, nor
impart unto him of my substance that he may not
suffer, for his punishments are just—
18 But I say unto you, O man, whosoever doeth
this the same hath great cause to repent; and ex-
cept he repenteth of that which he hath done
he perisheth forever, and hath no interest in the
kingdom of God.
19 For behold, are we not all beggars? Do we not
all depend upon the same Being, even God, for all
the substance which we have, for both food and
raiment, and for gold, and for silver, and for all
the riches which we have of every kind?
20 And behold, even at this time, ye have been
calling on his name, and begging for a remis-
sion of your sins. And has he suffered that ye
have begged in vain? Nay; he has poured out his
Spirit upon you, and has caused that your hearts
should be filled with joy, and has caused that your
mouths should be stopped that ye could not find
utterance, so exceedingly great was your joy.
21 And now, if God, who has created you, on
whom you are dependent for your lives and for
all that ye have and are, doth grant unto you
whatsoever ye ask that is right, in faith, believing
that ye shall receive, O then, how ye ought to im-
part of the substance that ye have one to another.
22 And if ye judge the man who putteth up his
petition to you for your substance that he perish
not, and condemn him, how much more just
will be your condemnation for withholding your
substance, which doth not belong to you but to
God, to whom also your life belongeth; and yet ye
put up no petition, nor repent of the thing which
thou hast done.
23 I say unto you, wo be unto that man, for his
substance shall perish with him; and now, I say
these things unto those who are rich as pertaining
to the things of this world.
26 And now, for the sake of these things which
I have spoken unto you—that is, for the sake of
retaining a remission of your sins from day to day,
that ye may walk guiltless before God—I would
that ye should impart of your substance to the
poor, every man according to that which he hath,
such as feeding the hungry, clothing the naked,
visiting the sick and administering to their relief,
both spiritually and temporally, according to their
wants.
27 And see that all these things are done in
wisdom and order; for it is not requisite that a
man should run faster than he has strength. And
again, it is expedient that he should be diligent,
that thereby he might win the prize; therefore, all
things must be done in order.

According to King Benjamin, how are we all "beggars"? What is our "substance" and what are we told to do with it? What can you do this week to share your time and substance with others?

KING BENJAMIN'S PEOPLE ENTER INTO A COVENANT WITH GOD AND TAKE UPON THEMSELVES THE NAME OF CHRIST

At the conclusion of King Benjamin's remarks from atop the tower, the Nephites responded with one voice.

MOSIAH 5:1–2, 5–10, 12–13, 15

And now, it came to pass that when king Benjamin had thus spoken to his people, he sent among them, desiring to know of his people if they believed the words which he had spoken unto them.

2 And they all cried with one voice, saying: Yea, we believe all the words which thou hast spoken unto us; and also, we know of their surety and truth, because of the Spirit of the Lord Omnipotent, which has wrought a mighty change in us, or in our hearts, that we have no more disposition to do evil, but to do good continually.

5 And we are willing to enter into a covenant with our God to do his will, and to be obedient to his commandments in all things that he shall command us, all the remainder of our days, that we may not bring upon ourselves a never-ending torment, as has been spoken by the angel, that we may not drink out of the cup of the wrath of God.

6 And now, these are the words which king Benjamin desired of them; and therefore he said unto them: Ye have spoken the words that I desired; and the covenant which ye have made is a righteous covenant.

7 And now, because of the covenant which ye have made ye shall be called the children of Christ, his sons, and his daughters; for behold, this day he hath spiritually begotten you; for ye say that your hearts are changed through faith on his name; therefore, ye are born of him and have become his sons and his daughters.

8 And under this head ye are made free, and there is no other head whereby ye can be made free. There is no other name given whereby salvation cometh; therefore, I would that ye should take upon you the name of Christ, all you that have entered into the covenant with God that ye should be obedient unto the end of your lives.

9 And it shall come to pass that whosoever doeth this shall be found at the right hand of God, for he shall know the name by which he is called; for he shall be called by the name of Christ.

10 And now it shall come to pass, that whosoever shall not take upon him the name of Christ must be called by some other name; therefore, he findeth himself on the left hand of God.

12 I say unto you, I would that ye should remember to retain the name written always in your hearts, that ye are not found on the left hand of God, but that ye hear and know the voice by which ye shall be called, and also, the name by which he shall call you.

13 For how knoweth a man the master whom he has not served, and who is a stranger unto him, and is far from the thoughts and intents of his heart?

15 Therefore, I would that ye should be steadfast and immovable, always abounding in good works, that Christ, the Lord God Omnipotent, may seal you his, that you may be brought to heaven, that ye may have everlasting salvation and eternal life, through the wisdom, and power, and justice, and mercy of him who created all things, in heaven and in earth, who is God above all. Amen.

Describe the covenant the Nephites made with God. What blessings were promised to those who obeyed the covenant? How is that covenant similar to covenants we make with God today?

ABINADI CALLS KING NOAH AND HIS PEOPLE TO REPENTANCE

Three years after consecrating his son Mosiah to be king, King Benjamin died. Many years earlier, during the reign of King Benjamin, a man named Zeniff led a group of people from Zarehemla to the land of Nephi in the hopes of reestablishing their homeland. There Zeniff was met by Laman, the cunning king of the Lamanites, who offered to let Zeniff and his people live in the cities of Nephi-Lehi and Shilom. After several years, the Lamanites began to periodically make war against Zeniff's people. King Laman died, and his son further stirred up the Lamanites against Zeniff's people. Zeniff helped his people defend themselves, led his people in righteousness, and then conferred the kingdom upon his son Noah, who was very wicked. Noah replaced his father's righteous priests with wicked ones. He and his priests spent their time with harlots and instituted a heavy tax upon the people so they could live in extravagance. King Noah's wicked example led his people to become lazy, vain, drunk, and promiscuous. The Lord sent a prophet among the people to call them to repentance.

MOSIAH 11:20–29

And it came to pass that there was a man among them whose name was Abinadi; and he went forth among them, and began to prophesy, saying: Behold, thus saith the Lord, and thus hath he commanded me, saying, Go forth, and say unto this people, thus saith the Lord—Wo be unto this people, for I have seen their abominations, and their wickedness, and their whoredoms; and except they repent I will visit them in mine anger.

21 And except they repent and turn to the Lord their God, behold, I will deliver them into the hands of their enemies; yea, and they shall be brought into bondage; and they shall be afflicted by the hand of their enemies.

22 And it shall come to pass that they shall know that I am the Lord their God, and am a jealous God, visiting the iniquities of my people.

23 And it shall come to pass that except this people repent and turn unto the Lord their God, they shall be brought into bondage; and none shall deliver them, except it be the Lord the Almighty God.

24 Yea, and it shall come to pass that when they shall cry unto me I will be slow to hear their cries; yea, and I will suffer them that they be smitten by their enemies.

25 And except they repent in sackcloth and ashes, and cry mightily to the Lord their God, I will not hear their prayers, neither will I deliver them out of their afflictions; and thus saith the Lord, and thus hath he commanded me.

26 Now it came to pass that when Abinadi had spoken these words unto them they were wroth with him, and sought to take away his life; but the Lord delivered him out of their hands.

27 Now when king Noah had heard of the words which Abinadi had spoken unto the people, he was also wroth; and he said: Who is Abinadi, that I and my people should be judged of him, or who is the Lord, that shall bring upon my people such great affliction?

28 I command you to bring Abinadi hither, that I may slay him, for he has said these things that he might stir up my people to anger one with another, and to raise contentions among my people; therefore I will slay him.

29 Now the eyes of the people were blinded; therefore they hardened their hearts against the words of Abinadi, and they sought from that time forward to take him. And king Noah hardened his heart against the word of the Lord, and he did not repent of his evil doings.

What did Abinadi say would happen if King Noah's people did not repent? What warnings have latter-day prophets given to people today? (See, for example, "The Family: A Proclamation to the World" or recent general conference addresses.) What are you doing to heed today's prophetic warnings?

ABINADI CHASTISES KING NOAH AND HIS PRIESTS FOR FAILING TO LIVE WHAT THEY TEACH

After going into hiding for two years, Abinadi again began prophesying among the people of King Noah, saying that unless the people repented, they would be driven from their land, brought into bondage, and face famine and pestilence, and that King Noah himself would be destroyed. The people were angry with Abinadi, bound him, and took him to King Noah. The wicked priests questioned Abinadi about many things, including a prophecy from Isaiah about the Lord redeeming Zion.

MOSIAH 12:25–30, 33–37

And now Abinadi said unto them: Are you priests, and pretend to teach this people, and to understand the spirit of prophesying, and yet desire to know of me what these things mean?

26 I say unto you, wo be unto you for perverting the ways of the Lord! For if ye understand these things ye have not taught them; therefore, ye have perverted the ways of the Lord.

27 Ye have not applied your hearts to understanding; therefore, ye have not been wise. Therefore, what teach ye this people?

28 And they said: We teach the law of Moses.

29 And again he said unto them: If ye teach the law of Moses why do ye not keep it? Why do ye set your hearts upon riches? Why do ye commit whoredoms and spend your strength with harlots, yea, and cause this people to commit sin, that the Lord has cause to send me to prophesy against this people, yea, even a great evil against this people?

30 Know ye not that I speak the truth? Yea, ye know that I speak the truth; and you ought to tremble before God.

33 But now Abinadi said unto them: I know if ye keep the commandments of God ye shall be saved; yea, if ye keep the commandments which the Lord delivered unto Moses in the mount of Sinai, saying:

34 I am the Lord thy God, who hath brought thee out of the land of Egypt, out of the house of bondage.

35 Thou shalt have no other God before me.

36 Thou shalt not make unto thee any graven image, or any likeness of any thing in heaven above, or things which are in the earth beneath.

37 Now Abinadi said unto them, Have ye done all this? I say unto you, Nay, ye have not. And have ye taught this people that they should do all these things? I say unto you, Nay, ye have not.

What does it mean to "[apply] your hearts to understanding" in relation to the commandments? Why is it important not only to teach what is right but also to *do* what is right? Which commandments could you more fully obey in your deeds and not just your words?

ABINADI REBUKES KING NOAH AND HIS PRIESTS AND BOLDLY PROCLAIMS THE TRUTH

Upon hearing Abinadi's chastisement of King Noah's wickedness, the king responded.

Mosiah 13:1–11

And now when the king had heard these words, he said unto his priests: Away with this fellow, and slay him; for what have we to do with him, for he is mad.
2 And they stood forth and attempted to lay their hands on him; but he withstood them, and said unto them:
3 Touch me not, for God shall smite you if ye lay your hands upon me, for I have not delivered the message which the Lord sent me to deliver; neither have I told you that which ye requested that I should tell; therefore, God will not suffer that I shall be destroyed at this time.
4 But I must fulfil the commandments wherewith God has commanded me; and because I have told you the truth ye are angry with me. And again, because I have spoken the word of God ye have judged me that I am mad.
5 Now it came to pass after Abinadi had spoken these words that the people of king Noah durst not lay their hands on him, for the Spirit of the Lord was upon him; and his face shone with exceeding luster, even as Moses' did while in the mount of Sinai, while speaking with the Lord.
6 And he spake with power and authority from God; and he continued his words, saying:
7 Ye see that ye have not power to slay me, therefore I finish my message. Yea, and I perceive that it cuts you to your hearts because I tell you the truth concerning your iniquities.
8 Yea, and my words fill you with wonder and amazement, and with anger.
9 But I finish my message; and then it matters not whither I go, if it so be that I am saved.
10 But this much I tell you, what you do with me, after this, shall be as a type and a shadow of things which are to come.
11 And now I read unto you the remainder of the commandments of God, for I perceive that they are not written in your hearts; I perceive that ye have studied and taught iniquity the most part of your lives.

According to Abinadi, why did God protect him at this time and not allow King Noah to kill him? What examples have you seen of someone bravely defending God's truth?

ABINADI TEACHES THE TEN COMMANDMENTS AND SPEAKS OF CHRIST'S ATONING SACRIFICE

As he stood before the wicked King Noah and his priests, Abinadi taught the ten commandments that were originally given to the prophet Moses about 1,200 years before Abinadi's time.

Mosiah 13:12–28, 33–34

And now, ye remember that I said unto you: Thou shalt not make unto thee any graven image, or any likeness of things which are in heaven above, or which are in the earth beneath, or which are in the water under the earth.

13 And again: Thou shalt not bow down thyself unto them, nor serve them; for I the Lord thy God am a jealous God, visiting the iniquities of the fathers upon the children, unto the third and fourth generations of them that hate me;

14 And showing mercy unto thousands of them that love me and keep my commandments.

15 Thou shalt not take the name of the Lord thy God in vain; for the Lord will not hold him guiltless that taketh his name in vain.

16 Remember the sabbath day, to keep it holy.

17 Six days shalt thou labor, and do all thy work;

18 But the seventh day, the sabbath of the Lord thy God, thou shalt not do any work, thou, nor thy son, nor thy daughter, thy man-servant, nor thy maid-servant, nor thy cattle, nor thy stranger that is within thy gates;

19 For in six days the Lord made heaven and earth, and the sea, and all that in them is; wherefore the Lord blessed the sabbath day, and hallowed it.

20 Honor thy father and thy mother, that thy days may be long upon the land which the Lord thy God giveth thee.

21 Thou shalt not kill.

22 Thou shalt not commit adultery. Thou shalt not steal.

23 Thou shalt not bear false witness against thy neighbor.

24 Thou shalt not covet thy neighbor's house, thou shalt not covet thy neighbor's wife, nor his man-servant, nor his maid-servant, nor his ox, nor his ass, nor anything that is thy neighbor's.

25 And it came to pass that after Abinadi had made an end of these sayings that he said unto them: Have ye taught this people that they should observe to do all these things for to keep these commandments?

26 I say unto you, Nay; for if ye had, the Lord would not have caused me to come forth and to prophesy evil concerning this people.

27 And now ye have said that salvation cometh by the law of Moses. I say unto you that it is expedient that ye should keep the law of Moses as yet; but I say unto you, that the time shall come when it shall no more be expedient to keep the law of Moses.

28 And moreover, I say unto you, that salvation doth not come by the law alone; and were it not for the atonement, which God himself shall make for the sins and iniquities of his people, that they must unavoidably perish, notwithstanding the law of Moses.

33 For behold, did not Moses prophesy unto them concerning the coming of the Messiah, and that God should redeem his people? Yea, and even all the prophets who have prophesied ever since the world began—have they not spoken more or less concerning these things?

34 Have they not said that God himself should come down among the children of men, and take upon him the form of man, and go forth in mighty power upon the face of the earth?

What can you learn from the fact that Abinadi taught the same commandments given to Moses centuries earlier? What does it mean that "salvation doth not come by the law alone"?

ABINADI QUOTES ISAIAH'S PROPHECY OF THE SUFFERING AND SACRIFICE OF JESUS CHRIST

As Abinadi continued to stand before King Noah and his wicked priests, he taught of Christ's Atonement by quoting a prophecy of Isaiah, who lived about 600 years before Abinadi's time. As you read these verses, notice what Christ "carries" and "bears" for each of us.

MOSIAH 14:1–12

Yea, even doth not Isaiah say: Who hath believed our report, and to whom is the arm of the Lord revealed?

2 For he shall grow up before him as a tender plant, and as a root out of dry ground; he hath no form nor comeliness; and when we shall see him there is no beauty that we should desire him.

3 He is despised and rejected of men; a man of sorrows, and acquainted with grief; and we hid as it were our faces from him; he was despised, and we esteemed him not.

4 Surely he has borne our griefs, and carried our sorrows; yet we did esteem him stricken, smitten of God, and afflicted.

5 But he was wounded for our transgressions, he was bruised for our iniquities; the chastisement of our peace was upon him; and with his stripes we are healed.

6 All we, like sheep, have gone astray; we have turned every one to his own way; and the Lord hath laid on him the iniquities of us all.

7 He was oppressed, and he was afflicted, yet he opened not his mouth; he is brought as a lamb to the slaughter, and as a sheep before her shearers is dumb so he opened not his mouth.

8 He was taken from prison and from judgment; and who shall declare his generation? For he was cut off out of the land of the living; for the transgressions of my people was he stricken.

9 And he made his grave with the wicked, and with the rich in his death; because he had done no evil, neither was any deceit in his mouth.

10 Yet it pleased the Lord to bruise him; he hath put him to grief; when thou shalt make his soul an offering for sin he shall see his seed, he shall prolong his days, and the pleasure of the Lord shall prosper in his hand.

11 He shall see the travail of his soul, and shall be satisfied; by his knowledge shall my righteous servant justify many; for he shall bear their iniquities.

12 Therefore will I divide him a portion with the great, and he shall divide the spoil with the strong; because he hath poured out his soul unto death; and he was numbered with the transgressors; and he bore the sins of many, and made intercession for the transgressors.

In these verses, what has Christ "carried" and "borne" for us? How do you feel as you consider what Christ suffered for you? How does it make you want to act? Why was Christ willing to suffer so much for us?

ABINADI TEACHES OF CHRIST'S ATONEMENT BREAKING THE BANDS OF DEATH

Abinadi continued to stand before the wicked King Noah and his priests and teach of Jesus Christ.

MOSIAH 15:1–12

And now Abinadi said unto them: I would that ye should understand that God himself shall come down among the children of men, and shall redeem his people.

2 And because he dwelleth in flesh he shall be called the Son of God, and having subjected the flesh to the will of the Father, being the Father and the Son—

3 The Father, because he was conceived by the power of God; and the Son, because of the flesh; thus becoming the Father and Son—

4 And they are one God, yea, the very Eternal Father of heaven and of earth.

5 And thus the flesh becoming subject to the Spirit, or the Son to the Father, being one God, suffereth temptation, and yieldeth not to the temptation, but suffereth himself to be mocked, and scourged, and cast out, and disowned by his people.

6 And after all this, after working many mighty miracles among the children of men, he shall be led, yea, even as Isaiah said, as a sheep before the shearer is dumb, so he opened not his mouth.

7 Yea, even so he shall be led, crucified, and slain, the flesh becoming subject even unto death, the will of the Son being swallowed up in the will of the Father.

8 And thus God breaketh the bands of death, having gained the victory over death; giving the Son power to make intercession for the children of men—

9 Having ascended into heaven, having the bowels of mercy; being filled with compassion towards the children of men; standing betwixt them and justice; having broken the bands of death, taken upon himself their iniquity and their transgressions, having redeemed them, and satisfied the demands of justice.

10 And now I say unto you, who shall declare his generation? Behold, I say unto you, that when his soul has been made an offering for sin he shall see his seed. And now what say ye? And who shall be his seed?

11 Behold I say unto you, that whosoever has heard the words of the prophets, yea, all the holy prophets who have prophesied concerning the coming of the Lord—I say unto you, that all those who have hearkened unto their words, and believed that the Lord would redeem his people, and have looked forward to that day for a remission of their sins, I say unto you, that these are his seed, or they are the heirs of the kingdom of God.

12 For these are they whose sins he has borne; these are they for whom he has died, to redeem them from their transgressions. And now, are they not his seed?

How is Jesus Christ both "the Father and Son"? In what ways did Jesus Christ submit His will to Heavenly Father? How does Christ show that He is "filled with compassion" toward you?

ABINADI SPEAKS OF THE FIRST RESURRECTION GRANTED TO THE RIGHTEOUS FOLLOWERS OF CHRIST

Standing before the wicked King Noah and his priests, Abinadi continued to teach of Jesus Christ's role as Redeemer of mankind. As you read, look for Abinadi's descriptions of the people who would come forth in the First Resurrection and those who the Lord would not redeem.

Mosiah 15:19–31

For were it not for the redemption which
he hath made for his people, which was
prepared from the foundation of the world, I say
unto you, were it not for this, all mankind must
have perished.
20 But behold, the bands of death shall be bro-
ken, and the Son reigneth, and hath power over
the dead; therefore, he bringeth to pass the resur-
rection of the dead.
21 And there cometh a resurrection, even a first
resurrection; yea, even a resurrection of those that
have been, and who are, and who shall be, even
until the resurrection of Christ—for so shall he
be called.
22 And now, the resurrection of all the prophets,
and all those that have believed in their words,
or all those that have kept the commandments
of God, shall come forth in the first resurrection;
therefore, they are the first resurrection.
23 They are raised to dwell with God who has re-
deemed them; thus they have eternal life through
Christ, who has broken the bands of death.
24 And these are those who have part in the first
resurrection; and these are they that have died be-
fore Christ came, in their ignorance, not having
salvation declared unto them. And thus the Lord
bringeth about the restoration of these; and they
have a part in the first resurrection, or have eternal
life, being redeemed by the Lord.
25 And little children also have eternal life.
26 But behold, and fear, and tremble before God,
for ye ought to tremble; for the Lord redeemeth
none such that rebel against him and die in their
sins; yea, even all those that have perished in their
sins ever since the world began, that have wilfully
rebelled against God, that have known the com-
mandments of God, and would not keep them;
these are they that have no part in the first resur-
rection.
27 Therefore ought ye not to tremble? For sal-
vation cometh to none such; for the Lord hath
redeemed none such; yea, neither can the Lord
redeem such; for he cannot deny himself; for he
cannot deny justice when it has its claim.
28 And now I say unto you that the time shall
come that the salvation of the Lord shall be de-
clared to every nation, kindred, tongue, and
people.
29 Yea, Lord, thy watchmen shall lift up their
voice; with the voice together shall they sing;
for they shall see eye to eye, when the Lord shall
bring again Zion.
30 Break forth into joy, sing together, ye waste
places of Jerusalem; for the Lord hath comforted
his people, he hath redeemed Jerusalem.
31 The Lord hath made bare his holy arm in
the eyes of all the nations; and all the ends of the
earth shall see the salvation of our God.

According to Abinadi's teaching, who will come forth in the First Resurrection? What kind of people will not be redeemed by the Lord? What must we do to take part in the First Resurrection?

ABINADI WARNS THOSE WHO PERSIST IN WICKEDNESS AND SPEAKS OF CHRIST AS THE LIGHT AND LIFE OF THE WORLD

Abinadi continued his preaching before King Noah and his wicked priests.

MOSIAH 16:1–15

And now, it came to pass that after Abinadi had spoken these words he stretched forth his hand and said: The time shall come when all shall see the salvation of the Lord; when every nation, kindred, tongue, and people shall see eye to eye and shall confess before God that his judgments are just.

2 And then shall the wicked be cast out, and they shall have cause to howl, and weep, and wail, and gnash their teeth; and this because they would not hearken unto the voice of the Lord; therefore the Lord redeemeth them not.

3 For they are carnal and devilish, and the devil has power over them; yea, even that old serpent that did beguile our first parents, which was the cause of their fall; which was the cause of all mankind becoming carnal, sensual, devilish, knowing evil from good, subjecting themselves to the devil.

4 Thus all mankind were lost; and behold, they would have been endlessly lost were it not that God redeemed his people from their lost and fallen state.

5 But remember that he that persists in his own carnal nature, and goes on in the ways of sin and rebellion against God, remaineth in his fallen state and the devil hath all power over him. Therefore he is as though there was no redemption made, being an enemy to God; and also is the devil an enemy to God.

6 And now if Christ had not come into the world, speaking of things to come as though they had already come, there could have been no redemption.

7 And if Christ had not risen from the dead, or have broken the bands of death that the grave should have no victory, and that death should have no sting, there could have been no resurrection.

8 But there is a resurrection, therefore the grave hath no victory, and the sting of death is swallowed up in Christ.

9 He is the light and the life of the world; yea, a light that is endless, that can never be darkened; yea, and also a life which is endless, that there can be no more death.

10 Even this mortal shall put on immortality, and this corruption shall put on incorruption, and shall be brought to stand before the bar of God, to be judged of him according to their works whether they be good or whether they be evil—

11 If they be good, to the resurrection of endless life and happiness; and if they be evil, to the resurrection of endless damnation, being delivered up to the devil, who hath subjected them, which is damnation—

12 Having gone according to their own carnal wills and desires; having never called upon the Lord while the arms of mercy were extended towards them; for the arms of mercy were extended towards them, and they would not; they being warned of their iniquities and yet they would not depart from them; and they were commanded to repent and yet they would not repent.

13 And now, ought ye not to tremble and repent of your sins, and remember that only in and through Christ ye can be saved?

14 Therefore, if ye teach the law of Moses, also teach that it is a shadow of those things which are to come—

15 Teach them that redemption cometh through Christ the Lord, who is the very Eternal Father. Amen.

Abinadi taught that Jesus Christ "is the light and the life of the world; yea, a light that is endless, that can never be darkened." How is the light of Jesus Christ "endless"? In what ways is Jesus Christ a light to you now?

ABINADI REFUSES TO DENY HIS TESTIMONY OF CHRIST AND IS PUT TO DEATH

At the conclusion of Abinadi's testimony before King Noah and his wicked priests, the king responded.

MOSIAH 17:1–4, 7–10, 13–16, 18–20

And now it came to pass that when
Abinadi had finished these sayings, that
the king commanded that the priests should take
him and cause that he should be put to death.
2 But there was one among them whose name
was Alma, he also being a descendant of Nephi.
And he was a young man, and he believed the
words which Abinadi had spoken, for he knew
concerning the iniquity which Abinadi had tes-
tified against them; therefore he began to plead
with the king that he would not be angry with
Abinadi, but suffer that he might depart in peace.
3 But the king was more wroth, and caused that
Alma should be cast out from among them, and
sent his servants after him that they might slay him.
4 But he fled from before them and hid himself
that they found him not. And he being concealed
for many days did write all the words which
Abinadi had spoken.
7 And he said unto him: Abinadi, we have found
an accusation against thee, and thou art worthy
of death.
8 For thou hast said that God himself should
come down among the children of men; and now,
for this cause thou shalt be put to death unless
thou wilt recall all the words which thou hast spo-
ken evil concerning me and my people.
9 Now Abinadi said unto him: I say unto you,
I will not recall the words which I have spoken
unto you concerning this people, for they are
true; and that ye may know of their surety I have
suffered myself that I have fallen into your hands.
10 Yea, and I will suffer even until death, and I
will not recall my words, and they shall stand as
a testimony against you. And if ye slay me ye will
shed innocent blood, and this shall also stand as a
testimony against you at the last day.
13 And it came to pass that they took him and
bound him, and scourged his skin with faggots,
yea, even unto death.
14 And now when the flames began to scorch
him, he cried unto them, saying:
15 Behold, even as ye have done unto me, so
shall it come to pass that thy seed shall cause that
many shall suffer the pains that I do suffer, even
the pains of death by fire; and this because they
believe in the salvation of the Lord their God.
16 And it will come to pass that ye shall be af-
flicted with all manner of diseases because of your
iniquities.
18 And in that day ye shall be hunted, and ye shall
be taken by the hand of your enemies, and then ye
shall suffer, as I suffer, the pains of death by fire.
19 Thus God executeth ven-
geance upon those that destroy
his people. O God, receive my
soul.
20 And now, when Abinadi
had said these words, he
fell, having suffered death
by fire; yea, having been
put to death because he
would not deny the com-
mandments of God, hav-
ing sealed the truth of his
words by his death.

Abinadi remained loyal to his testimony of Christ even in the face of pain and death. As you face adversity, how can you remain loyal to your testimony of Christ?

ALMA REPENTS OF HIS WICKEDNESS AND ORGANIZES BELIEVERS IN CHRIST

After escaping from King Noah's servants and his fellow wicked priests, Alma repented of his sins and began privately sharing Abinadi's teachings among the people. Many people believed his words and began gathering at a place called Mormon, which had a fountain of water and a grove of trees where they could hide from the searches of King Noah. With a large number of believers gathered at Mormon, Alma taught the people of repentance and faith in Christ and invited them to be baptized.

MOSIAH 18:8–17

And it came to pass that he said unto them: Behold, here are the waters of Mormon (for thus were they called) and now, as ye are desirous to come into the fold of God, and to be called his people, and are willing to bear one another's burdens, that they may be light;
9 Yea, and are willing to mourn with those that mourn; yea, and comfort those that stand in need of comfort, and to stand as witnesses of God at all times and in all things, and in all places that ye may be in, even until death, that ye may be redeemed of God, and be numbered with those of the first resurrection, that ye may have eternal life—
10 Now I say unto you, if this be the desire of your hearts, what have you against being baptized in the name of the Lord, as a witness before him that ye have entered into a covenant with him, that ye will serve him and keep his commandments, that he may pour out his Spirit more abundantly upon you?
11 And now when the people had heard these words, they clapped their hands for joy, and exclaimed: This is the desire of our hearts.
12 And now it came to pass that Alma took Helam, he being one of the first, and went and stood forth in the water, and cried, saying: O Lord, pour out thy Spirit upon thy servant, that he may do this work with holiness of heart.
13 And when he had said these words, the Spirit of the Lord was upon him, and he said: Helam, I baptize thee, having authority from the Almighty God, as a testimony that ye have entered into a covenant to serve him until you are dead as to the mortal body; and may the Spirit of the Lord be poured out upon you; and may he grant unto you eternal life, through the redemption of Christ, whom he has prepared from the foundation of the world.
14 And after Alma had said these words, both Alma and Helam were buried in the water; and they arose and came forth out of the water rejoicing, being filled with the Spirit.
15 And again, Alma took another, and went forth a second time into the water, and baptized him according to the first, only he did not bury himself again in the water.
16 And after this manner he did baptize every one that went forth to the place of Mormon; and they were in number about two hundred and four souls; yea, and they were baptized in the waters of Mormon, and were filled with the grace of God.
17 And they were called the church of God, or the church of Christ, from that time forward. And it came to pass that whosoever was baptized by the power and authority of God was added to his church.

What covenants did the people in this passage—and each of us—make at baptism? How can you "stand as a witness of God" in your present circumstances? What can you do this week to "comfort those that stand in need of comfort"?

ALMA ORGANIZES A CHURCH AND TEACHES THE PEOPLE TO CARE FOR ONE ANOTHER

After baptizing those who believed, Alma organized the people into a church and gave them direction.

Mosiah 18:18–29

And it came to pass that Alma, having
authority from God, ordained priests;
even one priest to every fifty of their number did
he ordain to preach unto them, and to teach them
concerning the things pertaining to the kingdom
of God.
19 And he commanded them that they should
teach nothing save it were the things which he
had taught, and which had been spoken by the
mouth of the holy prophets.
20 Yea, even he commanded them that they
should preach nothing save it were repentance and
faith on the Lord, who had redeemed his people.
21 And he commanded them that there should
be no contention one with another, but that they
should look forward with one eye, having one
faith and one baptism, having their hearts knit
together in unity and in love one towards another.
22 And thus he commanded them to preach.
And thus they became the children of God.
23 And he commanded them that they should
observe the sabbath day, and keep it holy, and
also every day they should give thanks to the Lord
their God.
24 And he also commanded them that the priests
whom he had ordained should labor with their
own hands for their support.
25 And there was one day in every week that
was set apart that they should gather themselves
together to teach the people, and to worship the
Lord their God, and also, as often as it was in
their power, to assemble themselves together.
26 And the priests were not to depend upon the
people for their support; but for their labor they
were to receive the grace of God, that they might
wax strong in the Spirit, having the knowledge of
God, that they might teach with power and au-
thority from God.
27 And again Alma commanded that the people
of the church should impart of their substance,
every one according to that which he had; if he
have more abundantly he should impart more
abundantly; and of him that had but little, but
little should be required; and to him that had not
should be given.
28 And thus they should impart of their sub-
stance of their own free will and good desires
towards God, and to those priests that stood in
need, yea, and to every needy, naked soul.
29 And this he said unto them, having been com-
manded of God; and they did walk uprightly be-
fore God, imparting to one another both tempo-
rally and spiritually according to their needs and
their wants.

How are Alma's commandments to the followers of Christ similar to the counsel given to Church members today? What direction does Alma give about what we should teach and preach to one another? What can you do in your family, ward, and neighborhood to create "hearts [that] are knit together in unity and love"?

ALMA WARNS OF THE DANGERS OF WICKED LEADERS AND SPEAKS OF HIS OWN REPENTANCE

King Noah noticed a movement among his people and discovered Alma and his followers at the Waters of Mormon. He sent his army to destroy them, but Alma and his followers, who numbered about 450 people, escaped into the wilderness and began to prosper in a land they called Helam.

MOSIAH 23:6–15

And the people were desirous that Alma should be their king, for he was beloved by his people.
7 But he said unto them: Behold, it is not expedient that we should have a king; for thus saith the Lord: Ye shall not esteem one flesh above another, or one man shall not think himself above another; therefore I say unto you it is not expedient that ye should have a king.
8 Nevertheless, if it were possible that ye could always have just men to be your kings it would be well for you to have a king.
9 But remember the iniquity of king Noah and his priests; and I myself was caught in a snare, and did many things which were abominable in the sight of the Lord, which caused me sore repentance;
10 Nevertheless, after much tribulation, the Lord did hear my cries, and did answer my prayers, and has made me an instrument in his hands in bringing so many of you to a knowledge of his truth.
11 Nevertheless, in this I do not glory, for I am unworthy to glory of myself.
12 And now I say unto you, ye have been oppressed by king Noah, and have been in bondage to him and his priests, and have been brought into iniquity by them; therefore ye were bound with the bands of iniquity.
13 And now as ye have been delivered by the power of God out of these bonds; yea, even out of the hands of king Noah and his people, and also from the bonds of iniquity, even so I desire that ye should stand fast in this liberty wherewith ye have been made free, and that ye trust no man to be a king over you.
14 And also trust no one to be your teacher nor your minister, except he be a man of God, walking in his ways and keeping his commandments.
15 Thus did Alma teach his people, that every man should love his neighbor as himself, that there should be no contention among them.

Alma spoke of being "caught in a snare" due to the wicked example of King Noah and his priests. What "snares" of wickedness do you see in the world today? According to Alma, whom should we trust to teach us? How can you recognize such people?

AFTER BEING BROUGHT INTO BONDAGE, ALMA AND HIS PEOPLE ARE COMFORTED BY THE LORD

While Alma and his people were in the land of Helam, the Lamanites invaded King Noah's land and began killing and scattering the people. King Noah was executed by fire in the wilderness. Amulon, one of King Noah's wicked priests, pleaded with the Lamanites for his life and was spared. The Lamanite army discovered the land of Helam and placed guards around the city, putting Alma and his people in bondage. Laman, king of the Lamanites, allowed Amulon to rule over Alma and his people.

MOSIAH 24:8–15

And now it came to pass that Amulon began to exercise authority over Alma and his brethren, and began to persecute him, and cause that his children should persecute their children.

9 For Amulon knew Alma, that he had been one of the king's priests, and that it was he that believed the words of Abinadi and was driven out before the king, and therefore he was wroth with him; for he was subject to king Laman, yet he exercised authority over them, and put tasks upon them, and put task-masters over them.

10 And it came to pass that so great were their afflictions that they began to cry mightily to God.

11 And Amulon commanded them that they should stop their cries; and he put guards over them to watch them, that whosoever should be found calling upon God should be put to death.

12 And Alma and his people did not raise their voices to the Lord their God, but did pour out their hearts to him; and he did know the thoughts of their hearts.

13 And it came to pass that the voice of the Lord came to them in their afflictions, saying: Lift up your heads and be of good comfort, for I know of the covenant which ye have made unto me; and I will covenant with my people and deliver them out of bondage.

14 And I will also ease the burdens which are put upon your shoulders, that even you cannot feel them upon your backs, even while you are in bondage; and this will I do that ye may stand as witnesses for me hereafter, and that ye may know of a surety that I, the Lord God, do visit my people in their afflictions.

15 And now it came to pass that the burdens which were laid upon Alma and his brethren were made light; yea, the Lord did strengthen them that they could bear up their burdens with ease, and they did submit cheerfully and with patience to all the will of the Lord.

When Alma's people prayed for relief, how were their prayers answered? How has the Lord made you able to bear your burdens? What does the example of the people of Alma teach you about how to approach trials?

ALMA'S PEOPLE ARE DELIVERED FROM BONDAGE AND THEY POUR OUT THEIR THANKS TO GOD

After lifting up their hearts in prayer and receiving strength to endure their burdens, the people of Alma received additional blessings.

Mosiah 24:16–25

And it came to pass that so great was their
faith and their patience that the voice
of the Lord came unto them again, saying: Be of
good comfort, for on the morrow I will deliver
you out of bondage.
17 And he said unto Alma: Thou shalt go before
this people, and I will go with thee and deliver
this people out of bondage.
18 Now it came to pass that Alma and his people
in the night-time gathered their flocks together,
and also of their grain; yea, even all the night-time
were they gathering their flocks together.
19 And in the morning the Lord caused a deep
sleep to come upon the Lamanites, yea, and all
their task-masters were in a profound sleep.
20 And Alma and his people departed into the
wilderness; and when they had traveled all day
they pitched their tents in a valley, and they called
the valley Alma, because he led their way in the
wilderness.
21 Yea, and in the valley of Alma they poured out
their thanks to God because he had been merciful
unto them, and eased their burdens, and had
delivered them out of bondage; for they were in
bondage, and none could deliver them except it
were the Lord their God.
22 And they gave thanks to God, yea, all their
men and all their women and all their children
that could speak lifted their voices in the praises
of their God.
23 And now the Lord said unto Alma: Haste thee
and get thou and this people out of this land, for
the Lamanites have awakened and do pursue thee;
therefore get thee out of this land, and I will stop
the Lamanites in this valley that they come no
further in pursuit of this people.
24 And it came to pass that they departed out of
the valley, and took their journey into the wilder-
ness.
25 And after they had been in the wilderness
twelve days they arrived in the land of Zarahemla;
and king Mosiah did also receive them with joy.

After Alma's people escaped and found safety, what did they do first? In what ways has God delivered you from difficulty? For what blessings can you "pour out [your] thanks to God"?

ALMA IS TAUGHT THE CONDITIONS OF MEMBERSHIP IN THE LORD'S CHURCH

After Alma and his people arrived in the land of Zarahemla, King Mosiah directed Alma to organize churches throughout the land. Priests and teachers were ordained, many were baptized, and for a time the people lived in unity and peace. As time went on, many of the younger generation did not believe in Jesus Christ and refused to be baptized. They were little children at the time King Benjamin taught the people, and they had not understood his words. They were carnal and sinful and deceived many in the Church into following their example. Alma was greatly troubled by this and prayed to God for direction.

MOSIAH 26:14–23, 28–32

And it came to pass that after he had poured out his whole soul to God, the voice of the Lord came to him, saying:
15 Blessed art thou, Alma, and blessed are they who were baptized in the waters of Mormon. Thou art blessed because of thy exceeding faith in the words alone of my servant Abinadi.
16 And blessed are they because of their exceeding faith in the words alone which thou hast spoken unto them.
17 And blessed art thou because thou hast established a church among this people; and they shall be established, and they shall be my people.
18 Yea, blessed is this people who are willing to bear my name; for in my name shall they be called; and they are mine.
19 And because thou hast inquired of me concerning the transgressor, thou art blessed.
20 Thou art my servant; and I covenant with thee that thou shalt have eternal life; and thou shalt serve me and go forth in my name, and shalt gather together my sheep.
21 And he that will hear my voice shall be my sheep; and him shall ye receive into the church, and him will I also receive.
22 For behold, this is my church; whosoever is baptized shall be baptized unto repentance. And whomsoever ye receive shall believe in my name; and him will I freely forgive.
23 For it is I that taketh upon me the sins of the world; for it is I that hath created them; and it is I that granteth unto him that believeth unto the end a place at my right hand.
28 Therefore I say unto you, that he that will not hear my voice, the same shall ye not receive into my church, for him I will not receive at the last day.
29 Therefore I say unto you, Go; and whosoever transgresseth against me, him shall ye judge according to the sins which he has committed; and if he confess his sins before thee and me, and repenteth in the sincerity of his heart, him shall ye forgive, and I will forgive him also.
30 Yea, and as often as my people repent will I forgive them their trespasses against me.
31 And ye shall also forgive one another your trespasses; for verily I say unto you, he that forgiveth not his neighbor's trespasses when he says that he repents, the same hath brought himself under condemnation.
32 Now I say unto you, Go; and whosoever will not repent of his sins the same shall not be numbered among my people; and this shall be observed from this time forward.

What conditions did the Lord give for those who would receive membership in His Church? What blessings have you received as a member of Christ's Church? How often will the Lord forgive us? What does that teach us about forgiving others?

ALMA THE YOUNGER IS CALLED TO REPENTANCE BY AN ANGEL OF THE LORD

While Alma worked diligently to see that the Church was properly administered, he and his fellow leaders faced great persecution from those who did not belong to the Church. Among the unbelievers were the sons of King Mosiah and Alma's son, Alma, who was wicked, idolatrous, and flattered many people into committing sin. It was Alma the Younger's intent to destroy the Church of God. One day, in the company of the sons of Mosiah, Alma the younger was visited by an angel.

Mosiah 27:11–20

And as I said unto you, as they were going
about rebelling against God, behold, the
angel of the Lord appeared unto them; and he de-
scended as it were in a cloud; and he spake as it
were with a voice of thunder, which caused the
earth to shake upon which they stood;
12 And so great was their astonishment, that they
fell to the earth, and understood not the words
which he spake unto them.
13 Nevertheless he cried again, saying: Alma,
arise and stand forth, for why persecutest thou the
church of God? For the Lord hath said: This is
my church, and I will establish it; and nothing
shall overthrow it, save it is the transgression of
my people.
14 And again, the angel said: Behold, the Lord
hath heard the prayers of his people, and also
the prayers of his servant, Alma, who is thy fa-
ther; for he has prayed with much faith concern-
ing thee that thou mightest be brought to the
knowledge of the truth; therefore, for this pur-
pose have I come to convince thee of the power
and authority of God, that the prayers of his
servants might be answered according to their
faith.
15 And now behold, can ye dispute the power
of God? For behold, doth not my voice shake the
earth? And can ye not also behold me before you?
And I am sent from God.
16 Now I say unto thee: Go, and remember the
captivity of thy fathers in the land of Helam, and
in the land of Nephi; and remember how great
things he has done for them; for they were in
bondage, and he has delivered them. And now I
say unto thee, Alma, go thy way, and seek to de-
stroy the church no more, that their prayers may
be answered, and this even if thou wilt of thyself
be cast off.
17 And now it came to pass that these were the
last words which the angel spake unto Alma, and
he departed.
18 And now Alma and those that were with him
fell again to the earth, for great was their astonish-
ment; for with their own eyes they had beheld an
angel of the Lord; and his voice was as thunder,
which shook the earth; and they knew that there
was nothing save the power of God that could
shake the earth and cause it to tremble as though
it would part asunder.
19 And now the astonishment of Alma was so
great that he became dumb, that he could not
open his mouth; yea, and he became weak, even
that he could not move his hands; therefore he was
taken by those that were with him, and carried
helpless, even until he was laid before his father.
20 And they rehearsed unto his father all that had
happened unto them; and his father rejoiced, for
he knew that it was the power of God.

What prompted the angel's visit to Alma the Younger? Why do you think the angel commanded Alma to "remember the captivity of [his] fathers in the land of Helam"? What events and experiences can you remember to help strengthen your own testimony?

ALMA THE YOUNGER ARISES AND TESTIFIES OF BEING REDEEMED OF THE LORD

Following the visit from the angel, Alma the Younger lay unconscious. He was brought to his father, who commanded the people to gather together while he and the priests fasted for the return of his son's strength. As you read, consider the words Alma used to describe the pain he felt as a result of his sins and the relief he felt as the Lord forgave him.

Mosiah 27:23–32

And it came to pass after they had fasted and prayed for the space of two days and two nights, the limbs of Alma received their strength, and he stood up and began to speak unto them, bidding them to be of good comfort:

24 For, said he, I have repented of my sins, and have been redeemed of the Lord; behold I am born of the Spirit.

25 And the Lord said unto me: Marvel not that all mankind, yea, men and women, all nations, kindreds, tongues and people, must be born again; yea, born of God, changed from their carnal and fallen state, to a state of righteousness, being redeemed of God, becoming his sons and daughters;

26 And thus they become new creatures; and unless they do this, they can in nowise inherit the kingdom of God.

27 I say unto you, unless this be the case, they must be cast off; and this I know, because I was like to be cast off.

28 Nevertheless, after wading through much tribulation, repenting nigh unto death, the Lord in mercy hath seen fit to snatch me out of an everlasting burning, and I am born of God.

29 My soul hath been redeemed from the gall of bitterness and bonds of iniquity. I was in the darkest abyss; but now I behold the marvelous light of God. My soul was racked with eternal torment; but I am snatched, and my soul is pained no more.

30 I rejected my Redeemer, and denied that which had been spoken of by our fathers; but now that they may foresee that he will come, and that he remembereth every creature of his creating, he will make himself manifest unto all.

31 Yea, every knee shall bow, and every tongue confess before him. Yea, even at the last day, when all men shall stand to be judged of him, then shall they confess that he is God; then shall they confess, who live without God in the world, that the judgment of an everlasting punishment is just upon them; and they shall quake, and tremble, and shrink beneath the glance of his all-searching eye.

32 And now it came to pass that Alma began from this time forward to teach the people, and those who were with Alma at the time the angel appeared unto them, traveling round about through all the land, publishing to all the people the things which they had heard and seen, and preaching the word of God in much tribulation, being greatly persecuted by those who were unbelievers, being smitten by many of them.

How did Alma describe the pain from his sins and his relief as the Lord forgave him? What does Alma's conversion teach you about the Lord's desire and ability to forgive even those as wicked as Alma was? According to Alma, what must we do to "inherit the kingdom of God"?

THE SONS OF MOSIAH DESIRE TO PREACH SALVATION AMONG THE LAMANITES

Following their missionary efforts in the land of Zarahemla, the sons of Mosiah—Ammon, Aaron, Omner, and Himni—sought further opportunities to share the gospel.

Mosiah 28:1–8

Now it came to pass that after the sons of Mosiah had done all these things, they took a small number with them and returned to their father, the king, and desired of him that he would grant unto them that they might, with these whom they had selected, go up to the land of Nephi that they might preach the things which they had heard, and that they might impart the word of God to their brethren, the Lamanites—

2 That perhaps they might bring them to the knowledge of the Lord their God, and convince them of the iniquity of their fathers; and that perhaps they might cure them of their hatred towards the Nephites, that they might also be brought to rejoice in the Lord their God, that they might become friendly to one another, and that there should be no more contentions in all the land which the Lord their God had given them.

3 Now they were desirous that salvation should be declared to every creature, for they could not bear that any human soul should perish; yea, even the very thoughts that any soul should endure endless torment did cause them to quake and tremble.

4 And thus did the Spirit of the Lord work upon them, for they were the very vilest of sinners. And the Lord saw fit in his infinite mercy to spare them; nevertheless they suffered much anguish of soul because of their iniquities, suffering much and fearing that they should be cast off forever.

5 And it came to pass that they did plead with their father many days that they might go up to the land of Nephi.

6 And king Mosiah went and inquired of the Lord if he should let his sons go up among the Lamanites to preach the word.

7 And the Lord said unto Mosiah: Let them go up, for many shall believe on their words, and they shall have eternal life; and I will deliver thy sons out of the hands of the Lamanites.

8 And it came to pass that Mosiah granted that they might go and do according to their request.

Why did the sons of Mosiah want to share the gospel with the Lamanites? How can you develop a desire to share the gospel with others? What blessings did the Lord promise the sons of Mosiah for sharing the gospel with the Lamanites?

KING MOSIAH WARNS OF THE SPIRITUAL DANGERS OF WICKED KINGS

As King Mosiah became old, he began looking for someone to succeed him as king. When each of his sons refused the title, he advised his people that instead of a king, a system of judges would serve them better. The people appointed judges—including Alma the Younger as the first chief judge—and a period known as the "reign of judges" began. King Mosiah then counseled the people pertaining to kings and righteousness.

MOSIAH 29:12–13, 16–20, 26–27, 31–32

Now it is better that a man should be judged of God than of man, for the judgments of God are always just, but the judgments of man are not always just.

13 Therefore, if it were possible that you could have just men to be your kings, who would establish the laws of God, and judge this people according to his commandments, yea, if ye could have men for your kings who would do even as my father Benjamin did for this people—I say unto you, if this could always be the case then it would be expedient that ye should always have kings to rule over you.

16 Now I say unto you, that because all men are not just it is not expedient that ye should have a king or kings to rule over you.

17 For behold, how much iniquity doth one wicked king cause to be committed, yea, and what great destruction!

18 Yea, remember king Noah, his wickedness and his abominations, and also the wickedness and abominations of his people. Behold what great destruction did come upon them; and also because of their iniquities they were brought into bondage.

19 And were it not for the interposition of their all-wise Creator, and this because of their sincere repentance, they must unavoidably remain in bondage until now.

20 But behold, he did deliver them because they did humble themselves before him; and because they cried mightily unto him he did deliver them out of bondage; and thus doth the Lord work with his power in all cases among the children of men, extending the arm of mercy towards them that put their trust in him.

26 Now it is not common that the voice of the people desireth anything contrary to that which is right; but it is common for the lesser part of the people to desire that which is not right; therefore this shall ye observe and make it your law—to do your business by the voice of the people.

27 And if the time comes that the voice of the people doth choose iniquity, then is the time that the judgments of God will come upon you; yea, then is the time he will visit you with great destruction even as he has hitherto visited this land.

31 For behold I say unto you, the sins of many people have been caused by the iniquities of their kings; therefore their iniquities are answered upon the heads of their kings.

32 And now I desire that this inequality should be no more in this land, especially among this my people; but I desire that this land be a land of liberty, and every man may enjoy his rights and privileges alike, so long as the Lord sees fit that we may live and inherit the land, yea, even as long as any of our posterity remains upon the face of the land.

What are the consequences when the majority of people choose wickedness? How can a country or group of people qualify for the Lord's help and mercy? What can you do to be an influence for righteousness in your community?

The Book of Alma

NEHOR INTRODUCES PRIESTCRAFT AMONG THE NEPHITES AND IS PUT TO DEATH FOR MURDER

It had been 509 years since Lehi and his family left Jerusalem and was now about 91 years before the birth of Jesus Christ. Alma the Elder and King Mosiah both died in their old age, and a system of judges now governed the people of Zarahemla, with Alma the Younger as chief judge. At this time, a strong and persuasive man named Nehor began proclaiming that people need not fear and tremble, for God would redeem all men. He also taught that priests and teachers should be paid for their work. Many Nephites believed Nehor and gave him money, which he used to buy costly apparel and establish a church. During his preaching, Nehor contended with a righteous man named Gideon, slayed Gideon with the sword, and was brought before Alma to be judged.

ALMA 1:11–16

And it came to pass that he stood before Alma and pled for himself with much boldness.
12 But Alma said unto him: Behold, this is the first time that priestcraft has been introduced among this people. And behold, thou art not only guilty of priestcraft, but hast endeavored to enforce it by the sword; and were priestcraft to be enforced among this people it would prove their entire destruction.
13 And thou hast shed the blood of a righteous man, yea, a man who has done much good among this people; and were we to spare thee his blood would come upon us for vengeance.
14 Therefore thou art condemned to die, according to the law which has been given us by Mosiah, our last king; and it has been acknowledged by this people; therefore this people must abide by the law.
15 And it came to pass that they took him; and his name was Nehor; and they carried him upon the top of the hill Manti, and there he was caused, or rather did acknowledge, between the heavens and the earth, that what he had taught to the people was contrary to the word of God; and there he suffered an ignominious death.
16 Nevertheless, this did not put an end to the spreading of priestcraft through the land; for there were many who loved the vain things of the world, and they went forth preaching false doctrines; and this they did for the sake of riches and honor.

The Bible Dictionary defines priestcraft as "men preaching and setting themselves up for a light to the world that they may get gain and praise of the world." What examples of priestcraft have you seen in the world today? What should we desire if we are called to teach and lead in Christ's Church?

NEPHITE CHURCH MEMBERS ENDURE PERSECUTION AND SUPPORT ONE ANOTHER IN HUMILITY

In Zarahemla, vanity and pride increased among those who did not belong to the Church as they sought for riches and honor.

ALMA 1:19–20, 25–27, 29–30

But it came to pass that whosoever did
not belong to the church of God began
to persecute those that did belong to the church
of God, and had taken upon them the name of
Christ.
20 Yea, they did persecute them, and afflict them
with all manner of words, and this because of
their humility; because they were not proud in
their own eyes, and because they did impart the
word of God, one with another, without money
and without price.
25 Now this was a great trial to those that did
stand fast in the faith; nevertheless, they were
steadfast and immovable in keeping the com-
mandments of God, and they bore with patience
the persecution which was heaped upon them.
26 And when the priests left their labor to im-
part the word of God unto the people, the people
also left their labors to hear the word of God. And
when the priest had imparted unto them the word
of God they all returned again diligently unto
their labors; and the priest, not esteeming himself
above his hearers, for the preacher was no better
than the hearer, neither was the teacher any bet-
ter than the learner; and thus they were all equal,
and they did all labor, every man according to his
strength.
27 And they did impart of their substance, every
man according to that which he had, to the poor,
and the needy, and the sick, and the afflicted; and
they did not wear costly apparel, yet they were
neat and comely.
29 And now, because of the steadiness of the
church they began to be exceedingly rich, having
abundance of all things whatsoever they stood in
need—an abundance of flocks and herds, and fat-
lings of every kind, and also abundance of grain,
and of gold, and of silver, and of precious things,
and abundance of silk and fine-twined linen, and
all manner of good homely cloth.
30 And thus, in their prosperous circumstances,
they did not send away any who were naked, or
that were hungry, or that were athirst, or that
were sick, or that had not been nourished; and
they did not set their hearts upon riches; there-
fore they were liberal to all, both old and young,
both bond and free, both male and female,
whether out of the church or in the church, hav-
ing no respect to persons as to those who stood
in need.

What persecutions might you face because of your beliefs? How can you be "steadfast and immovable" like the Nephites when persecutions come? What persecutions do others experience? How can we be sensitive to them and defend them? When the Nephites were blessed with riches, what did they do with those riches?

ALMA EXORTS PRIDEFUL CHURCH MEMBERS TO REMEMBER THE DELIVERANCE OF THEIR FATHERS

In the fifth year of the reign of the judges, a wicked man named Amlici attempted to establish himself as king over the Nephites. Those who supported Amlici broke off from the Nephites, made Amlici their king, and joined the Lamanites in war against the Nephites. Alma led the Nephite forces and slew Amlici in battle. Tens of thousands of people were killed, and the Lamanite army was driven out of Zarahemla. Peace was established in the land, but Church members soon began to be lifted up in pride and contention due to their many riches. Alma was troubled, designated Nephihah to be the chief judge, and began traveling throughout Zarahemla to stir the Church members up in remembrance of their duty.

Alma 5:2–8

And these are the words which he spake
to the people in the church which was
established in the city of Zarahemla, according to
his own record, saying:
3 I, Alma, having been consecrated by my father,
Alma, to be a high priest over the church of God,
he having power and authority from God to do
these things, behold, I say unto you that he began
to establish a church in the land which was in the
borders of Nephi; yea, the land which was called
the land of Mormon; yea, and he did baptize his
brethren in the waters of Mormon.
4 And behold, I say unto you, they were deliv-
ered out of the hands of the people of king Noah,
by the mercy and power of God.
5 And behold, after that, they were brought
into bondage by the hands of the Lamanites in
the wilderness; yea, I say unto you, they were in
captivity, and again the Lord did deliver them
out of bondage by the power of his word; and we
were brought into this land, and here we began to
establish the church of God throughout this land
also.
6 And now behold, I say unto you, my breth-
ren, you that belong to this church, have you
sufficiently retained in remembrance the captiv-
ity of your fathers? Yea, and have you sufficiently
retained in remembrance his mercy and long-
suffering towards them? And moreover, have ye
sufficiently retained in remembrance that he has
delivered their souls from hell?
7 Behold, he changed their hearts; yea, he awak-
ened them out of a deep sleep, and they awoke
unto God. Behold, they were in the midst of
darkness; nevertheless, their souls were illumi-
nated by the light of the everlasting word; yea,
they were encircled about by the bands of death,
and the chains of hell, and an everlasting destruc-
tion did await them.
8 And now I ask of you, my brethren, were they
destroyed? Behold, I say unto you, Nay, they were
not.

Alma pleaded with the Nephites to remember how their ancestors had been delivered by the Lord. What blessings of deliverance have you and your family experienced? How can remembering blessings from the Lord help you remain humble and committed to God?

ALMA ASKS CHURCH MEMBERS IF THEY HAVE EXPERIENCED A MIGHTY CHANGE IN THEIR HEARTS

As Alma stirred the Church members up in remembrance of their duty, he continued by speaking of the experiences of their fathers.

ALMA 5:9–15

And again I ask, were the bands of death
broken, and the chains of hell which en-
circled them about, were they loosed? I say unto
you, Yea, they were loosed, and their souls did ex-
pand, and they did sing redeeming love. And I say
unto you that they are saved.
10 And now I ask of you on what conditions are
they saved? Yea, what grounds had they to hope
for salvation? What is the cause of their being
loosed from the bands of death, yea, and also the
chains of hell?
11 Behold, I can tell you—did not my father
Alma believe in the words which were delivered
by the mouth of Abinadi? And was he not a holy
prophet? Did he not speak the words of God, and
my father Alma believe them?
12 And according to his faith there was a mighty
change wrought in his heart. Behold I say unto
you that this is all true.
13 And behold, he preached the word unto your
fathers, and a mighty change was also wrought in
their hearts, and they humbled themselves and
put their trust in the true and living God. And
behold, they were faithful until the end; therefore
they were saved.
14 And now behold, I ask of you, my brethren of
the church, have ye spiritually been born of God?
Have ye received his image in your countenances?
Have ye experienced this mighty change in your
hearts?
15 Do ye exercise faith in the redemption of him
who created you? Do you look forward with an
eye of faith, and view this mortal body raised in
immortality, and this corruption raised in incor-
ruption, to stand before God to be judged ac-
cording to the deeds which have been done in the
mortal body?

What did Alma's father do that allowed a mighty change to take place in his heart? Alma asks the Church members many questions to assess their faith and testimony (see verses 14 and 15). Answer these questions for yourself and discuss what you can do to strengthen each area.

ALMA TEACHES OF THE NEED TO BE PURIFIED FROM ALL SIN IN ORDER TO ENTER THE KINGDOM OF GOD

Alma continued to speak to the Church members in Zarahemla as he called them to repentance.

ALMA 5:16–25

I say unto you, can you imagine to your-
selves that ye hear the voice of the Lord,
saying unto you, in that day: Come unto me ye
blessed, for behold, your works have been the
works of righteousness upon the face of the earth?
17 Or do ye imagine to yourselves that ye can
lie unto the Lord in that day, and say—Lord, our
works have been righteous works upon the face of
the earth—and that he will save you?
18 Or otherwise, can ye imagine yourselves
brought before the tribunal of God with your
souls filled with guilt and remorse, having a re-
membrance of all your guilt, yea, a perfect remem-
brance of all your wickedness, yea, a remembrance
that ye have set at defiance the commandments
of God?
19 I say unto you, can ye look up to God at that
day with a pure heart and clean hands? I say unto
you, can you look up, having the image of God
engraven upon your countenances?
20 I say unto you, can ye think of being saved
when you have yielded yourselves to become sub-
jects to the devil?
21 I say unto you, ye will know at that day that
ye cannot be saved; for there can no man be saved
except his garments are washed white; yea, his
garments must be purified until they are cleansed
from all stain, through the blood of him of whom
it has been spoken by our fathers, who should
come to redeem his people from their sins.
22 And now I ask of you, my brethren, how will
any of you feel, if ye shall stand before the bar
of God, having your garments stained with blood
and all manner of filthiness? Behold, what will
these things testify against you?
23 Behold will they not testify that ye are mur-
derers, yea, and also that ye are guilty of all man-
ner of wickedness?
24 Behold, my brethren, do ye suppose that
such an one can have a place to sit down in the
kingdom of God, with Abraham, with Isaac, and
with Jacob, and also all the holy prophets, whose
garments are cleansed and are spotless, pure and
white?
25 I say unto you, Nay; except ye make our
Creator a liar from the beginning, or suppose that
he is a liar from the beginning, ye cannot sup-
pose that such can have place in the kingdom of
heaven; but they shall be cast out for they are the
children of the kingdom of the devil.

Picture yourself standing before the judgment bar of God. Knowing that event will actually take place one day, how do you want to act today? How can you have clean hands and a pure heart in a world filled with temptation and wickedness?

ALMA COMMANDS CHURCH MEMBERS TO BE STRIPPED OF PRIDE AND ENVY

Alma continued his discourse to the prideful Church members in Zarahemla.

ALMA 5:26–36

And now behold, I say unto you, my
brethren, if ye have experienced a change
of heart, and if ye have felt to sing the song of re-
deeming love, I would ask, can ye feel so now?
27 Have ye walked, keeping yourselves blameless
before God? Could ye say, if ye were called to die
at this time, within yourselves, that ye have been
sufficiently humble? That your garments have
been cleansed and made white through the blood
of Christ, who will come to redeem his people
from their sins?
28 Behold, are ye stripped of pride? I say unto
you, if ye are not ye are not prepared to meet
God. Behold ye must prepare quickly; for the
kingdom of heaven is soon at hand, and such an
one hath not eternal life.
29 Behold, I say, is there one among you who is
not stripped of envy? I say unto you that such an
one is not prepared; and I would that he should
prepare quickly, for the hour is close at hand, and
he knoweth not when the time shall come; for
such an one is not found guiltless.
30 And again I say unto you, is there one among
you that doth make a mock of his brother, or that
heapeth upon him persecutions?
31 Wo unto such an one, for he is not prepared,
and the time is at hand that he must repent or he
cannot be saved!
32 Yea, even wo unto all ye workers of iniquity;
repent, repent, for the Lord God hath spoken it!
33 Behold, he sendeth an invitation unto all
men, for the arms of mercy are extended towards
them, and he saith: Repent, and I will receive you.
34 Yea, he saith: Come unto me and ye shall par-
take of the fruit of the tree of life; yea, ye shall
eat and drink of the bread and the waters of life
freely;
35 Yea, come unto me and bring forth works of
righteousness, and ye shall not be hewn down and
cast into the fire—
36 For behold, the time is at hand that whoso-
ever bringeth forth not good fruit, or whosoever
doeth not the works of righteousness, the same
have cause to wail and mourn.

According to Alma, what does the Lord require of people in order to be received by Him? What can you do to become stripped of envy and pride? What promises does the Lord make to those who accept His invitation to repent?

ALMA COMMANDS CHURCH MEMBERS TO HEED THE VOICE OF THE GOOD SHEPHERD

Alma continued his discourse to the prideful Church members in Zarahemla.

ALMA 5:37–40, 43–48

O ye workers of iniquity; ye that are puffed
up in the vain things of the world, ye that
have professed to have known the ways of righ-
teousness nevertheless have gone astray, as sheep
having no shepherd, notwithstanding a shepherd
hath called after you and is still calling after you,
but ye will not hearken unto his voice!
38 Behold, I say unto you, that the good shep-
herd doth call you; yea, and in his own name he
doth call you, which is the name of Christ; and
if ye will not hearken unto the voice of the good
shepherd, to the name by which ye are called, be-
hold, ye are not the sheep of the good shepherd.
39 And now if ye are not the sheep of the good
shepherd, of what fold are ye? Behold, I say unto
you, that the devil is your shepherd, and ye are of
his fold; and now, who can deny this? Behold, I
say unto you, whosoever denieth this is a liar and
a child of the devil.
40 For I say unto you that whatsoever is good
cometh from God, and whatsoever is evil cometh
from the devil.
43 And now, my brethren, I would that ye should
hear me, for I speak in the energy of my soul; for
behold, I have spoken unto you plainly that ye
cannot err, or have spoken according to the com-
mandments of God.
44 For I am called to speak after this manner,
according to the holy order of God, which is in
Christ Jesus; yea, I am commanded to stand and
testify unto this people the things which have
been spoken by our fathers concerning the things
which are to come.
45 And this is not all. Do ye not suppose that
I know of these things myself? Behold, I testify
unto you that I do know that these things whereof
I have spoken are true. And how do ye suppose
that I know of their surety?
46 Behold, I say unto you they are made known
unto me by the Holy Spirit of God. Behold, I
have fasted and prayed many days that I might
know these things of myself. And now I do know
of myself that they are true; for the Lord God
hath made them manifest unto me by his Holy
Spirit; and this is the spirit of revelation which is
in me.
47 And moreover, I say unto you that it has thus
been revealed unto me, that the words which have
been spoken by our fathers are true, even so ac-
cording to the spirit of prophecy which is in me,
which is also by the manifestation of the Spirit of
God.
48 I say unto you, that I know of myself that
whatsoever I shall say unto you, concerning that
which is to come, is true; and I say unto you, that
I know that Jesus Christ shall come, yea, the Son,
the Only Begotten of the Father, full of grace, and
mercy, and truth. And behold, it is he that cometh
to take away the sins of the world, yea, the sins of
every man who steadfastly believeth on his name.

How did Alma gain his own understanding of Jesus Christ and His Atonement? What tools are available to help you gain your own testimony of Jesus Christ? What influence has the testimony of prophets and apostles had on strengthening your testimony?

ALMA COMMANDS CHURCH MEMBERS TO CEASE FROM PRIDE AND VANITY

Alma concluded his discourse to the prideful Church members in Zarahemla. As you read, look for the sins that Alma condemns and asks whether the people will "persist in."

ALMA 5:49, 53–57, 60–62

And now I say unto you that this is the
order after which I am called, yea, to
preach unto my beloved brethren, yea, and every
one that dwelleth in the land; yea, to preach unto
all, both old and young, both bond and free; yea,
I say unto you the aged, and also the middle aged,
and the rising generation; yea, to cry unto them
that they must repent and be born again.
53 And now my beloved brethren, I say unto you,
can ye withstand these sayings; yea, can ye lay aside
these things, and trample the Holy One under
your feet; yea, can ye be puffed up in the pride of
your hearts; yea, will ye still persist in the wearing
of costly apparel and setting your hearts upon the
vain things of the world, upon your riches?
54 Yea, will ye persist in supposing that ye are
better one than another; yea, will ye persist in
the persecution of your brethren, who humble
themselves and do walk after the holy order of
God, wherewith they have been brought into this
church, having been sanctified by the Holy Spirit,
and they do bring forth works which are meet for
repentance—
55 Yea, and will you persist in turning your backs
upon the poor, and the needy, and in withholding
your substance from them?
56 And finally, all ye that will persist in your
wickedness, I say unto you that these are they
who shall be hewn down and cast into the fire ex-
cept they speedily repent.
57 And now I say unto you, all you that are de-
sirous to follow the voice of the good shepherd,
come ye out from the wicked, and be ye separate,
and touch not their unclean things; and behold,
their names shall be blotted out, that the names
of the wicked shall not be numbered among the
names of the righteous, that the word of God
may be fulfilled, which saith: The names of the
wicked shall not be mingled with the names of
my people;
60 And now I say unto you that the good shep-
herd doth call after you; and if you will hearken
unto his voice he will bring you into his fold, and
ye are his sheep; and he commandeth you that ye
suffer no ravenous wolf to enter among you, that
ye may not be destroyed.
61 And now I, Alma, do command you in the
language of him who hath commanded me, that
ye observe to do the words which I have spoken
unto you.
62 I speak by way of command unto you that
belong to the church; and unto those who do not
belong to the church I speak by way of invitation,
saying: Come and be baptized unto repentance,
that ye also may be partakers of the fruit of the
tree of life.

Identify and discuss the sins that Alma invited the people to turn from. What examples of those same sins do you see in the world today? How can you avoid and overcome those temptations?

ALMA SPEAKS OF CHRIST SUFFERING THE TEMPTATIONS, INFIRMITIES, PAINS, AND DEATH OF MANKIND

After preaching repentance to Church members, Alma set the Church in order. Priests and elders were ordained, new members were baptized, and unrepentant members were removed. Alma then traveled to the city of Gideon and spoke to Church members of future events to come.

ALMA 7:7–13

For behold, I say unto you there be many
things to come; and behold, there is one
thing which is of more importance than they
all—for behold, the time is not far distant that the
Redeemer liveth and cometh among his people.
8 Behold, I do not say that he will come among
us at the time of his dwelling in his mortal taber-
nacle; for behold, the Spirit hath not said unto me
that this should be the case. Now as to this thing
I do not know; but this much I do know, that the
Lord God hath power to do all things which are
according to his word.
9 But behold, the Spirit hath said this much unto
me, saying: Cry unto this people, saying—Repent
ye, and prepare the way of the Lord, and walk in
his paths, which are straight; for behold, the king-
dom of heaven is at hand, and the Son of God
cometh upon the face of the earth.
10 And behold, he shall be born of Mary, at
Jerusalem which is the land of our forefathers, she
being a virgin, a precious and chosen vessel, who
shall be overshadowed and conceive by the power
of the Holy Ghost, and bring forth a son, yea,
even the Son of God.
11 And he shall go forth, suffering pains and af-
flictions and temptations of every kind; and this
that the word might be fulfilled which saith he
will take upon him the pains and the sicknesses
of his people.
12 And he will take upon him death, that he may
loose the bands of death which bind his people;
and he will take upon him their infirmities, that
his bowels may be filled with mercy, according to
the flesh, that he may know according to the flesh
how to succor his people according to their infir-
mities.
13 Now the Spirit knoweth all things; neverthe-
less the Son of God suffereth according to the
flesh that he might take upon him the sins of his
people, that he might blot out their transgressions
according to the power of his deliverance; and
now behold, this is the testimony which is in me.

Alma taught that Christ would take upon Himself many things for us. What are they, and why did Christ do this for us? What do you learn from this passage about Christ's ability to help you in all things? Share experiences when you have felt Christ's help in various types of trials.

ALMA INVITES CHURCH MEMBERS TO BE HUMBLE, SUBMISSIVE, AND GENTLE

Alma continued his address to the Church members in Gideon. As you read these verses, look for a list of attributes Alma invited the people to adopt.

ALMA 7:14–17, 19–20, 23–25

Now I say unto you that ye must repent, and be born again; for the Spirit saith if ye are not born again ye cannot inherit the kingdom of heaven; therefore come and be baptized unto repentance, that ye may be washed from your sins, that ye may have faith on the Lamb of God, who taketh away the sins of the world, who is mighty to save and to cleanse from all unrighteousness.

15 Yea, I say unto you come and fear not, and lay aside every sin, which easily doth beset you, which doth bind you down to destruction, yea, come and go forth, and show unto your God that ye are willing to repent of your sins and enter into a covenant with him to keep his commandments, and witness it unto him this day by going into the waters of baptism.

16 And whosoever doeth this, and keepeth the commandments of God from thenceforth, the same will remember that I say unto him, yea, he will remember that I have said unto him, he shall have eternal life, according to the testimony of the Holy Spirit, which testifieth in me.

17 And now my beloved brethren, do you believe these things? Behold, I say unto you, yea, I know that ye believe them; and the way that I know that ye believe them is by the manifestation of the Spirit which is in me. And now because your faith is strong concerning that, yea, concerning the things which I have spoken, great is my joy.

19 For I perceive that ye are in the paths of righteousness; I perceive that ye are in the path which leads to the kingdom of God; yea, I perceive that ye are making his paths straight.

20 I perceive that it has been made known unto you, by the testimony of his word, that he cannot walk in crooked paths; neither doth he vary from that which he hath said; neither hath he a shadow of turning from the right to the left, or from that which is right to that which is wrong; therefore, his course is one eternal round.

23 And now I would that ye should be humble, and be submissive and gentle; easy to be entreated; full of patience and long-suffering; being temperate in all things; being diligent in keeping the commandments of God at all times; asking for whatsoever things ye stand in need, both spiritual and temporal; always returning thanks unto God for whatsoever things ye do receive.

24 And see that ye have faith, hope, and charity, and then ye will always abound in good works.

25 And may the Lord bless you, and keep your garments spotless, that ye may at last be brought to sit down with Abraham, Isaac, and Jacob, and the holy prophets who have been ever since the world began, having your garments spotless even as their garments are spotless, in the kingdom of heaven to go no more out.

What attributes did Alma invite his listeners to adopt? Discuss the meaning of each one. What are some ways you can develop and show these qualities in your life?

ALMA AND AMULEK PREACH REPENTANCE TO THE PEOPLE OF AMMONIHAH

After departing from the city of Gideon, Alma preached the gospel in the land of Melek and baptized many people. He then journeyed to the land of Ammonihah, where the people reviled him, spit on him, and cast him out. Alma was greatly saddened by the people's wickedness and was visited by the same angel that had called him to repentance. The angel praised Alma for his diligence in keeping God's commandments and told him to return to the city of Ammonihah. Upon entering the city, Alma was met by a man named Amulek who took Alma into his house, fed him, and told him that an angel had foretold Alma's arrival. Together, Alma and Amulek began preaching repentance among the people of Ammonihah. Alma was the first to speak to a gathering of people.

Alma 9:8–14

Behold, O ye wicked and perverse generation, how have ye forgotten the tradition of your fathers; yea, how soon ye have forgotten the commandments of God.

9 Do ye not remember that our father, Lehi, was brought out of Jerusalem by the hand of God? Do ye not remember that they were all led by him through the wilderness?

10 And have ye forgotten so soon how many times he delivered our fathers out of the hands of their enemies, and preserved them from being destroyed, even by the hands of their own brethren?

11 Yea, and if it had not been for his matchless power, and his mercy, and his long-suffering towards us, we should unavoidably have been cut off from the face of the earth long before this period of time, and perhaps been consigned to a state of endless misery and woe.

12 Behold, now I say unto you that he commandeth you to repent; and except ye repent, ye can in nowise inherit the kingdom of God. But behold, this is not all—he has commanded you to repent, or he will utterly destroy you from off the face of the earth; yea, he will visit you in his anger, and in his fierce anger he will not turn away.

13 Behold, do ye not remember the words which he spake unto Lehi, saying that: Inasmuch as ye shall keep my commandments, ye shall prosper in the land? And again it is said that: Inasmuch as ye will not keep my commandments ye shall be cut off from the presence of the Lord.

14 Now I would that ye should remember, that inasmuch as the Lamanites have not kept the commandments of God, they have been cut off from the presence of the Lord. Now we see that the word of the Lord has been verified in this thing, and the Lamanites have been cut off from his presence, from the beginning of their transgressions in the land.

What events and truths did Alma say the people needed to remember? Alma spoke of the Lamanites being "cut off from the presence of the Lord." What does that mean? How can we ensure we are not cut off from the Lord's presence?

ALMA REMINDS THE PEOPLE OF AMMONIHAH OF THEIR OBLIGATIONS TO THE LORD

Alma continued his address to the wicked people of Ammonihah. As you read, consider the many ways the Lord had blessed and delivered the people before they became wicked.

Alma 9:18–23, 28

But behold, I say unto you that if ye
persist in your wickedness that your
days shall not be prolonged in the land, for the
Lamanites shall be sent upon you; and if ye repent
not they shall come in a time when you know
not, and ye shall be visited with utter destruction;
and it shall be according to the fierce anger of the
Lord.
19 For he will not suffer you that ye shall live
in your iniquities, to destroy his people. I say
unto you, Nay; he would rather suffer that the
Lamanites might destroy all his people who are
called the people of Nephi, if it were possible that
they could fall into sins and transgressions, after
having had so much light and so much knowledge
given unto them of the Lord their God;
20 Yea, after having been such a highly favored
people of the Lord; yea, after having been favored
above every other nation, kindred, tongue, or
people; after having had all things made known
unto them, according to their desires, and their
faith, and prayers, of that which has been, and
which is, and which is to come;
21 Having been visited by the Spirit of God; hav-
ing conversed with angels, and having been spo-
ken unto by the voice of the Lord; and having the
spirit of prophecy, and the spirit of revelation, and
also many gifts, the gift of speaking with tongues,
and the gift of preaching, and the gift of the Holy
Ghost, and the gift of translation;
22 Yea, and after having been delivered of God
out of the land of Jerusalem, by the hand of the
Lord; having been saved from famine, and from
sickness, and all manner of diseases of every kind;
and they having waxed strong in battle, that they
might not be destroyed; having been brought out
of bondage time after time, and having been kept
and preserved until now; and they have been pros-
pered until they are rich in all manner of things—
23 And now behold I say unto you, that if this
people, who have received so many blessings from
the hand of the Lord, should transgress contrary
to the light and knowledge which they do have, I
say unto you that if this be the case, that if they
should fall into transgression, it would be far
more tolerable for the Lamanites than for them.
28 Therefore, prepare ye the way of the Lord, for
the time is at hand that all men shall reap a re-
ward of their works, according to that which they
have been—if they have been righteous they shall
reap the salvation of their souls, according to the
power and deliverance of Jesus Christ; and if they
have been evil they shall reap the damnation of
their souls, according to the power and captiva-
tion of the devil.

How had the Lord favored, blessed, and delivered the people of Ammonihah? Why do you think it would be better for the Lamanites to transgress than those who had been richly blessed? How are we obligated to the Lord for the blessings He has given us?

AMULEK SPEAKS OF BEING BLESSED BY EMBRACING THE LORD'S WORD

After Alma boldly declared repentance to the people of Ammonihah, the people were angry and attempted to seize him, but the Lord protected him from being taken. Amulek then spoke to the people.

Alma 10:1, 4–12

Now these are the words which Amulek
preached unto the people who were in
the land of Ammonihah, saying:
4 And behold, I am also a man of no small rep-
utation among all those who know me; yea, and
behold, I have many kindreds and friends, and I
have also acquired much riches by the hand of my
industry.
5 Nevertheless, after all this, I never have known
much of the ways of the Lord, and his mysteries
and marvelous power. I said I never had known
much of these things; but behold, I mistake, for
I have seen much of his mysteries and his mar-
velous power; yea, even in the preservation of the
lives of this people.
6 Nevertheless, I did harden my heart, for I was
called many times and I would not hear; there-
fore I knew concerning these things, yet I would
not know; therefore I went on rebelling against
God, in the wickedness of my heart, even until
the fourth day of this seventh month, which is in
the tenth year of the reign of the judges.
7 As I was journeying to see a very near kindred,
behold an angel of the Lord appeared unto me
and said: Amulek, return to thine own house,
for thou shalt feed a prophet of the Lord; yea, a
holy man, who is a chosen man of God; for he
has fasted many days because of the sins of this
people, and he is an hungered, and thou shalt re-
ceive him into thy house and feed him, and he
shall bless thee and thy house; and the blessing of
the Lord shall rest upon thee and thy house.
8 And it came to pass that I obeyed the voice of
the angel, and returned towards my house. And
as I was going thither I found the man whom the
angel said unto me: Thou shalt receive into thy
house—and behold it was this same man who has
been speaking unto you concerning the things of
God.
9 And the angel said unto me he is a holy man;
wherefore I know he is a holy man because it was
said by an angel of God.
10 And again, I know that the things whereof
he hath testified are true; for behold I say unto
you, that as the Lord liveth, even so has he sent
his angel to make these things manifest unto me;
and this he has done while this Alma hath dwelt
at my house.
11 For behold, he hath blessed mine house, he
hath blessed me, and my women, and my chil-
dren, and my father and my kinsfolk; yea, even
all my kindred hath he blessed, and the blessing
of the Lord hath rested upon us according to the
words which he spake.
12 And now, when Amulek had spoken these
words the people began to be astonished, seeing
there was more than one witness who testified of
the things whereof they were accused, and also of
the things which were to come, according to the
spirit of prophecy which was in them.

Though he had seen the marvelous power of God, Amulek initially hardened his heart against the truth. What can you do to see, hear, and embrace evidence of God's "marvelous works" in your own life? What difference does it make when you not only hear God's words but act on them?

AMULEK CONDEMNS HYPOCRISY AND SPEAKS OF THE PRAYERS OF THE RIGHTEOUS

As Amulek proclaimed his testimony to the wicked people of Ammonihah, many began to be astonished. But others sought to question Amulek in hopes he would contradict himself or say something unlawful and could therefore be cast into prison.

ALMA 10:17–27

Now they knew not that Amulek could
know of their designs. But it came to
pass as they began to question him, he perceived
their thoughts, and he said unto them: O ye
wicked and perverse generation, ye lawyers and
hypocrites, for ye are laying the foundations of
the devil; for ye are laying traps and snares to
catch the holy ones of God.
18 Ye are laying plans to pervert the ways of the
righteous, and to bring down the wrath of God
upon your heads, even to the utter destruction of
this people.
19 Yea, well did Mosiah say, who was our last
king, when he was about to deliver up the king-
dom, having no one to confer it upon, causing
that this people should be governed by their
own voices—yea, well did he say that if the time
should come that the voice of this people should
choose iniquity, that is, if the time should come
that this people should fall into transgression,
they would be ripe for destruction.
20 And now I say unto you that well doth the
Lord judge of your iniquities; well doth he cry
unto this people, by the voice of his angels: Repent
ye, repent, for the kingdom of heaven is at hand.
21 Yea, well doth he cry, by the voice of his an-
gels that: I will come down among my people,
with equity and justice in my hands.
22 Yea, and I say unto you that if it were not for
the prayers of the righteous, who are now in the
land, that ye would even now be visited with utter
destruction; yet it would not be by flood, as were
the people in the days of Noah, but it would be
by famine, and by pestilence, and the sword.
23 But it is by the prayers of the righteous that
ye are spared; now therefore, if ye will cast out the
righteous from among you then will not the Lord
stay his hand; but in his fierce anger he will come
out against you; then ye shall be smitten by fam-
ine, and by pestilence, and by the sword; and the
time is soon at hand except ye repent.
24 And now it came to pass that the people were
more angry with Amulek, and they cried out, say-
ing: This man doth revile against our laws which
are just, and our wise lawyers whom we have se-
lected.
25 But Amulek stretched forth his hand, and
cried the mightier unto them, saying: O ye
wicked and perverse generation, why hath Satan
got such great hold upon your hearts? Why will ye
yield yourselves unto him that he may have power
over you, to blind your eyes, that ye will not un-
derstand the words which are spoken, according
to their truth?
26 For behold, have I testified against your law?
Ye do not understand; ye say that I have spoken
against your law; but I have not, but I have spo-
ken in favor of your law, to your condemnation.
27 And now behold, I say unto you, that the
foundation of the destruction of this people is be-
ginning to be laid by the unrigh-
teousness of your lawyers
and your judges.

According to Amulek, what effect did righteous people and their prayers have upon the wicked? What consequences would come upon the wicked people if they were to cast out the righteous? How have the prayers of righteous people blessed your life? How have your prayers helped others?

AMULEK THWARTS ZEEZROM AND SPEAKS OF THE SON OF GOD SAVING PEOPLE FROM THEIR SINS

After being chastised by Amulek, the people of Ammonihah became angry. A wicked man named Zeezrom confronted Amulek with the intent to trick him into saying something contradictory to the law. Zeezrom offered Amulek a large sum of money to deny his testimony. As you read, look closely for the words Amulek used to describe how God would save His people.

ALMA 11:21–37

And this Zeezrom began to question
Amulek, saying: Will ye answer me
a few questions which I shall ask you? Now
Zeezrom was a man who was expert in the devices
of the devil, that he might destroy that which was
good; therefore, he said unto Amulek: Will ye an-
swer the questions which I shall put unto you?
22 And Amulek said unto him: Yea, if it be ac-
cording to the Spirit of the Lord, which is in me;
for I shall say nothing which is contrary to the
Spirit of the Lord. And Zeezrom said unto him:
Behold, here are six onties of silver, and all these
will I give thee if thou wilt deny the existence of a
Supreme Being.
23 Now Amulek said: O thou child of hell, why
tempt ye me? Knowest thou that the righteous
yieldeth to no such temptations?
24 Believest thou that there is no God? I say unto
you, Nay, thou knowest that there is a God, but
thou lovest that lucre more than him.
25 And now thou hast lied before God unto me.
Thou saidst unto me—Behold these six onties,
which are of great worth, I will give unto thee—
when thou hadst it in thy heart to retain them
from me; and it was only thy desire that I should
deny the true and living God, that thou mightest
have cause to destroy me. And now behold, for
this great evil thou shalt have thy reward.
26 And Zeezrom said unto him: Thou sayest
there is a true and living God?
27 And Amulek said: Yea, there is a true and liv-
ing God.
28 Now Zeezrom said: Is there more than one
God?
29 And he answered, No.
30 Now Zeezrom said unto him again: How
knowest thou these things?
31 And he said: An angel hath made them known
unto me.
32 And Zeezrom said again: Who is he that shall
come? Is it the Son of God?
33 And he said unto him, Yea.
34 And Zeezrom said again: Shall he save his
people in their sins? And Amulek answered and
said unto him: I say unto you he shall not, for it is
impossible for him to deny his word.
35 Now Zeezrom said unto the people: See that
ye remember these things; for he said there is but
one God; yet he saith that the Son of God shall
come, but he shall not save his people—as though
he had authority to command God.
36 Now Amulek saith again unto him: Behold
thou hast lied, for thou sayest that I spake as
though I had authority to command God because
I said he shall not save his people in their sins.
37 And I say unto you again that he cannot save
them in their sins; for I cannot deny his word,
and he hath said that no unclean thing can inherit
the kingdom of heaven; therefore, how can ye be
saved, except ye inherit the kingdom of heaven?
Therefore, ye cannot be saved in your sins.

Amulek taught that the Son of God would save people *from* their sins, not *in* their sins. What is the difference? Why is it significant? Zeezrom used many methods to try to trick Amulek, tempt him, and misinterpret his words. How can you respond to those who may criticize your beliefs or try to twist your words?

AMULEK TEACHES THE CONDITIONS OF REDEMPTION AND RESURRECTION

Amulek continued his debate with the wicked Zeezrom before the crowd of people in Ammonihah. As you read, look for Amulek's description of who will receive eternal life and who will be resurrected, as well as what happens when someone is resurrected.

Alma 11:38–46

Now Zeezrom saith again unto him: Is
the Son of God the very Eternal Father?
39 And Amulek said unto him: Yea, he is the
very Eternal Father of heaven and of earth, and all
things which in them are; he is the beginning and
the end, the first and the last;
40 And he shall come into the world to redeem
his people; and he shall take upon him the trans-
gressions of those who believe on his name; and
these are they that shall have eternal life, and sal-
vation cometh to none else.
41 Therefore the wicked remain as though there
had been no redemption made, except it be the
loosing of the bands of death; for behold, the day
cometh that all shall rise from the dead and stand
before God, and be judged according to their
works.
42 Now, there is a death which is called a tem-
poral death; and the death of Christ shall loose
the bands of this temporal death, that all shall be
raised from this temporal death.
43 The spirit and the body shall be reunited again
in its perfect form; both limb and joint shall be
restored to its proper frame, even as we now are at
this time; and we shall be brought to stand before
God, knowing even as we know now, and have a
bright recollection of all our guilt.
44 Now, this restoration shall come to all, both
old and young, both bond and free, both male
and female, both the wicked and the righteous;
and even there shall not so much as a hair of their
heads be lost; but every thing shall be restored
to its perfect frame, as it is now, or in the body,
and shall be brought and be arraigned before the
bar of Christ the Son, and God the Father, and
the Holy Spirit, which is one Eternal God, to be
judged according to their works, whether they be
good or whether they be evil.
45 Now, behold, I have spoken unto you con-
cerning the death of the mortal body, and also
concerning the resurrection of the mortal body.
I say unto you that this mortal body is raised
to an immortal body, that is from death, even
from the first death unto life, that they can die
no more; their spirits uniting with their bodies,
never to be divided; thus the whole becoming
spiritual and immortal, that they can no more
see corruption.
46 Now, when Amulek had finished these words
the people began again to be astonished, and
also Zeezrom began to tremble. And thus ended
the words of Amulek, or this is all that I have
written.

According to this passage, who will be resurrected? What happens when a mortal body is resurrected? Who does Amulek say will receive eternal life? What do we learn from these scriptures about the difference between the resurrection of the mortal body and receiving eternal life?

ALMA TEACHES THE PATTERN OF LEARNING THE MYSTERIES OF GOD

After Amulek had thwarted Zeezrom's attempt to trick him into contradicting himself, Zeezrom began to tremble with guilt. Alma then expounded on Amulek's teachings.

ALMA 12:2–11

Now the words that Alma spake unto
Zeezrom were heard by the people
round about; for the multitude was great, and he
spake on this wise:
3 Now Zeezrom, seeing that thou hast been
taken in thy lying and craftiness, for thou hast not
lied unto men only but thou hast lied unto God;
for behold, he knows all thy thoughts, and thou
seest that thy thoughts are made known unto us
by his Spirit;
4 And thou seest that we know that thy plan was
a very subtle plan, as to the subtlety of the devil,
for to lie and to deceive this people that thou
mightest set them against us, to revile us and to
cast us out—
5 Now this was a plan of thine adversary, and he
hath exercised his power in thee. Now I would
that ye should remember that what I say unto
thee I say unto all.
6 And behold I say unto you all that this was a
snare of the adversary, which he has laid to catch
this people, that he might bring you into subjec-
tion unto him, that he might encircle you about
with his chains, that he might chain you down to
everlasting destruction, according to the power of
his captivity.
7 Now when Alma had spoken these words,
Zeezrom began to tremble more exceedingly, for
he was convinced more and more of the power of
God; and he was also convinced that Alma and
Amulek had a knowledge of him, for he was con-
vinced that they knew the thoughts and intents
of his heart; for power was given unto them that
they might know of these things according to the
spirit of prophecy.
8 And Zeezrom began to inquire of them dili-
gently, that he might know more concerning the
kingdom of God. And he said unto Alma: What
does this mean which Amulek hath spoken con-
cerning the resurrection of the dead, that all shall
rise from the dead, both the just and the unjust,
and are brought to stand before God to be judged
according to their works?
9 And now Alma began to expound these things
unto him, saying: It is given unto many to know
the mysteries of God; nevertheless they are laid
under a strict command that they shall not im-
part only according to the portion of his word
which he doth grant unto the children of men,
according to the heed and diligence which they
give unto him.
10 And therefore, he that will harden his heart,
the same receiveth the lesser portion of the word;
and he that will not harden his heart, to him is
given the greater portion of the word, until it is
given unto him to know the mysteries of God
until he know them in full.
11 And they that will harden their hearts, to
them is given the lesser portion of the word until
they know nothing concerning his mysteries; and
then they are taken captive by the devil, and led
by his will down to destruction. Now this is what
is meant by the chains of hell.

Alma taught that those who obey the word of God are blessed with a greater understanding of God and His works. How is that evident in Alma and Amulek's teachings? How have you experienced that principle in your own life?

ALMA WARNS OF THE JUDGMENT TO COME TO THOSE WHO REJECT GOD'S WORD

Standing before the wicked crowd at Ammonihah, Alma continued to expound on Amulek's teachings.

ALMA 12:12–19

And Amulek hath spoken plainly concerning death, and being raised from this mortality to a state of immortality, and being brought before the bar of God, to be judged according to our works.

13 Then if our hearts have been hardened, yea, if we have hardened our hearts against the word, insomuch that it has not been found in us, then will our state be awful, for then we shall be condemned.

14 For our words will condemn us, yea, all our works will condemn us; we shall not be found spotless; and our thoughts will also condemn us; and in this awful state we shall not dare to look up to our God; and we would fain be glad if we could command the rocks and the mountains to fall upon us to hide us from his presence.

15 But this cannot be; we must come forth and stand before him in his glory, and in his power, and in his might, majesty, and dominion, and acknowledge to our everlasting shame that all his judgments are just; that he is just in all his works, and that he is merciful unto the children of men, and that he has all power to save every man that believeth on his name and bringeth forth fruit meet for repentance.

16 And now behold, I say unto you then cometh a death, even a second death, which is a spiritual death; then is a time that whosoever dieth in his sins, as to a temporal death, shall also die a spiritual death; yea, he shall die as to things pertaining unto righteousness.

17 Then is the time when their torments shall be as a lake of fire and brimstone, whose flame ascendeth up forever and ever; and then is the time that they shall be chained down to an everlasting destruction, according to the power and captivity of Satan, he having subjected them according to his will.

18 Then, I say unto you, they shall be as though there had been no redemption made; for they cannot be redeemed according to God's justice; and they cannot die, seeing there is no more corruption.

19 Now it came to pass that when Alma had made an end of speaking these words, the people began to be more astonished;

How did Alma define and describe the "second death" or "spiritual death"? How is it similar to physical death? How can you ensure that your heart is not hardened against the word of God?

ALMA EXPLAINS THE NEED FOR A PLAN OF REDEMPTION

Alma continued to expound on the teachings of Amulek as he taught the wicked crowd gathered in Ammonihah.

ALMA 12:24–30, 34–37

And we see that death comes upon mankind, yea, the death which has been spoken of by Amulek, which is the temporal death; nevertheless there was a space granted unto man in which he might repent; therefore this life became a probationary state; a time to prepare to meet God; a time to prepare for that endless state which has been spoken of by us, which is after the resurrection of the dead.

25 Now, if it had not been for the plan of redemption, which was laid from the foundation of the world, there could have been no resurrection of the dead; but there was a plan of redemption laid, which shall bring to pass the resurrection of the dead, of which has been spoken.

26 And now behold, if it were possible that our first parents could have gone forth and partaken of the tree of life they would have been forever miserable, having no preparatory state; and thus the plan of redemption would have been frustrated, and the word of God would have been void, taking none effect.

27 But behold, it was not so; but it was appointed unto men that they must die; and after death, they must come to judgment, even that same judgment of which we have spoken, which is the end.

28 And after God had appointed that these things should come unto man, behold, then he saw that it was expedient that man should know concerning the things whereof he had appointed unto them;

29 Therefore he sent angels to converse with them, who caused men to behold of his glory.

30 And they began from that time forth to call on his name; therefore God conversed with men, and made known unto them the plan of redemption, which had been prepared from the foundation of the world; and this he made known unto them according to their faith and repentance and their holy works.

34 Therefore, whosoever repenteth, and hardeneth not his heart, he shall have claim on mercy through mine Only Begotten Son, unto a remission of his sins; and these shall enter into my rest.

35 And whosoever will harden his heart and will do iniquity, behold, I swear in my wrath that he shall not enter into my rest.

36 And now, my brethren, behold I say unto you, that if ye will harden your hearts ye shall not enter into the rest of the Lord; therefore your iniquity provoketh him that he sendeth down his wrath upon you as in the first provocation, yea, according to his word in the last provocation as well as the first, to the everlasting destruction of your souls; therefore, according to his word, unto the last death, as well as the first.

37 And now, my brethren, seeing we know these things, and they are true, let us repent, and harden not our hearts, that we provoke not the Lord our God to pull down his wrath upon us in these his second commandments which he has given unto us; but let us enter into the rest of God, which is prepared according to his word.

According to Alma, why was a plan of redemption necessary? What events and blessings are made possible through the plan of redemption? Who are those who "shall have claim on mercy through mine Only Begotten Son"?

ALMA EXPLAINS THE HISTORY AND PURPOSE OF MEN BEING CALLED AS HIGH PRIESTS

Alma continued his discourse to the wicked crowd gathered in Ammonihah. As you read, look for the description of the kind of men who are entrusted with God's priesthood.

ALMA 13:1–9

And again, my brethren, I would cite your minds forward to the time when the Lord God gave these commandments unto his children; and I would that ye should remember that the Lord God ordained priests, after his holy order, which was after the order of his Son, to teach these things unto the people.

2 And those priests were ordained after the order of his Son, in a manner that thereby the people might know in what manner to look forward to his Son for redemption.

3 And this is the manner after which they were ordained—being called and prepared from the foundation of the world according to the foreknowledge of God, on account of their exceeding faith and good works; in the first place being left to choose good or evil; therefore they having chosen good, and exercising exceedingly great faith, are called with a holy calling, yea, with that holy calling which was prepared with, and according to, a preparatory redemption for such.

4 And thus they have been called to this holy calling on account of their faith, while others would reject the Spirit of God on account of the hardness of their hearts and blindness of their minds, while, if it had not been for this they might have had as great privilege as their brethren.

5 Or in fine, in the first place they were on the same standing with their brethren; thus this holy calling being prepared from the foundation of the world for such as would not harden their hearts, being in and through the atonement of the Only Begotten Son, who was prepared—

6 And thus being called by this holy calling, and ordained unto the high priesthood of the holy order of God, to teach his commandments unto the children of men, that they also might enter into his rest—

7 This high priesthood being after the order of his Son, which order was from the foundation of the world; or in other words, being without beginning of days or end of years, being prepared from eternity to all eternity, according to his foreknowledge of all things—

8 Now they were ordained after this manner—being called with a holy calling, and ordained with a holy ordinance, and taking upon them the high priesthood of the holy order, which calling, and ordinance, and high priesthood, is without beginning or end—

9 Thus they become high priests forever, after the order of the Son, the Only Begotten of the Father, who is without beginning of days or end of years, who is full of grace, equity, and truth. And thus it is. Amen.

According to Alma, what kind of men have been entrusted with God's priesthood? Who do you know who holds the priesthood and has these attributes? How have you been blessed through righteous priesthood holders?

ALMA SPEAKS OF MELCHIZEDEK'S EXAMPLE OF RIGHTEOUS PRIESTHOOD SERVICE

Alma continued to speak to the wicked crowd gathered in Ammonihah.

ALMA 13:10–19

Now, as I said concerning the holy order, or this high priesthood, there were many who were ordained and became high priests of God; and it was on account of their exceeding faith and repentance, and their righteousness before God, they choosing to repent and work righteousness rather than to perish;

11 Therefore they were called after this holy order, and were sanctified, and their garments were washed white through the blood of the Lamb.

12 Now they, after being sanctified by the Holy Ghost, having their garments made white, being pure and spotless before God, could not look upon sin save it were with abhorrence; and there were many, exceedingly great many, who were made pure and entered into the rest of the Lord their God.

13 And now, my brethren, I would that ye should humble yourselves before God, and bring forth fruit meet for repentance, that ye may also enter into that rest.

14 Yea, humble yourselves even as the people in the days of Melchizedek, who was also a high priest after this same order which I have spoken, who also took upon him the high priesthood forever.

15 And it was this same Melchizedek to whom Abraham paid tithes; yea, even our father Abraham paid tithes of one-tenth part of all he possessed.

16 Now these ordinances were given after this manner, that thereby the people might look forward on the Son of God, it being a type of his order, or it being his order, and this that they might look forward to him for a remission of their sins, that they might enter into the rest of the Lord.

17 Now this Melchizedek was a king over the land of Salem; and his people had waxed strong in iniquity and abomination; yea, they had all gone astray; they were full of all manner of wickedness;

18 But Melchizedek having exercised mighty faith, and received the office of the high priesthood according to the holy order of God, did preach repentance unto his people. And behold, they did repent; and Melchizedek did establish peace in the land in his days; therefore he was called the prince of peace, for he was the king of Salem; and he did reign under his father.

19 Now, there were many before him, and also there were many afterwards, but none were greater; therefore, of him they have more particularly made mention.

Melchizedek used the priesthood to serve and teach the people in his day. What latter-day priesthood and auxiliary leaders of the Church have had a personal impact on your life? What can you do to serve like these righteous men and women?

ALMA PLEADS WITH THE PEOPLE TO BE HUMBLE AND CAST OFF THEIR SINS

Alma concluded his remarks to the wicked people of Ammonihah.

ALMA 13:21–30

And now it came to pass that when Alma had said these words unto them, he stretched forth his hand unto them and cried with a mighty voice, saying: Now is the time to repent, for the day of salvation draweth nigh;

22 Yea, and the voice of the Lord, by the mouth of angels, doth declare it unto all nations; yea, doth declare it, that they may have glad tidings of great joy; yea, and he doth sound these glad tidings among all his people, yea, even to them that are scattered abroad upon the face of the earth; wherefore they have come unto us.

23 And they are made known unto us in plain terms, that we may understand, that we cannot err; and this because of our being wanderers in a strange land; therefore, we are thus highly favored, for we have these glad tidings declared unto us in all parts of our vineyard.

24 For behold, angels are declaring it unto many at this time in our land; and this is for the purpose of preparing the hearts of the children of men to receive his word at the time of his coming in his glory.

25 And now we only wait to hear the joyful news declared unto us by the mouth of angels, of his coming; for the time cometh, we know not how soon. Would to God that it might be in my day; but let it be sooner or later, in it I will rejoice.

26 And it shall be made known unto just and holy men, by the mouth of angels, at the time of his coming, that the words of our fathers may be fulfilled, according to that which they have spoken concerning him, which was according to the spirit of prophecy which was in them.

27 And now, my brethren, I wish from the inmost part of my heart, yea, with great anxiety even unto pain, that ye would hearken unto my words, and cast off your sins, and not procrastinate the day of your repentance;

28 But that ye would humble yourselves before the Lord, and call on his holy name, and watch and pray continually, that ye may not be tempted above that which ye can bear, and thus be led by the Holy Spirit, becoming humble, meek, submissive, patient, full of love and all long-suffering;

29 Having faith on the Lord; having a hope that ye shall receive eternal life; having the love of God always in your hearts, that ye may be lifted up at the last day and enter into his rest.

30 And may the Lord grant unto you repentance, that ye may not bring down his wrath upon you, that ye may not be bound down by the chains of hell, that ye may not suffer the second death.

What did Alma say would be the result of being humble and continually praying to God? Though many people in Ammonihah hated Alma, he patiently taught them and invited them to repent and find joy. What can you learn from this? How can you follow Alma's example in your life?

ALMA AND AMULEK WITNESS THE BURNING OF MANY BELIEVERS

At the conclusion of Alma's preaching, many people believed on his words and repented. But the majority of the people were angry because Alma and Amulek had spoken plainly of their wickedness. They bound Alma and Amulek, took them before the chief judge, and falsely accused them of reviling the law and speaking false doctrines. Zeezrom, who had repented, spoke in defense of Alma and Amulek but was cast out of the city with many other believers.

ALMA 14:8–17

And they brought their wives and chil-
dren together, and whosoever believed
or had been taught to believe in the word of God
they caused that they should be cast into the fire;
and they also brought forth their records which
contained the holy scriptures, and cast them into
the fire also, that they might be burned and de-
stroyed by fire.
9 And it came to pass that they took Alma and
Amulek, and carried them forth to the place of
martyrdom, that they might witness the destruc-
tion of those who were consumed by fire.
10 And when Amulek saw the pains of the
women and children who were consuming in the
fire, he also was pained; and he said unto Alma:
How can we witness this awful scene? Therefore
let us stretch forth our hands, and exercise the
power of God which is in us, and save them from
the flames.
11 But Alma said unto him: The Spirit con-
straineth me that I must not stretch forth mine
hand; for behold the Lord receiveth them up
unto himself, in glory; and he doth suffer that
they may do this thing, or that the people may do
this thing unto them, according to the hardness
of their hearts, that the judgments which he shall
exercise upon them in his wrath may be just; and
the blood of the innocent shall stand as a witness
against them, yea, and cry mightily against them
at the last day.
12 Now Amulek said unto Alma: Behold, per-
haps they will burn us also.
13 And Alma said: Be it according to the will of
the Lord. But, behold, our work is not finished;
therefore they burn us not.
14 Now it came to pass that when the bodies
of those who had been cast into the fire were
consumed, and also the records which were cast
in with them, the chief judge of the land came
and stood before Alma and Amulek, as they were
bound; and he smote them with his hand upon
their cheeks, and said unto them: After what ye
have seen, will ye preach again unto this people,
that they shall be cast into a lake of fire and brim-
stone?
15 Behold, ye see that ye had not power to save
those who had been cast into the fire; neither has
God saved them because they were of thy faith.
And the judge smote them again upon their
cheeks, and asked: What say ye for yourselves?
16 Now this judge was after the order and faith
of Nehor, who slew Gideon.
17 And it came to pass that Alma and Amulek
answered him nothing; and he smote them again,
and delivered them to the officers to be cast into
prison.

What reason did Alma give for not using the power of God to save the believers from being burned? What does this event teach you about agency and justice in the plan of salvation? How can you feel peace even amid persecution and trial?

ALMA AND AMULEK ARE DELIVERED FROM PRISON BY THE POWER OF GOD

After the believers in Ammonihah were burned by fire, Alma and Amulek were bound and cast into prison. They were stripped of their clothes and denied food and water. Wicked lawyers, judges, and priests came to the prison, beat Alma and Amulek, and mockingly asked why their God could not deliver them. This went on for many days as Alma and Amulek silently refused to respond to the taunting.

Alma 14:22–29

And many such things, yea, all manner
of such things did they say unto them;
and thus they did mock them for many days.
And they did withhold food from them that they
might hunger, and water that they might thirst;
and they also did take from them their clothes
that they were naked; and thus they were bound
with strong cords, and confined in prison.
23 And it came to pass after they had thus suf-
fered for many days, (and it was on the twelfth
day, in the tenth month, in the tenth year of the
reign of the judges over the people of Nephi) that
the chief judge over the land of Ammonihah and
many of their teachers and their lawyers went in
unto the prison where Alma and Amulek were
bound with cords.
24 And the chief judge stood before them, and
smote them again, and said unto them: If ye have
the power of God deliver yourselves from these
bands, and then we will believe that the Lord will
destroy this people according to your words.
25 And it came to pass that they all went forth
and smote them, saying the same words, even
until the last; and when the last had spoken unto
them the power of God was upon Alma and
Amulek, and they rose and stood upon their feet.
26 And Alma cried, saying: How long shall we
suffer these great afflictions, O Lord? O Lord,
give us strength according to our faith which is in
Christ, even unto deliverance. And they broke the
cords with which they were bound; and when the
people saw this, they began to flee, for the fear of
destruction had come upon them.
27 And it came to pass that so great was their
fear that they fell to the earth, and did not obtain
the outer door of the prison; and the earth shook
mightily, and the walls of the prison were rent in
twain, so that they fell to the earth; and the chief
judge, and the lawyers, and priests, and teachers,
who smote upon Alma and Amulek, were slain by
the fall thereof.
28 And Alma and Amulek came forth out of the
prison, and they were not hurt; for the Lord had
granted unto them power, according to their faith
which was in Christ. And they straightway came
forth out of the prison; and they were loosed
from their bands; and the prison had fallen to
the earth, and every soul within the walls thereof,
save it were Alma and Amulek, was slain; and they
straightway came forth into the city.
29 Now the people having heard a great noise
came running together by multitudes to know the
cause of it; and when they saw Alma and Amulek
coming forth out of the prison, and the walls
thereof had fallen to the earth, they were struck
with great fear, and fled from the presence of
Alma and Amulek even as a goat fleeth with her
young from two lions; and thus they did flee from
the presence of Alma and Amulek.

What words did Alma speak as he prayed to God for deliverance? How had Alma and Amulek shown faith in Christ? What experiences have you had in asking God to deliver you from trials?

ALMA HEALS ZEEZROM THROUGH FAITH IN JESUS CHRIST

After emerging from the fallen prison in Ammonihah, Alma and Amulek continued their journey.

ALMA 15:1–12

And it came to pass that Alma and
Amulek were commanded to depart
out of that city; and they departed, and came out
even into the land of Sidom; and behold, there
they found all the people who had departed out of
the land of Ammonihah, who had been cast out
and stoned, because they believed in the words of
Alma.
2 And they related unto them all that had hap-
pened unto their wives and children, and also
concerning themselves, and of their power of de-
liverance.
3 And also Zeezrom lay sick at Sidom, with a
burning fever, which was caused by the great trib-
ulations of his mind on account of his wickedness,
for he supposed that Alma and Amulek were no
more; and he supposed that they had been slain
because of his iniquity. And this great sin, and his
many other sins, did harrow up his mind until
it did become exceedingly sore, having no deliv-
erance; therefore he began to be scorched with a
burning heat.
4 Now, when he heard that Alma and Amulek
were in the land of Sidom, his heart began to take
courage; and he sent a message immediately unto
them, desiring them to come unto him.
5 And it came to pass that they went immedi-
ately, obeying the message which he had sent
unto them; and they went in unto the house unto
Zeezrom; and they found him upon his bed, sick,
being very low with a burning fever; and his mind
also was exceedingly sore because of his iniqui-
ties; and when he saw them he stretched forth his
hand, and besought them that they would heal
him.
6 And it came to pass that Alma said unto him,
taking him by the hand: Believest thou in the
power of Christ unto salvation?
7 And he answered and said: Yea, I believe all the
words that thou hast taught.
8 And Alma said: If thou believest in the redemp-
tion of Christ thou canst be healed.
9 And he said: Yea, I believe according to thy
words.
10 And then Alma cried unto the Lord, saying:
O Lord our God, have mercy on this man, and
heal him according to his faith which is in Christ.
11 And when Alma had said these words,
Zeezrom leaped upon his feet, and began to walk;
and this was done to the great astonishment of all
the people; and the knowledge of this went forth
throughout all the land of Sidom.
12 And Alma baptized Zeezrom unto the Lord;
and he began from that time forth to preach unto
the people.

What allowed Zeezrom to be healed? Alma, Amulek, and Zeezrom were each wicked and disobedient before their conversions. What do you learn from their repentance and their leadership after they were converted? What can this teach you about doing missionary work?

ALMA ESTABLISHES A CHURCH IN SIDOM AND ADMINISTERS TO AMULEK IN HIS HOUSE

After healing Zeezrom from his sickness, Alma organized a church in Sidom.

ALMA 15:13–18

And Alma established a church in the land of Sidom, and consecrated priests and teachers in the land, to baptize unto the Lord whosoever were desirous to be baptized.

14 And it came to pass that they were many; for they did flock in from all the region round about Sidom, and were baptized.

15 But as to the people that were in the land of Ammonihah, they yet remained a hard-hearted and a stiffnecked people; and they repented not of their sins, ascribing all the power of Alma and Amulek to the devil; for they were of the profession of Nehor, and did not believe in the repentance of their sins.

16 And it came to pass that Alma and Amulek, Amulek having forsaken all his gold, and silver, and his precious things, which were in the land of Ammonihah, for the word of God, he being rejected by those who were once his friends and also by his father and his kindred;

17 Therefore, after Alma having established the church at Sidom, seeing a great check, yea, seeing that the people were checked as to the pride of their hearts, and began to humble themselves before God, and began to assemble themselves together at their sanctuaries to worship God before the altar, watching and praying continually, that they might be delivered from Satan, and from death, and from destruction—

18 Now as I said, Alma having seen all these things, therefore he took Amulek and came over to the land of Zarahemla, and took him to his own house, and did administer unto him in his tribulations, and strengthened him in the Lord.

Amulek's commitment to his faith caused him to lose his wealth and many friends and family members. How can similar losses and trials happen today? What can you do to withstand trials and rejection?

THE PEOPLE OF AMMONIHAH ARE DESTROYED AND THE RIGHTEOUS NEPHITES PROSPER

About a year after Alma and Amulek departed from Ammonihah, an army of Lamanites invaded Ammonihah and destroyed the city. Alma inquired of the Lord, learned the plans of the Lamanite army, and advised the leader of the Nephite army to drive the Lamanites out of the land.

ALMA 16:9–11, 13–21

And thus ended the eleventh year of
the judges, the Lamanites having
been driven out of the land, and the people of
Ammonihah were destroyed; yea, every living soul
of the Ammonihahites was destroyed, and also
their great city, which they said God could not
destroy, because of its greatness.
10 But behold, in one day it was left desolate;
and the carcasses were mangled by dogs and wild
beasts of the wilderness.
11 Nevertheless, after many days their dead bod-
ies were heaped up upon the face of the earth, and
they were covered with a shallow covering. And
now so great was the scent thereof that the people
did not go in to possess the land of Ammonihah
for many years. And it was called Desolation of
Nehors; for they were of the profession of Nehor,
who were slain; and their lands remained desolate.
13 And Alma and Amulek went forth preaching
repentance to the people in their temples, and in
their sanctuaries, and also in their synagogues,
which were built after the manner of the Jews.
14 And as many as would hear their words, unto
them they did impart the word of God, without
any respect of persons, continually.
15 And thus did Alma and Amulek go forth,
and also many more who had been chosen for the
work, to preach the word throughout all the land.
And the establishment of the church became gen-
eral throughout the land, in all the region round
about, among all the people of the Nephites.
16 And there was no inequality among them;
the Lord did pour out his Spirit on all the face of
the land to prepare the minds of the children of
men, or to prepare their hearts to receive the word
which should be taught among them at the time
of his coming—
17 That they might not be hardened against the
word, that they might not be unbelieving, and go
on to destruction, but that they might receive the
word with joy, and as a branch be grafted into the
true vine, that they might enter into the rest of
the Lord their God.
18 Now those priests who did go forth among
the people did preach against all lyings, and de-
ceivings, and envyings, and strifes, and malice,
and revilings, and stealing, robbing, plundering,
murdering, committing adultery, and all manner
of lasciviousness, crying that these things ought
not so to be—
19 Holding forth things which must shortly
come; yea, holding forth the coming of the Son of
God, his sufferings and death, and also the resur-
rection of the dead.
20 And many of the people did inquire concern-
ing the place where the Son of God should come;
and they were taught that he would appear unto
them after his resurrection; and this the people
did hear with great joy and gladness.
21 And now after the church had been estab-
lished throughout all the land—having got the
victory over the devil, and the word of God being
preached in its purity in all the land, and the Lord
pouring out his blessings upon the people—thus
ended the fourteenth year of the reign of the
judges over the people of Nephi.

What did the priests teach the righteous Nephites? What can you do today to follow that counsel? Abinadi and Alma both warned of the destruction of the people if they did not repent, and their prophecies were fulfilled. What modern-day prophecies have you witnessed being fulfilled today?

THE SONS OF MOSIAH PREPARE SPIRITUALLY TO PREACH AMONG THE LAMANITES

As Alma was journeying through the land, he was reunited with the sons of Mosiah, who were traveling toward Zarahemla. The sons of Mosiah had been preaching among the Lamanites for fourteen years, during which Alma was serving as chief judge, high priest, and missionary in the lands surrounding Zarahemla.

ALMA 17:2–4, 6, 9–12

Now these sons of Mosiah were with
Alma at the time the angel first ap-
peared unto him; therefore Alma did rejoice
exceedingly to see his brethren; and what added
more to his joy, they were still his brethren in
the Lord; yea, and they had waxed strong in the
knowledge of the truth; for they were men of a
sound understanding and they had searched the
scriptures diligently, that they might know the
word of God.
3 But this is not all; they had given themselves to
much prayer, and fasting; therefore they had the
spirit of prophecy, and the spirit of revelation, and
when they taught, they taught with power and au-
thority of God.
4 And they had been teaching the word of
God for the space of fourteen years among the
Lamanites, having had much success in bringing
many to the knowledge of the truth; yea, by the
power of their words many were brought before
the altar of God, to call on his name and confess
their sins before him.
6 Now these were their journeyings: Having
taken leave of their father, Mosiah, in the first year
of the judges; having refused the kingdom which
their father was desirous to confer upon them,
and also this was the minds of the people;
9 And it came to pass that they journeyed many
days in the wilderness, and they fasted much and
prayed much that the Lord would grant unto them
a portion of his Spirit to go with them, and abide
with them, that they might be an instrument in
the hands of God to bring, if it were possible, their
brethren, the Lamanites, to the knowledge of the
truth, to the knowledge of the baseness of the tra-
ditions of their fathers, which were not correct.
10 And it came to pass that the Lord did visit
them with his Spirit, and said unto them: Be
comforted. And they were comforted.
11 And the Lord said unto them also: Go forth
among the Lamanites, thy brethren, and establish
my word; yet ye shall be patient in long-suffering
and afflictions, that ye may show forth good
examples unto them in me, and I will make an
instrument of thee in my hands unto the salvation
of many souls.
12 And it came to pass that the hearts of the sons
of Mosiah, and also those who were with them,
took courage to go forth unto the Lamanites to
declare unto them the word of God.

How did the sons of Mosiah prepare to preach among the Lamanites? The sons of Mosiah were described as "men of a sound understanding." What do you think that means? How can you attain this quality?

AMMON BECOMES A SERVANT TO KING LAMONI AND DEFENDS HIS FLOCKS

After the sons of Mosiah prepared themselves spiritually, they went their separate ways to preach among the Lamanites—who had become a wild and ferocious people who worshipped idols, sought for riches, and delighted in robbing and murdering the Nephites. Ammon, the leader of the sons of Mosiah, entered the land of Ishmael, was taken captive by the guards of King Lamoni, and offered to be the king's servant. While Ammon worked with the king's servants, other men came and scattered the king's flocks in an attempt to steal them. Ammon led the servants in gathering the flocks and then single-handedly battled the thieves when they returned—slaying a number of them with his sling, killing their leader with his sword, and cutting off the arms of many others. The servants presented the severed arms to King Lamoni and told him of Ammon's power.

ALMA 18:2–3, 8–10

And when they had all testified to the
things which they had seen, and he had
learned of the faithfulness of Ammon in preserv-
ing his flocks, and also of his great power in con-
tending against those who sought to slay him, he
was astonished exceedingly, and said: Surely, this
is more than a man. Behold, is not this the Great
Spirit who doth send such great punishments
upon this people, because of their murders?
3 And they answered the king, and said: Whether
he be the Great Spirit or a man, we know not; but
this much we do know, that he cannot be slain by
the enemies of the king; neither can they scatter
the king's flocks when he is with us, because of
his expertness and great strength; therefore, we
know that he is a friend to the king. And now, O
king, we do not believe that a man has such great
power, for we know he cannot be slain.
8 And it came to pass that king Lamoni inquired
of his servants, saying: Where is this man that has
such great power?
9 And they said unto him: Behold, he is feeding
thy horses. Now the king had commanded his ser-
vants, previous to the time of the watering of their
flocks, that they should prepare his horses and
chariots, and conduct him forth to the land of
Nephi; for there had been a great feast appointed
at the land of Nephi, by the father of Lamoni,
who was king over all the land.
10 Now when king Lamoni heard that Ammon
was preparing his horses and his chariots he was
more astonished, because of the faithfulness of
Ammon, saying: Surely there has not been any
servant among all my servants that has been so
faithful as this man; for even he doth remember
all my commandments to execute them.

Ammon's diligent service helped prepare King Lamoni to hear the gospel. What can you do to offer service? How can serving others lead to opportunities to share the gospel?

AMMON TEACHES KING LAMONI OF THE NATURE OF GOD AND HIS CREATIONS

King Lamoni was astonished to hear of Ammon's power in defending the king's flocks. Ammon was invited to speak to the king, discerned his thoughts through the Spirit, and assured the king that he was not the Great Spirit but merely a man who desired to serve him. Further astonished, King Lamoni promised Ammon whatever he desired if he would explain his power. Ammon asked if the king would hearken to his words in return for explaining the source of his power. King Lamoni said he would believe all of Ammon's words. As you read, pay attention to the questions and answers Ammon offered as he taught the king.

ALMA 18:24–35

And Ammon began to speak unto him with boldness, and said unto him: Believest thou that there is a God?
25 And he answered, and said unto him: I do not know what that meaneth.
26 And then Ammon said: Believest thou that there is a Great Spirit?
27 And he said, Yea.
28 And Ammon said: This is God. And Ammon said unto him again: Believest thou that this Great Spirit, who is God, created all things which are in heaven and in the earth?
29 And he said: Yea, I believe that he created all things which are in the earth; but I do not know the heavens.
30 And Ammon said unto him: The heavens is a place where God dwells and all his holy angels.
31 And king Lamoni said: Is it above the earth?
32 And Ammon said: Yea, and he looketh down upon all the children of men; and he knows all the thoughts and intents of the heart; for by his hand were they all created from the beginning.
33 And king Lamoni said: I believe all these things which thou hast spoken. Art thou sent from God?
34 Ammon said unto him: I am a man; and man in the beginning was created after the image of God, and I am called by his Holy Spirit to teach these things unto this people, that they may be brought to a knowledge of that which is just and true;
35 And a portion of that Spirit dwelleth in me, which giveth me knowledge, and also power according to my faith and desires which are in God.

What kinds of questions and answers did Ammon offer as he taught the king? How can asking questions lead to teaching opportunities? How can you follow Ammon's example as you teach the gospel?

KING LAMONI LEARNS OF THE PLAN OF REDEMPTION AND PLEADS FOR GOD'S MERCY

After explaining the nature of God and His creations, Alma continued to teach King Lamoni.

ALMA 18:36–43

Now when Ammon had said these words,
he began at the creation of the world,
and also the creation of Adam, and told him all
the things concerning the fall of man, and re-
hearsed and laid before him the records and the
holy scriptures of the people, which had been spo-
ken by the prophets, even down to the time that
their father, Lehi, left Jerusalem.
37 And he also rehearsed unto them (for it was
unto the king and to his servants) all the journey-
ings of their fathers in the wilderness, and all their
sufferings with hunger and thirst, and their tra-
vail, and so forth.
38 And he also rehearsed unto them concerning
the rebellions of Laman and Lemuel, and the sons
of Ishmael, yea, all their rebellions did he relate
unto them; and he expounded unto them all the
records and scriptures from the time that Lehi left
Jerusalem down to the present time.
39 But this is not all; for he expounded unto
them the plan of redemption, which was prepared
from the foundation of the world; and he also
made known unto them concerning the coming
of Christ, and all the works of the Lord did he
make known unto them.
40 And it came to pass that after he had said all
these things, and expounded them to the king,
that the king believed all his words.
41 And he began to cry unto the Lord, saying:
O Lord, have mercy; according to thy abundant
mercy which thou hast had upon the people of
Nephi, have upon me, and my people.
42 And now, when he had said this, he fell unto
the earth, as if he were dead.
43 And it came to pass that his servants took him
and carried him in unto his wife, and laid him
upon a bed; and he lay as if he were dead for the
space of two days and two nights; and his wife,
and his sons, and his daughters mourned over
him, after the manner of the Lamanites, greatly
lamenting his loss.

Before Ammon's arrival, King Lamoni knew very little about God. What are some things that prepared King Lamoni to believe in God and pray for mercy? What can you learn from Ammon's example of how to teach the gospel?

KING LAMONI ARISES AND SPEAKS OF HIS VISION OF THE SAVIOR

Upon hearing Ammon's teachings about the plan of redemption, King Lamoni had cried aloud for God's mercy and fell to the earth as if he were dead. After two days, some servants felt the king should be buried, but the queen felt her husband was not dead and invited Ammon to see her husband as he lay upon his bed. Consider Ammon's description of God's power, light, and glory.

Alma 19:6, 8–14

Now, this was what Ammon desired, for he knew that king Lamoni was under the power of God; he knew that the dark veil of unbelief was being cast away from his mind, and the light which did light up his mind, which was the light of the glory of God, which was a marvelous light of his goodness—yea, this light had infused such joy into his soul, the cloud of darkness having been dispelled, and that the light of everlasting life was lit up in his soul, yea, he knew that this had overcome his natural frame, and he was carried away in God—

8 And he said unto the queen: He is not dead, but he sleepeth in God, and on the morrow he shall rise again; therefore bury him not.

9 And Ammon said unto her: Believest thou this? And she said unto him: I have had no witness save thy word, and the word of our servants; nevertheless I believe that it shall be according as thou hast said.

10 And Ammon said unto her: Blessed art thou because of thy exceeding faith; I say unto thee, woman, there has not been such great faith among all the people of the Nephites.

11 And it came to pass that she watched over the bed of her husband, from that time even until that time on the morrow which Ammon had appointed that he should rise.

12 And it came to pass that he arose, according to the words of Ammon; and as he arose, he stretched forth his hand unto the woman, and said: Blessed be the name of God, and blessed art thou.

13 For as sure as thou livest, behold, I have seen my Redeemer; and he shall come forth, and be born of a woman, and he shall redeem all mankind who believe on his name. Now, when he had said these words, his heart was swollen within him, and he sunk again with joy; and the queen also sunk down, being overpowered by the Spirit.

14 Now Ammon seeing the Spirit of the Lord poured out according to his prayers upon the Lamanites, his brethren, who had been the cause of so much mourning among the Nephites, or among all the people of God because of their iniquities and their traditions, he fell upon his knees, and began to pour out his soul in prayer and thanksgiving to God for what he had done for his brethren; and he was also overpowered with joy; and thus they all three had sunk to the earth.

How was the queen's faith a blessing to her and to King Lamoni? How are we blessed when we believe even without having a perfect understanding? What joyful event did King Lamoni prophesy of?

KING LAMONI'S HOUSEHOLD AND MANY LAMANITES EXPERIENCE A SPIRITUAL REBIRTH

After King Lamoni had arisen and proclaimed his vision of the Savior, he was again overpowered by the Spirit and he and his wife fell unconscious. Praying in gratitude for the outpouring of the spirit, Ammon too fell unconscious, as did all of the king's servants except for a woman named Abish, who had been converted early in her life. Abish gathered Lamanites from their homes to witness the scene in hopes they too would be converted. One Lamanite attempted to slay Ammon as he lay unconscious, but the man was struck dead as he lifted up his sword. The people were astonished and argued about whether Ammon was good or evil.

Alma 19:28–36

And thus the contention began to be exceedingly sharp among them. And while they were thus contending, the woman servant who had caused the multitude to be gathered together came, and when she saw the contention which was among the multitude she was exceedingly sorrowful, even unto tears.
29 And it came to pass that she went and took the queen by the hand, that perhaps she might raise her from the ground; and as soon as she touched her hand she arose and stood upon her feet, and cried with a loud voice, saying: O blessed Jesus, who has saved me from an awful hell! O blessed God, have mercy on this people!
30 And when she had said this, she clasped her hands, being filled with joy, speaking many words which were not understood; and when she had done this, she took the king, Lamoni, by the hand, and behold he arose and stood upon his feet.
31 And he, immediately, seeing the contention among his people, went forth and began to rebuke them, and to teach them the words which he had heard from the mouth of Ammon; and as many as heard his words believed, and were converted unto the Lord.
32 But there were many among them who would not hear his words; therefore they went their way.
33 And it came to pass that when Ammon arose he also administered unto them, and also did all the servants of Lamoni; and they did all declare unto the people the selfsame thing—that their hearts had been changed; that they had no more desire to do evil.
34 And behold, many did declare unto the people that they had seen angels and had conversed with them; and thus they had told them things of God, and of his righteousness.
35 And it came to pass that there were many that did believe in their words; and as many as did believe were baptized; and they became a righteous people, and they did establish a church among them.
36 And thus the work of the Lord did commence among the Lamanites; thus the Lord did begin to pour out his Spirit upon them; and we see that his arm is extended to all people who will repent and believe on his name.

The wicked Lamanites experienced a change of heart and "had no more desire to do evil." What can you do when you are tempted to do something wrong? How can you develop a heart that desires to choose the right?

AMMON BATTLES THE KING OF ALL LAMANITES AND SPARES HIS LIFE

After King Lamoni's household and many other Lamanites were converted through Ammon's efforts, a Church was established in that part of the land. Ammon was then commanded by the Lord to go to Middoni, where his fellow missionaries Aaron, Muloki, and Ammah were being held in prison. King Lamoni offered to travel with Ammon to help secure the missionaries' release. As they traveled toward Middoni, they met King Lamoni's father, who was king over all the land and hated all Nephites. The king commanded his son to slay Ammon. Lamoni refused, and the king attempted to slay Lamoni. Ammon intervened, withstood an attack from the old king, and wounded the old king's arm.

ALMA 20:21–28

Now when the king saw that Ammon could slay him, he began to plead with Ammon that he would spare his life.

22 But Ammon raised his sword, and said unto him: Behold, I will smite thee except thou wilt grant unto me that my brethren may be cast out of prison.

23 Now the king, fearing he should lose his life, said: If thou wilt spare me I will grant unto thee whatsoever thou wilt ask, even to half of the kingdom.

24 Now when Ammon saw that he had wrought upon the old king according to his desire, he said unto him: If thou wilt grant that my brethren may be cast out of prison, and also that Lamoni may retain his kingdom, and that ye be not displeased with him, but grant that he may do according to his own desires in whatsoever thing he thinketh, then will I spare thee; otherwise I will smite thee to the earth.

25 Now when Ammon had said these words, the king began to rejoice because of his life.

26 And when he saw that Ammon had no desire to destroy him, and when he also saw the great love he had for his son Lamoni, he was astonished exceedingly, and said: Because this is all that thou hast desired, that I would release thy brethren, and suffer that my son Lamoni should retain his kingdom, behold, I will grant unto you that my son may retain his kingdom from this time and forever; and I will govern him no more—

27 And I will also grant unto thee that thy brethren may be cast out of prison, and thou and thy brethren may come unto me, in my kingdom; for I shall greatly desire to see thee. For the king was greatly astonished at the words which he had spoken, and also at the words which had been spoken by his son Lamoni, therefore he was desirous to learn them.

28 And it came to pass that Ammon and Lamoni proceeded on their journey towards the land of Middoni. And Lamoni found favor in the eyes of the king of the land; therefore the brethren of Ammon were brought forth out of prison.

King Lamoni's father offered to give Ammon half of his kingdom. What did Ammon request instead? What attributes of Ammon helped turn a contentious situation into a positive one? What can you learn about greed and humility from Ammon's experience?

AARON, MULOKI, AND AMMAH PREACH THE GOSPEL AND ARE IMPRISONED

When Ammon and his fellow missionaries separated into the lands of the Lamanites, Aaron journeyed to the city of Jerusalem. There he began preaching among the Amalekites—a people who were even more wicked and hardened than the Lamanites.

ALMA 21:5–14

Therefore, as Aaron entered into one of their synagogues to preach unto the people, and as he was speaking unto them, behold there arose an Amalekite and began to contend with him, saying: What is that thou hast testified? Hast thou seen an angel? Why do not angels appear unto us? Behold are not this people as good as thy people?
6 Thou also sayest, except we repent we shall per-
ish. How knowest thou the thought and intent of our hearts? How knowest thou that we have cause to repent? How knowest thou that we are not a righteous people? Behold, we have built sanctuaries, and we do assemble ourselves together to worship God. We do believe that God will save all men.
7 Now Aaron said unto him: Believest thou that the Son of God shall come to redeem mankind from their sins?
8 And the man said unto him: We do not believe that thou knowest any such thing. We do not believe in these foolish traditions. We do not believe that thou knowest of things to come, neither do we believe that thy fathers and also that our fathers did know concerning the things which they spake, of that which is to come.
9 Now Aaron began to open the scriptures unto them concerning the coming of Christ, and also concerning the resurrection of the dead, and that there could be no redemption for mankind save it were through the death and sufferings of Christ, and the atonement of his blood.
10 And it came to pass as he began to expound these things unto them they were angry with him, and began to mock him; and they would not hear the words which he spake.
11 Therefore, when he saw that they would not hear his words, he departed out of their synagogue, and came over to a village which was called Ani-Anti, and there he found Muloki preaching the word unto them; and also Ammah and his brethren. And they contended with many about the word.
12 And it came to pass that they saw that the people would harden their hearts, therefore they departed and came over into the land of Middoni. And they did preach the word unto many, and few believed on the words which they taught.
13 Nevertheless, Aaron and a certain number of his brethren were taken and cast into prison, and the remainder of them fled out of the land of Middoni unto the regions round about.
14 And those who were cast into prison suffered many things, and they were delivered by the hand of Lamoni and Ammon, and they were fed and clothed.

Despite their best effort, Aaron and his fellow missionaries' initial attempts to share the gospel appeared to fail—and even caused them great suffering. What can you do to follow their example in your own missionary efforts?

AARON TEACHES KING LAMONI'S FATHER THE PLAN OF REDEMPTION

After Ammon helped free Aaron from the prison in Middoni, Ammon returned to the land of Ishmael to teach King Lamoni's people. Meanwhile, Aaron and his fellow missionaries journeyed to the land of Nephi, where they taught King Lamoni's father, whose heart had been softened by Ammon's teachings.

Alma 22:5–14

Now the king said unto them: What is
this that ye have said concerning the
Spirit of the Lord? Behold, this is the thing which
doth trouble me.
6 And also, what is this that Ammon said—If
ye will repent ye shall be saved, and if ye will not
repent, ye shall be cast off at the last day?
7 And Aaron answered him and said unto him:
Believest thou that there is a God? And the king
said: I know that the Amalekites say that there is
a God, and I have granted unto them that they
should build sanctuaries, that they may assemble
themselves together to worship him. And if now
thou sayest there is a God, behold I will believe.
8 And now when Aaron heard this, his heart
began to rejoice, and he said: Behold, assuredly as
thou livest, O king, there is a God.
9 And the king said: Is God that Great Spirit that
brought our fathers out of the land of Jerusalem?
10 And Aaron said unto him: Yea, he is that
Great Spirit, and he created all things both in
heaven and in earth. Believest thou this?
11 And he said: Yea, I believe that the Great Spirit
created all things, and I desire that ye should tell
me concerning all these things, and I will believe
thy words.
12 And it came to pass that when Aaron saw
that the king would believe his words, he began
from the creation of Adam, reading the scriptures
unto the king—how God created man after his
own image, and that God gave him command-
ments, and that because of transgression, man
had fallen.
13 And Aaron did expound unto him the scrip-
tures from the creation of Adam, laying the fall of
man before him, and their carnal state and also
the plan of redemption, which was prepared from
the foundation of the world, through Christ, for
all whosoever would believe on his name.
14 And since man had fallen he could not merit
anything of himself; but the sufferings and death
of Christ atone for their sins, through faith and
repentance, and so forth; and that he breaketh the
bands of death, that the grave shall have no vic-
tory, and that the sting of death should be swal-
lowed up in the hopes of glory; and Aaron did
expound all these things unto the king.

What tool did Aaron use to teach King Lamoni's father the plan of salvation? What does Aaron's example teach you about how to share the gospel with others? Discuss some scriptures you can share as you teach the plan of salvation (you may want to use the Topical Guide or index in your scriptures).

KING LAMONI'S FATHER EXPERIENCES A SPIRITUAL REBIRTH

After being taught by Aaron of the plan of redemption, King Lamoni's father responded.

Alma 22:15–26

And it came to pass that after Aaron had
expounded these things unto him, the
king said: What shall I do that I may have this
eternal life of which thou hast spoken? Yea, what
shall I do that I may be born of God, having this
wicked spirit rooted out of my breast, and receive
his Spirit, that I may be filled with joy, that I may
not be cast off at the last day? Behold, said he, I
will give up all that I possess, yea, I will forsake
my kingdom, that I may receive this great joy.
16 But Aaron said unto him: If thou desirest this
thing, if thou wilt bow down before God, yea,
if thou wilt repent of all thy sins, and will bow
down before God, and call on his name in faith,
believing that ye shall receive, then shalt thou re-
ceive the hope which thou desirest.
17 And it came to pass that when Aaron had said
these words, the king did bow down before the
Lord, upon his knees; yea, even he did prostrate
himself upon the earth, and cried mightily, saying:
18 O God, Aaron hath told me that there is a
God; and if there is a God, and if thou art God,
wilt thou make thyself known unto me, and I will
give away all my sins to know thee, and that I
may be raised from the dead, and be saved at the
last day. And now when the king had said these
words, he was struck as if he were dead.
19 And it came to pass that his servants ran and
told the queen all that had happened unto the
king. And she came in unto the king; and when
she saw him lay as if he were dead, and also Aaron
and his brethren standing as though they had been
the cause of his fall, she was angry with them, and
commanded that her servants, or the servants of
the king, should take them and slay them.
20 Now the servants had seen the cause of the
king's fall, therefore they durst not lay their hands
on Aaron and his brethren; and they pled with
the queen saying: Why commandest thou that we
should slay these men, when behold one of them
is mightier than us all? Therefore we shall fall be-
fore them.
21 Now when the queen saw the fear of the ser-
vants she also began to fear exceedingly, lest there
should some evil come upon her. And she com-
manded her servants that they should go and call
the people, that they might slay Aaron and his
brethren.
22 Now when Aaron saw the determination of the
queen, he, also knowing the hardness of the hearts
of the people, feared lest that a multitude should
assemble themselves together, and there should be
a great contention and a disturbance among them;
therefore he put forth his hand and raised the king
from the earth, and said unto him: Stand. And he
stood upon his feet, receiving his strength.
23 Now this was done in the presence of the queen
and many of the servants. And when they saw it
they greatly marveled, and began to fear. And the
king stood forth, and began to minister unto them.
And he did minister unto them, insomuch that his
whole household were converted unto the Lord.
24 Now there was a multitude gathered together
because of the commandment of the queen, and
there began to be great murmurings among them
because of Aaron and his brethren.
25 But the king stood forth among them and
administered unto them. And they were pacified
towards Aaron and those who were with him.
26 And it came to pass that when the king saw
that the people were pacified, he caused that
Aaron and his brethren should stand forth in
the midst of the multitude, and that they should
preach the word unto them.

What was King Lamoni's father willing to do in order to be filled with joy and receive eternal life? What did Aaron tell the king to do to receive his desire? King Lamoni's father said to God, "I will give away all my sins to know thee." Consider in your own heart the sins you are willing to "give away" in order to be closer to God.

THOUSANDS OF LAMANITES ARE CONVERTED AND CALL THEMSELVES ANTI-NEPHI-LEHIES

After King Lamoni's father was converted, he made an announcement to all the Lamanites.

Alma 23:1–7, 16–17

Behold, now it came to pass that the king of the Lamanites sent a proclamation among all his people, that they should not lay their hands on Ammon, or Aaron, or Omner, or Himni, nor either of their brethren who should go forth preaching the word of God, in whatsoever place they should be, in any part of their land.

2 Yea, he sent a decree among them, that they should not lay their hands on them to bind them, or to cast them into prison; neither should they spit upon them, nor smite them, nor cast them out of their synagogues, nor scourge them; neither should they cast stones at them, but that they should have free access to their houses, and also their temples, and their sanctuaries.

3 And thus they might go forth and preach the word according to their desires, for the king had been converted unto the Lord, and all his household; therefore he sent his proclamation throughout the land unto his people, that the word of God might have no obstruction, but that it might go forth throughout all the land, that his people might be convinced concerning the wicked traditions of their fathers, and that they might be convinced that they were all brethren, and that they ought not to murder, nor to plunder, nor to steal, nor to commit adultery, nor to commit any manner of wickedness.

4 And now it came to pass that when the king had sent forth this proclamation, that Aaron and his brethren went forth from city to city, and from one house of worship to another, establishing churches, and consecrating priests and teachers throughout the land among the Lamanites, to preach and to teach the word of God among them; and thus they began to have great success.

5 And thousands were brought to the knowledge of the Lord, yea, thousands were brought to believe in the traditions of the Nephites; and they were taught the records and prophecies which were handed down even to the present time.

6 And as sure as the Lord liveth, so sure as many as believed, or as many as were brought to the knowledge of the truth, through the preaching of Ammon and his brethren, according to the spirit of revelation and of prophecy, and the power of God working miracles in them—yea, I say unto you, as the Lord liveth, as many of the Lamanites as believed in their preaching, and were converted unto the Lord, never did fall away.

7 For they became a righteous people; they did lay down the weapons of their rebellion, that they did not fight against God any more, neither against any of their brethren.

16 And now it came to pass that the king and those who were converted were desirous that they might have a name, that thereby they might be distinguished from their brethren; therefore the king consulted with Aaron and many of their priests, concerning the name that they should take upon them, that they might be distinguished.

17 And it came to pass that they called their names Anti-Nephi-Lehies; and they were called by this name and were no more called Lamanites.

What law did the king of the Lamanites declare to his people? What was the result of that law? How can you help protect religious freedoms where you live?

KING ANTI-NEPHI-LEHI COUNSELS HIS PEOPLE TO NOT BATTLE THE LAMANITES AS A TESTIMONY OF THEIR CONVERSION

While thousands of Lamanites were converted and became known as Anti-Nephi-Lehies, the Amalakites and the Amulonites resisted the truth and stirred the unconverted Lamanites up in hatred toward their brethren. King Lamoni's father conferred the kingdom upon his son—who was known as Anti-Nephi-Lehi—and died in the same year the wicked Lamanites began to make preparations for war against the Anti-Nephi-Lehies. Ammon and his fellow missionaries held a counsel with King Anti-Nephi-Lehi and Lamoni about what they should do.

ALMA 24:6–15

Now there was not one soul among all the people who had been converted unto the Lord that would take up arms against their brethren; nay, they would not even make any preparations for war; yea, and also their king commanded them that they should not.

7 Now, these are the words which he said unto the people concerning the matter: I thank my God, my beloved people, that our great God has in goodness sent these our brethren, the Nephites, unto us to preach unto us, and to convince us of the traditions of our wicked fathers.

8 And behold, I thank my great God that he has given us a portion of his Spirit to soften our hearts, that we have opened a correspondence with these brethren, the Nephites.

9 And behold, I also thank my God, that by opening this correspondence we have been convinced of our sins, and of the many murders which we have committed.

10 And I also thank my God, yea, my great God, that he hath granted unto us that we might repent of these things, and also that he hath forgiven us of those our many sins and murders which we have committed, and taken away the guilt from our hearts, through the merits of his Son.

11 And now behold, my brethren, since it has been all that we could do (as we were the most lost of all mankind) to repent of all our sins and the many murders which we have committed, and to get God to take them away from our hearts, for it was all we could do to repent sufficiently before God that he would take away our stain—

12 Now, my best beloved brethren, since God hath taken away our stains, and our swords have become bright, then let us stain our swords no more with the blood of our brethren.

13 Behold, I say unto you, Nay, let us retain our swords that they be not stained with the blood of our brethren; for perhaps, if we should stain our swords again they can no more be washed bright through the blood of the Son of our great God, which shall be shed for the atonement of our sins.

14 And the great God has had mercy on us, and made these things known unto us that we might not perish; yea, and he has made these things known unto us beforehand, because he loveth our souls as well as he loveth our children; therefore, in his mercy he doth visit us by his angels, that the plan of salvation might be made known unto us as well as unto future generations.

15 Oh, how merciful is our God! And now behold, since it has been as much as we could do to get our stains taken away from us, and our swords are made bright, let us hide them away that they may be kept bright, as a testimony to our God at the last day, or at the day that we shall be brought to stand before him to be judged, that we have not stained our swords in the blood of our brethren since he imparted his word unto us and has made us clean thereby.

What blessings did the king thank God for? What did the king ask his people to do in order retain those blessings? What does the Anti-Nephi-Lehies' promise teach you about repentance?

THE ANTI-NEPHI-LEHIES BURY THEIR WEAPONS, AND OVER A THOUSAND ARE SLAIN

As the wicked Lamanites prepared to come upon the Anti-Nephi-Lehies in battle, King Anti-Nephi-Lehi continued to counsel his people.

ALMA 24:16–26

And now, my brethren, if our brethren seek to destroy us, behold, we will hide away our swords, yea, even we will bury them deep in the earth, that they may be kept bright, as a testimony that we have never used them, at the last day; and if our brethren destroy us, behold, we shall go to our God and shall be saved.

17 And now it came to pass that when the king had made an end of these sayings, and all the people were assembled together, they took their swords, and all the weapons which were used for the shedding of man's blood, and they did bury them up deep in the earth.

18 And this they did, it being in their view a testimony to God, and also to men, that they never would use weapons again for the shedding of man's blood; and this they did, vouching and covenanting with God, that rather than shed the blood of their brethren they would give up their own lives; and rather than take away from a brother they would give unto him; and rather than spend their days in idleness they would labor abundantly with their hands.

19 And thus we see that, when these Lamanites were brought to believe and to know the truth, they were firm, and would suffer even unto death rather than commit sin; and thus we see that they buried their weapons of peace, or they buried the weapons of war, for peace.

20 And it came to pass that their brethren, the Lamanites, made preparations for war, and came up to the land of Nephi for the purpose of destroying the king, and to place another in his stead, and also of destroying the people of Anti-Nephi-Lehi out of the land.

21 Now when the people saw that they were coming against them they went out to meet them, and prostrated themselves before them to the earth, and began to call on the name of the Lord; and thus they were in this attitude when the Lamanites began to fall upon them, and began to slay them with the sword.

22 And thus without meeting any resistance, they did slay a thousand and five of them; and we know that they are blessed, for they have gone to dwell with their God.

23 Now when the Lamanites saw that their brethren would not flee from the sword, neither would they turn aside to the right hand or to the left, but that they would lie down and perish, and praised God even in the very act of perishing under the sword—

24 Now when the Lamanites saw this they did forbear from slaying them; and there were many whose hearts had swollen in them for those of their brethren who had fallen under the sword, for they repented of the things which they had done.

25 And it came to pass that they threw down their weapons of war, and they would not take them again, for they were stung for the murders which they had committed; and they came down even as their brethren, relying upon the mercies of those whose arms were lifted to slay them.

26 And it came to pass that the people of God were joined that day by more than the number who had been slain; and those who had been slain were righteous people, therefore we have no reason to doubt but what they were saved.

Why did the Anti-Nephi-Lehies bury their weapons? What sins or weaknesses can you symbolically bury as you remain committed to your conversion? What good came from so many of the Anti-Nephi-Lehies sacrificing their lives?

AMMON REJOICES IN THE LORD AND CELEBRATES THE CONVERSION OF THE LAMANITES

After they had slain over a thousand of the submissive Anti-Nephi-Lehies, many of the wicked Lamanites repented and were converted. A number of unrepentant Lamanites then battled with the Nephites. Many were killed, and others returned and joined peacefully with the people of Anti-Nephi-Lehi. Ammon, reflecting on the great conversion that had taken place among the Lamanites, then spoke to his fellow missionaries.

ALMA 26:1–9

And now, these are the words of Ammon
to his brethren, which say thus: My
brothers and my brethren, behold I say unto you,
how great reason have we to rejoice; for could we
have supposed when we started from the land of
Zarahemla that God would have granted unto us
such great blessings?
2 And now, I ask, what great blessings has he be-
stowed upon us? Can ye tell?
3 Behold, I answer for you; for our brethren,
the Lamanites, were in darkness, yea, even in the
darkest abyss, but behold, how many of them are
brought to behold the marvelous light of God!
And this is the blessing which hath been bestowed
upon us, that we have been made instruments in
the hands of God to bring about this great work.
4 Behold, thousands of them do rejoice, and have
been brought into the fold of God.
5 Behold, the field was ripe, and blessed are ye,
for ye did thrust in the sickle, and did reap with
your might, yea, all the day long did ye labor; and
behold the number of your sheaves! And they
shall be gathered into the garners, that they are
not wasted.
6 Yea, they shall not be beaten down by the storm
at the last day; yea, neither shall they be harrowed
up by the whirlwinds; but when the storm com-
eth they shall be gathered together in their place,
that the storm cannot penetrate to them; yea, nei-
ther shall they be driven with fierce winds whith-
ersoever the enemy listeth to carry them.
7 But behold, they are in the hands of the Lord
of the harvest, and they are his; and he will raise
them up at the last day.
8 Blessed be the name of our God; let us sing to
his praise, yea, let us give thanks to his holy name,
for he doth work righteousness forever.
9 For if we had not come up out of the land of
Zarahemla, these our dearly beloved brethren,
who have so dearly beloved us, would still have
been racked with hatred against us, yea, and they
would also have been strangers to God.

How did Ammon respond to the events that had occurred among the Anti-Nephi-Lehies? According to this passage, what reasons did he have to rejoice? Think of someone you know who has been converted to the gospel. How has that person's conversion brought joy? How has your own conversion brought you joy?

AMMON REJOICES IN THE STRENGTH OF THE LORD AND IN HIS OWN CONVERSION

Ammon continued to speak to his fellow missionaries as he reflected on the conversion of the Lamanites. As you read, look for Ammon's description of the Lamanites before and after their conversion.

ALMA 26:10–22

And it came to pass that when Ammon
had said these words, his brother Aaron
rebuked him, saying: Ammon, I fear that thy joy
doth carry thee away unto boasting.
11 But Ammon said unto him: I do not boast
in my own strength, nor in my own wisdom; but
behold, my joy is full, yea, my heart is brim with
joy, and I will rejoice in my God.
12 Yea, I know that I am nothing; as to my
strength I am weak; therefore I will not boast
of myself, but I will boast of my God, for in his
strength I can do all things; yea, behold, many
mighty miracles we have wrought in this land, for
which we will praise his name forever.
13 Behold, how many thousands of our brethren
has he loosed from the pains of hell; and they are
brought to sing redeeming love, and this because
of the power of his word which is in us, therefore
have we not great reason to rejoice?
14 Yea, we have reason to praise him forever,
for he is the Most High God, and has loosed our
brethren from the chains of hell.
15 Yea, they were encircled about with everlast-
ing darkness and destruction; but behold, he has
brought them into his everlasting light, yea, into
everlasting salvation; and they are encircled about
with the matchless bounty of his love; yea, and we
have been instruments in his hands of doing this
great and marvelous work.
16 Therefore, let us glory, yea, we will glory in
the Lord; yea, we will rejoice, for our joy is full;
yea, we will praise our God forever. Behold, who
can glory too much in the Lord? Yea, who can say
too much of his great power, and of his mercy,
and of his long-suffering towards the children of
men? Behold, I say unto you, I cannot say the
smallest part which I feel.
17 Who could have supposed that our God
would have been so merciful as to have snatched
us from our awful, sinful, and polluted state?
18 Behold, we went forth even in wrath, with
mighty threatenings to destroy his church.
19 Oh then, why did he not consign us to an
awful destruction, yea, why did he not let the
sword of his justice fall upon us, and doom us to
eternal despair?
20 Oh, my soul, almost as it were, fleeth at the
thought. Behold, he did not exercise his justice
upon us, but in his great mercy hath brought us
over that everlasting gulf of death and misery,
even to the salvation of our souls.
21 And now behold, my brethren, what natural
man is there that knoweth these things? I say unto
you, there is none that knoweth these things, save
it be the penitent.
22 Yea, he that repenteth and exerciseth faith,
and bringeth forth good works, and prayeth con-
tinually without ceasing—unto such it is given to
know the mysteries of God; yea, unto such it shall
be given to reveal things which never have been
revealed; yea, and it shall be given unto such to
bring thousands of souls to repentance, even as it
has been given unto us to bring these our brethren
to repentance.

How did Ammon describe the Lamanites before and after their conversion? Of what did Ammon boast? What does he teach you about God's strength?

AMMON RECALLS THE DOUBTS AND CHALLENGES OF PREACHING AMONG THE LAMANITES

Ammon continued to speak to his fellow missionaries as he reflected on their success among the Lamanites.

ALMA 26:23–32

Now do ye remember, my brethren, that we said unto our brethren in the land of Zarahemla, we go up to the land of Nephi, to preach unto our brethren, the Lamanites, and they laughed us to scorn?
24 For they said unto us: Do ye suppose that ye can bring the Lamanites to the knowledge of the truth? Do ye suppose that ye can convince the Lamanites of the incorrectness of the traditions of their fathers, as stiffnecked a people as they are; whose hearts delight in the shedding of blood; whose days have been spent in the grossest iniquity; whose ways have been the ways of a transgressor from the beginning? Now my brethren, ye remember that this was their language.
25 And moreover they did say: Let us take up arms against them, that we destroy them and their iniquity out of the land, lest they overrun us and destroy us.
26 But behold, my beloved brethren, we came into the wilderness not with the intent to destroy our brethren, but with the intent that perhaps we might save some few of their souls.
27 Now when our hearts were depressed, and we were about to turn back, behold, the Lord comforted us, and said: Go amongst thy brethren, the Lamanites, and bear with patience thine afflictions, and I will give unto you success.
28 And now behold, we have come, and been forth amongst them; and we have been patient in our sufferings, and we have suffered every privation; yea, we have traveled from house to house, relying upon the mercies of the world—not upon the mercies of the world alone but upon the mercies of God.
29 And we have entered into their houses and taught them, and we have taught them in their streets; yea, and we have taught them upon their hills; and we have also entered into their temples and their synagogues and taught them; and we have been cast out, and mocked, and spit upon, and smote upon our cheeks; and we have been stoned, and taken and bound with strong cords, and cast into prison; and through the power and wisdom of God we have been delivered again.
30 And we have suffered all manner of afflictions, and all this, that perhaps we might be the means of saving some soul; and we supposed that our joy would be full if perhaps we could be the means of saving some.
31 Now behold, we can look forth and see the fruits of our labors; and are they few? I say unto you, Nay, they are many; yea, and we can witness of their sincerity, because of their love towards their brethren and also towards us.
32 For behold, they had rather sacrifice their lives than even to take the life of their enemy; and they have buried their weapons of war deep in the earth, because of their love towards their brethren.

What can make it difficult to share the gospel? How can you overcome challenges to doing missionary work? How did Ammon know of the sincerity of the Lamanites' conversion?

AMMON REJOICES IN GOD'S WISDOM AND POWER AND MERCY

Ammon concluded his remarks to his fellow missionaries, recounting the great conversion among the Lamanites.

Alma 26:33–37

And now behold I say unto you, has
there been so great love in all the land?
Behold, I say unto you, Nay, there has not, even
among the Nephites.
34 For behold, they would take up arms against
their brethren; they would not suffer themselves
to be slain. But behold how many of these have
laid down their lives; and we know that they have
gone to their God, because of their love and of
their hatred to sin.
35 Now have we not reason to rejoice? Yea, I
say unto you, there never were men that had
so great reason to rejoice as we, since the world
began; yea, and my joy is carried away, even unto
boasting in my God; for he has all power, all wis-
dom, and all understanding; he comprehendeth
all things, and he is a merciful Being, even unto
salvation, to those who will repent and believe on
his name.
36 Now if this is boasting, even so will I boast;
for this is my life and my light, my joy and my
salvation, and my redemption from everlasting
wo. Yea, blessed is the name of my God, who has
been mindful of this people, who are a branch of
the tree of Israel, and has been lost from its body
in a strange land; yea, I say, blessed be the name of
my God, who has been mindful of us, wanderers
in a strange land.
37 Now my brethren, we see that God is mindful
of every people, whatsoever land they may be in;
yea, he numbereth his people, and his bowels of
mercy are over all the earth. Now this is my joy,
and my great thanksgiving; yea, and I will give
thanks unto my God forever. Amen.

Ammon said, "There never were men that had so great reason to rejoice as we." What reasons did he give for his rejoicing? When have you felt joy in your life? What is the difference between "joy" and "fun"?

ALMA DESIRES TO PREACH REPENTANCE WITH ANGELIC FORCE

Soon the wicked Lamanites were again stirred up in anger toward the Anti-Nephi-Lehies and began again to kill many of them as they still refused to defend themselves. Ammon sought counsel from the Lord and led the Anti-Nephi-Lehies to safety in the land of Zarahemla. There the Nephites offered the land of Jershon as a place for the Anti-Nephi-Lehies to permanently live and also offered to defend them from the Lamanites. The Lamanite army had pursued the Anti-Nephi-Lehies—who began to call themselves the people of Ammon—and the Nephite army met them in the deadliest battle since the time of Lehi's arrival in the promised land. Tens of thousands of Lamanites were slain and scattered. The Nephites were victorious, but many of them were slain. The surviving Nephites greatly mourned the loss of their loved ones. Alma reflected on his desires to preach the gospel to all the world.

Alma 29:1–8

O that I were an angel, and could have the wish of mine heart, that I might go forth and speak with the trump of God, with a voice to shake the earth, and cry repentance unto every people!
2 Yea, I would declare unto every soul, as with the voice of thunder, repentance and the plan of redemption, that they should repent and come unto our God, that there might not be more sorrow upon all the face of the earth.
3 But behold, I am a man, and do sin in my wish; for I ought to be content with the things which the Lord hath allotted unto me.
4 I ought not to harrow up in my desires the firm decree of a just God, for I know that he granteth unto men according to their desire, whether it be unto death or unto life; yea, I know that he allotteth unto men, yea, decreeth unto them decrees which are unalterable, according to their wills, whether they be unto salvation or unto destruction.
5 Yea, and I know that good and evil have come before all men; he that knoweth not good from evil is blameless; but he that knoweth good and evil, to him it is given according to his desires, whether he desireth good or evil, life or death, joy or remorse of conscience.
6 Now, seeing that I know these things, why should I desire more than to perform the work to which I have been called?
7 Why should I desire that I were an angel, that I could speak unto all the ends of the earth?
8 For behold, the Lord doth grant unto all nations, of their own nation and tongue, to teach his word, yea, in wisdom, all that he seeth fit that they should have; therefore we see that the Lord doth counsel in wisdom, according to that which is just and true.

What is the desire of Alma's heart? What does he say would happen if everyone on earth repented and learned the plan of redemption? Alma teaches that God "granteth unto men according to their desire" and speaks of men desiring good or evil. What choices can you make to show God you desire good?

ALMA REJOICES IN THE LORD'S MERCY TO HIS ANCESTORS AND HIS BRETHREN

Alma continued to reflect upon his missionary experiences and the deliverance of the Lord.

ALMA 29:9–17

I know that which the Lord hath commanded me, and I glory in it. I do not glory of myself, but I glory in that which the Lord hath commanded me; yea, and this is my glory, that perhaps I may be an instrument in the hands of God to bring some soul to repentance; and this is my joy.

10 And behold, when I see many of my brethren truly penitent, and coming to the Lord their God, then is my soul filled with joy; then do I remember what the Lord has done for me, yea, even that he hath heard my prayer; yea, then do I remember his merciful arm which he extended towards me.

11 Yea, and I also remember the captivity of my fathers; for I surely do know that the Lord did deliver them out of bondage, and by this did establish his church; yea, the Lord God, the God of Abraham, the God of Isaac, and the God of Jacob, did deliver them out of bondage.

12 Yea, I have always remembered the captivity of my fathers; and that same God who delivered them out of the hands of the Egyptians did deliver them out of bondage.

13 Yea, and that same God did establish his church among them; yea, and that same God hath called me by a holy calling, to preach the word unto this people, and hath given me much success, in the which my joy is full.

14 But I do not joy in my own success alone, but my joy is more full because of the success of my brethren, who have been up to the land of Nephi.

15 Behold, they have labored exceedingly, and have brought forth much fruit; and how great shall be their reward!

16 Now, when I think of the success of these my brethren my soul is carried away, even to the separation of it from the body, as it were, so great is my joy.

17 And now may God grant unto these, my brethren, that they may sit down in the kingdom of God; yea, and also all those who are the fruit of their labors that they may go no more out, but that they may praise him forever. And may God grant that it may be done according to my words, even as I have spoken. Amen.

What caused Alma's soul to be "filled with joy"? Beyond his own missionary experiences, what made his joy "more full"? Alma rejoiced as he recalled the Lord's deliverance of His people and the establishment of His Church. In what ways has the Lord delivered your family or your ancestors?

KORIHOR PREACHES AGAINST A BELIEF IN JESUS CHRIST AND THE HOLY PROPHETS

It was now about seventy-five years before the birth of Jesus Christ. The Nephites buried the countless numbers of those killed in their great battle with the Lamanites. Peace was established, and the Nephites were strictly obedient to the commandments and the law of Moses. A man named Korihor entered the land of Zarahemla and began teaching against a belief in Jesus Christ.

ALMA 30:12–18

And this Anti-Christ, whose name was
Korihor, (and the law could have no
hold upon him) began to preach unto the people
that there should be no Christ. And after this
manner did he preach, saying:
13 O ye that are bound down under a foolish and
a vain hope, why do ye yoke yourselves with such
foolish things? Why do ye look for a Christ? For
no man can know of anything which is to come.
14 Behold, these things which ye call prophecies,
which ye say are handed down by holy prophets,
behold, they are foolish traditions of your fathers.
15 How do ye know of their surety? Behold, ye
cannot know of things which ye do not see; there-
fore ye cannot know that there shall be a Christ.
16 Ye look forward and say that ye see a remis-
sion of your sins. But behold, it is the effect of
a frenzied mind; and this derangement of your
minds comes because of the traditions of your fa-
thers, which lead you away into a belief of things
which are not so.
17 And many more such things did he say unto
them, telling them that there could be no atone-
ment made for the sins of men, but every man
fared in this life according to the management of
the creature; therefore every man prospered ac-
cording to his genius, and that every man con-
quered according to his strength; and whatsoever
a man did was no crime.
18 And thus he did preach unto them, leading
away the hearts of many, causing them to lift
up their heads in their wickedness, yea, leading
away many women, and also men, to commit
whoredoms—telling them that when a man was
dead, that was the end thereof.

What arguments and criticisms does Korihor try to make against the members of the Church? What similar attacks do you see against religious believers in the world today? How might you respond to such criticism?

ALMA TESTIFIES OF GOD'S EXISTENCE AS KORIHOR DEMANDS A SIGN

After preaching against a belief in Christ to the people in Zarahemla, Korihor attempted to preach in Jershon and in Gideon. He was bound by the people, taken to Zarahemla, and presented to Alma and the chief judge.

Alma 30:30, 37–45

And it came to pass that when he was
brought before Alma and the chief
judge, he did go on in the same manner as he did
in the land of Gideon; yea, he went on to blas-
pheme.
37 And then Alma said unto him: Believest thou
that there is a God?
38 And he answered, Nay.
39 Now Alma said unto him: Will ye deny again
that there is a God, and also deny the Christ? For
behold, I say unto you, I know there is a God,
and also that Christ shall come.
40 And now what evidence have ye that there is
no God, or that Christ cometh not? I say unto
you that ye have none, save it be your word only.
41 But, behold, I have all things as a testimony
that these things are true; and ye also have all
things as a testimony unto you that they are true;
and will ye deny them? Believest thou that these
things are true?
42 Behold, I know that thou believest, but thou
art possessed with a lying spirit, and ye have put
off the Spirit of God that it may have no place
in you; but the devil has power over you, and he
doth carry you about, working devices that he
may destroy the children of God.
43 And now Korihor said unto Alma: If thou
wilt show me a sign, that I may be convinced that
there is a God, yea, show unto me that he hath
power, and then will I be convinced of the truth
of thy words.
44 But Alma said unto him: Thou hast had signs
enough; will ye tempt your God? Will ye say,
Show unto me a sign, when ye have the testimony
of all these thy brethren, and also all the holy
prophets? The scriptures are laid before thee, yea,
and all things denote there is a God; yea, even the
earth, and all things that are upon the face of it,
yea, and its motion, yea, and also all the planets
which move in their regular form do witness that
there is a Supreme Creator.
45 And yet do ye go about, leading away the
hearts of this people, testifying unto them there
is no God? And yet will ye deny against all these
witnesses? And he said: Yea, I will deny, except ye
shall show me a sign.

In response to Korihor, Alma said there were many things that proved God's existence. What were they? What experiences have taught you that Heavenly Father and Jesus Christ are real?

KORIHOR CONTINUES TO DEMAND A SIGN AND IS STRUCK DUMB AND KILLED

Alma had testified of the existence of God and warned Korihor not to tempt God in asking for a sign of things he already knew were true. Korihor said again that unless he was shown a sign, he would continue to deny the existence of God.

ALMA 30:46–53, 56, 59–60

And now it came to pass that Alma said unto him: Behold, I am grieved because of the hardness of your heart, yea, that ye will still resist the spirit of the truth, that thy soul may be destroyed.
47 But behold, it is better that thy soul should be lost than that thou shouldst be the means of bringing many souls down to destruction, by thy lying and by thy flattering words; therefore if thou shalt deny again, behold God shall smite thee, that thou shalt become dumb, that thou shalt never open thy mouth any more, that thou shalt not deceive this people any more.
48 Now Korihor said unto him: I do not deny the existence of a God, but I do not believe that there is a God; and I say also, that ye do not know that there is a God; and except ye show me a sign, I will not believe.
49 Now Alma said unto him: This will I give unto thee for a sign, that thou shalt be struck dumb, according to my words; and I say, that in the name of God, ye shall be struck dumb, that ye shall no more have utterance.
50 Now when Alma had said these words, Korihor was struck dumb, that he could not have utterance, according to the words of Alma.
51 And now when the chief judge saw this, he put forth his hand and wrote unto Korihor, saying: Art thou convinced of the power of God? In whom did ye desire that Alma should show forth his sign? Would ye that he should afflict others, to show unto thee a sign? Behold, he has showed unto you a sign; and now will ye dispute more?
52 And Korihor put forth his hand and wrote, saying: I know that I am dumb, for I cannot speak; and I know that nothing save it were the power of God could bring this upon me; yea, and I always knew that there was a God.
53 But behold, the devil hath deceived me; for he appeared unto me in the form of an angel, and said unto me: Go and reclaim this people, for they have all gone astray after an unknown God. And he said unto me: There is no God; yea, and he taught me that which I should say. And I have taught his words; and I taught them because they were pleasing unto the carnal mind; and I taught them, even until I had much success, insomuch that I verily believed that they were true; and for this cause I withstood the truth, even until I have brought this great curse upon me.
56 And it came to pass that the curse was not taken off of Korihor; but he was cast out, and went about from house to house begging for his food.
59 And it came to pass that as he went forth among the people, yea, among a people who had separated themselves from the Nephites and called themselves Zoramites, being led by a man whose name was Zoram—and as he went forth amongst them, behold, he was run upon and trodden down, even until he was dead.
60 And thus we see the end of him who perverteth the ways of the Lord; and thus we see that the devil will not support his children at the last day, but doth speedily drag them down to hell.

Korihor successfully led people astray by teaching false doctrines that "were pleasing unto the carnal mind." What are some false doctrines in today's world that are "pleasing unto the carnal mind"? What does Korihor's fate teach you about seeking happiness from false teachings?

ALMA AND HIS BRETHREN WITNESS THE PRIDEFUL ZORAMITES ATOP THE RAMEUMPTOM

Following the death of Korihor, Alma heard of idolatry and iniquity taking place among the Zoramites, who were dissenters from the Nephites. Alma took Ammon, Aaron, Omner, Amulek, Zeezrom, and his sons Shiblon and Corianton and traveled to the land of Antionum to preach to the Zoramites.

ALMA 31:12–21, 23–25

Now, when they had come into the land, behold, to their astonishment they found that the Zoramites had built synagogues, and that they did gather themselves together on one day of the week, which day they did call the day of the Lord; and they did worship after a manner which Alma and his brethren had never beheld;

13 For they had a place built up in the center of their synagogue, a place for standing, which was high above the head; and the top thereof would only admit one person.

14 Therefore, whosoever desired to worship must go forth and stand upon the top thereof, and stretch forth his hands towards heaven, and cry with a loud voice, saying:

15 Holy, holy God; we believe that thou art God, and we believe that thou art holy, and that thou wast a spirit, and that thou art a spirit, and that thou wilt be a spirit forever.

16 Holy God, we believe that thou hast separated us from our brethren; and we do not believe in the tradition of our brethren, which was handed down to them by the childishness of their fathers; but we believe that thou hast elected us to be thy holy children; and also thou hast made it known unto us that there shall be no Christ.

17 But thou art the same yesterday, today, and forever; and thou hast elected us that we shall be saved, whilst all around us are elected to be cast by thy wrath down to hell; for the which holiness, O God, we thank thee; and we also thank thee that thou hast elected us, that we may not be led away after the foolish traditions of our brethren, which doth bind them down to a belief of Christ, which doth lead their hearts to wander far from thee, our God.

18 And again we thank thee, O God, that we are a chosen and a holy people. Amen.

19 Now it came to pass that after Alma and his brethren and his sons had heard these prayers, they were astonished beyond all measure.

20 For behold, every man did go forth and offer up these same prayers.

21 Now the place was called by them Rameumptom, which, being interpreted, is the holy stand.

23 Now, after the people had all offered up thanks after this manner, they returned to their homes, never speaking of their God again until they had assembled themselves together again to the holy stand, to offer up thanks after their manner.

24 Now when Alma saw this his heart was grieved; for he saw that they were a wicked and a perverse people; yea, he saw that their hearts were set upon gold, and upon silver, and upon all manner of fine goods.

25 Yea, and he also saw that their hearts were lifted up unto great boasting, in their pride.

Why did the Zoramites' prayer cause Alma to grieve? The Zoramites prayed only on one day and never spoke of God the rest of the week. What can you do to sincerely live according to your belief in God throughout the week?

ALMA PRAYS FOR PATIENCE AND SUCCESS IN PREACHING TO THE WICKED ZORAMITES

After witnessing the prideful prayers of the Zoramites atop the Rameumptom, Alma's heart was grieved and he prayed to God for guidance. As you read, look for the specific blessings Alma asked God to give him.

ALMA 31:26–36

And he lifted up his voice to heaven, and cried, saying: O, how long, O Lord, wilt thou suffer that thy servants shall dwell here below in the flesh, to behold such gross wickedness among the children of men?

27 Behold, O God, they cry unto thee, and yet their hearts are swallowed up in their pride. Behold, O God, they cry unto thee with their mouths, while they are puffed up, even to greatness, with the vain things of the world.

28 Behold, O my God, their costly apparel, and their ringlets, and their bracelets, and their ornaments of gold, and all their precious things which they are ornamented with; and behold, their hearts are set upon them, and yet they cry unto thee and say—We thank thee, O God, for we are a chosen people unto thee, while others shall perish.

29 Yea, and they say that thou hast made it known unto them that there shall be no Christ.

30 O Lord God, how long wilt thou suffer that such wickedness and infidelity shall be among this people? O Lord, wilt thou give me strength, that I may bear with mine infirmities. For I am infirm, and such wickedness among this people doth pain my soul.

31 O Lord, my heart is exceedingly sorrowful; wilt thou comfort my soul in Christ. O Lord, wilt thou grant unto me that I may have strength, that I may suffer with patience these afflictions which shall come upon me, because of the iniquity of this people.

32 O Lord, wilt thou comfort my soul, and give unto me success, and also my fellow laborers who are with me—yea, Ammon, and Aaron, and Omner, and also Amulek and Zeezrom, and also my two sons—yea, even all these wilt thou comfort, O Lord. Yea, wilt thou comfort their souls in Christ.

33 Wilt thou grant unto them that they may have strength, that they may bear their afflictions which shall come upon them because of the iniquities of this people.

34 O Lord, wilt thou grant unto us that we may have success in bringing them again unto thee in Christ.

35 Behold, O Lord, their souls are precious, and many of them are our brethren; therefore, give unto us, O Lord, power and wisdom that we may bring these, our brethren, again unto thee.

36 Now it came to pass that when Alma had said these words, that he clapped his hands upon all them who were with him. And behold, as he clapped his hands upon them, they were filled with the Holy Spirit.

What blessings did Alma ask for in prayer? For what ultimate purpose did he desire these blessings? What differences do you notice between the prayers of the wicked Zoramites and the prayers of Alma?

ALMA TEACHES OF THE BLESSINGS THAT COME TO THOSE WHO ARE HUMBLE

After praying for patience and success, Alma and his fellow missionaries went among the Zoramites to preach the gospel. They began to have success among the poorest of the people, who had been cast out of the synagogues—a type of church building—due to their poor clothing. While preaching, Alma was approached by a group of these poor people. Their leader asked Alma how they could worship God if they were not permitted to enter a synagogue.

ALMA 32:6–16

And now when Alma heard this, he
turned him about, his face immediately
towards him, and he beheld with great joy; for he
beheld that their afflictions had truly humbled
them, and that they were in a preparation to hear
the word.
7 Therefore he did say no more to the other mul-
titude; but he stretched forth his hand, and cried
unto those whom he beheld, who were truly pen-
itent, and said unto them:
8 I behold that ye are lowly in heart; and if so,
blessed are ye.
9 Behold thy brother hath said, What shall we
do?—for we are cast out of our synagogues, that
we cannot worship our God.
10 Behold I say unto you, do ye suppose that ye
cannot worship God save it be in your synagogues
only?
11 And moreover, I would ask, do ye suppose
that ye must not worship God only once in a
week?
12 I say unto you, it is well that ye are cast out
of your synagogues, that ye may be humble, and
that ye may learn wisdom; for it is necessary that
ye should learn wisdom; for it is because that ye
are cast out, that ye are despised of your brethren
because of your exceeding poverty, that ye are
brought to a lowliness of heart; for ye are neces-
sarily brought to be humble.
13 And now, because ye are compelled to be
humble blessed are ye; for a man sometimes, if he
is compelled to be humble, seeketh repentance;
and now surely, whosoever repenteth shall find
mercy; and he that findeth mercy and endureth to
the end the same shall be saved.
14 And now, as I said unto you, that because ye
were compelled to be humble ye were blessed, do
ye not suppose that they are more blessed who
truly humble themselves because of the word?
15 Yea, he that truly humbleth himself, and re-
penteth of his sins, and endureth to the end, the
same shall be blessed—yea, much more blessed
than they who are compelled to be humble be-
cause of their exceeding poverty.
16 Therefore, blessed are they who humble them-
selves without being compelled to be humble; or
rather, in other words, blessed is he that believeth
in the word of God, and is baptized without stub-
bornness of heart, yea, without being brought to
know the word, or even compelled to know, be-
fore they will believe.

According to Alma, what are some of the blessings of being humble? Alma spoke of the difference between those who are forced to be humble and those who choose to be humble. In what ways can you *choose* to be humble?

ALMA INVITES THE PEOPLE TO PLANT THE WORD OF GOD IN THEIR HEARTS

Alma continued to teach the group of humbled Zoramites who had been cast out of the synagogues because of their poor status. As you read, consider the words Alma uses to describe what faith is.

ALMA 32:17–18, 21–23, 26–32

Yea, there are many who do say: If thou wilt show unto us a sign from heaven, then we shall know of a surety; then we shall believe.
18 Now I ask, is this faith? Behold, I say unto you, Nay; for if a man knoweth a thing he hath no cause to believe, for he knoweth it.
21 And now as I said concerning faith—faith is not to have a perfect knowledge of things; therefore if ye have faith ye hope for things which are not seen, which are true.
22 And now, behold, I say unto you, and I would that ye should remember, that God is merciful unto all who believe on his name; therefore he desireth, in the first place, that ye should believe, yea, even on his word.
23 And now, he imparteth his word by angels unto men, yea, not only men but women also. Now this is not all; little children do have words given unto them many times, which confound the wise and the learned.
26 Now, as I said concerning faith—that it was not a perfect knowledge—even so it is with my words. Ye cannot know of their surety at first, unto perfection, any more than faith is a perfect knowledge.
27 But behold, if ye will awake and arouse your faculties, even to an experiment upon my words, and exercise a particle of faith, yea, even if ye can no more than desire to believe, let this desire work in you, even until ye believe in a manner that ye can give place for a portion of my words.
28 Now, we will compare the word unto a seed. Now, if ye give place, that a seed may be planted in your heart, behold, if it be a true seed, or a good seed, if ye do not cast it out by your unbelief, that ye will resist the Spirit of the Lord, behold, it will begin to swell within your breasts; and when you feel these swelling motions, ye will begin to say within yourselves—It must needs be that this is a good seed, or that the word is good, for it beginneth to enlarge my soul; yea, it beginneth to enlighten my understanding, yea, it beginneth to be delicious to me.
29 Now behold, would not this increase your faith? I say unto you, Yea; nevertheless it hath not grown up to a perfect knowledge.
30 But behold, as the seed swelleth, and sprouteth, and beginneth to grow, then you must needs say that the seed is good; for behold it swelleth, and sprouteth, and beginneth to grow. And now, behold, will not this strengthen your faith? Yea, it will strengthen your faith: for ye will say I know that this is a good seed; for behold it sprouteth and beginneth to grow.
31 And now, behold, are ye sure that this is a good seed? I say unto you, Yea; for every seed bringeth forth unto its own likeness.
32 Therefore, if a seed groweth it is good, but if it groweth not, behold it is not good, therefore it is cast away.

How did Alma describe faith? Alma taught that if we allow God's word to be planted in our hearts like a seed, our understanding of God's word would increase. According to Alma, what do we have to do to nourish and grow the seed of God's word? What role does faith play?

ALMA TEACHES THE PEOPLE TO CONTINUALLY NOURISH THE WORD OF GOD IN THEIR HEARTS

Alma continued to speak to the poor Zoramites about planting the word of God in their hearts and nourishing it through faith. He compared the process to nourishing a seed as it takes root and grows into a strong tree.

ALMA 32:33–43

And now, behold, because ye have tried the experiment, and planted the seed, and it swelleth and sprouteth, and beginneth to grow, ye must needs know that the seed is good.

34 And now, behold, is your knowledge perfect? Yea, your knowledge is perfect in that thing, and your faith is dormant; and this because you know, for ye know that the word hath swelled your souls, and ye also know that it hath sprouted up, that your understanding doth begin to be enlightened, and your mind doth begin to expand.

35 O then, is not this real? I say unto you, Yea, because it is light; and whatsoever is light, is good, because it is discernible, therefore ye must know that it is good; and now behold, after ye have tasted this light is your knowledge perfect?

36 Behold I say unto you, Nay; neither must ye lay aside your faith, for ye have only exercised your faith to plant the seed that ye might try the experiment to know if the seed was good.

37 And behold, as the tree beginneth to grow, ye will say: Let us nourish it with great care, that it may get root, that it may grow up, and bring forth fruit unto us. And now behold, if ye nourish it with much care it will get root, and grow up, and bring forth fruit.

38 But if ye neglect the tree, and take no thought for its nourishment, behold it will not get any root; and when the heat of the sun cometh and scorcheth it, because it hath no root it withers away, and ye pluck it up and cast it out.

39 Now, this is not because the seed was not good, neither is it because the fruit thereof would not be desirable; but it is because your ground is barren, and ye will not nourish the tree, therefore ye cannot have the fruit thereof.

40 And thus, if ye will not nourish the word, looking forward with an eye of faith to the fruit thereof, ye can never pluck of the fruit of the tree of life.

41 But if ye will nourish the word, yea, nourish the tree as it beginneth to grow, by your faith with great diligence, and with patience, looking forward to the fruit thereof, it shall take root; and behold it shall be a tree springing up unto everlasting life.

42 And because of your diligence and your faith and your patience with the word in nourishing it, that it may take root in you, behold, by and by ye shall pluck the fruit thereof, which is most precious, which is sweet above all that is sweet, and which is white above all that is white, yea, and pure above all that is pure; and ye shall feast upon this fruit even until ye are filled, that ye hunger not, neither shall ye thirst.

43 Then, my brethren, ye shall reap the rewards of your faith, and your diligence, and patience, and long-suffering, waiting for the tree to bring forth fruit unto you.

Alma spoke of the need to carefully nourish understanding of God's word through faith. What are things you can do to nourish the seed of God's word in your heart? What might diminish it? What "fruit" or blessings have you seen as a result of your faith?

ALMA QUOTES ZENOS' EXPERIENCE OF PRAYING TO GOD IN ALL PLACES

After teaching the importance of nourishing God's word, Alma continued to teach the poor Zoramites by quoting the prophet Zenos, whose words were contained in the brass plates. Consider the many different situations in which Zenos prayed and the specific things he prayed for.

Alma 33:1–13

Now after Alma had spoken these words, they sent forth unto him desiring to know whether they should believe in one God, that they might obtain this fruit of which he had spoken, or how they should plant the seed, or the word of which he had spoken, which he said must be planted in their hearts; or in what manner they should begin to exercise their faith.

2 And Alma said unto them: Behold, ye have said that ye could not worship your God because ye are cast out of your synagogues. But behold, I say unto you, if ye suppose that ye cannot worship God, ye do greatly err, and ye ought to search the scriptures; if ye suppose that they have taught you this, ye do not understand them.

3 Do ye remember to have read what Zenos, the prophet of old, has said concerning prayer or worship?

4 For he said: Thou art merciful, O God, for thou hast heard my prayer, even when I was in the wilderness; yea, thou wast merciful when I prayed concerning those who were mine enemies, and thou didst turn them to me.

5 Yea, O God, and thou wast merciful unto me when I did cry unto thee in my field; when I did cry unto thee in my prayer, and thou didst hear me.

6 And again, O God, when I did turn to my house thou didst hear me in my prayer.

7 And when I did turn unto my closet, O Lord, and prayed unto thee, thou didst hear me.

8 Yea, thou art merciful unto thy children when they cry unto thee, to be heard of thee and not of men, and thou wilt hear them.

9 Yea, O God, thou hast been merciful unto me, and heard my cries in the midst of thy congregations.

10 Yea, and thou hast also heard me when I have been cast out and have been despised by mine enemies; yea, thou didst hear my cries, and wast angry with mine enemies, and thou didst visit them in thine anger with speedy destruction.

11 And thou didst hear me because of mine afflictions and my sincerity; and it is because of thy Son that thou hast been thus merciful unto me, therefore I will cry unto thee in all mine afflictions, for in thee is my joy; for thou hast turned thy judgments away from me, because of thy Son.

12 And now Alma said unto them: Do ye believe those scriptures which have been written by them of old?

13 Behold, if ye do, ye must believe what Zenos said; for, behold he said: Thou hast turned away thy judgments because of thy Son.

When and where did Zenos pray? What examples does he give of things he prayed for? In your typical week, what are some situations when you could take the opportunity to pray? How has God answered one of your prayers recently?

ALMA INVITES PEOPLE TO LOOK TO JESUS CHRIST AND BELIEVE

As Alma continued to teach the humbled Zoramites, he quoted Zenock, another prophet whose words were contained in the brass plates. Alma also referred to Moses guiding the children of Israel toward the promised land. God had sent serpents among the wicked Israelites. Many were bitten and died. God told Moses to make a brass serpent and set it upon a pole—and promised that those who looked at the serpent would be healed from the poisonous bites.

ALMA 33:14–23

Now behold, my brethren, I would ask if
ye have read the scriptures? If ye have,
how can ye disbelieve on the Son of God?
15 For it is not written that Zenos alone spake
of these things, but Zenock also spake of these
things—
16 For behold, he said: Thou art angry, O Lord,
with this people, because they will not understand
thy mercies which thou hast bestowed upon them
because of thy Son.
17 And now, my brethren, ye see that a second
prophet of old has testified of the Son of God,
and because the people would not understand his
words they stoned him to death.
18 But behold, this is not all; these are not the
only ones who have spoken concerning the Son
of God.
19 Behold, he was spoken of by Moses; yea, and
behold a type was raised up in the wilderness, that
whosoever would look upon it might live. And
many did look and live.
20 But few understood the meaning of those
things, and this because of the hardness of their
hearts. But there were many who were so hard-
ened that they would not look, therefore they
perished. Now the reason they would not look
is because they did not believe that it would heal
them.
21 O my brethren, if ye could be healed by
merely casting about your eyes that ye might be
healed, would ye not behold quickly, or would
ye rather harden your hearts in unbelief, and be
slothful, that ye would not cast about your eyes,
that ye might perish?
22 If so, wo shall come upon you; but if not so,
then cast about your eyes and begin to believe in
the Son of God, that he will come to redeem his
people, and that he shall suffer and die to atone
for their sins; and that he shall rise again from the
dead, which shall bring to pass the resurrection,
that all men shall stand before him, to be judged
at the last and judgment day, according to their
works.
23 And now, my brethren, I desire that ye shall
plant this word in your hearts, and as it beginneth
to swell even so nourish it by your faith. And be-
hold, it will become a tree, springing up in you
unto everlasting life. And then may God grant
unto you that your burdens may be light, through
the joy of his Son. And even all this can ye do if
ye will. Amen.

Why did some of the Israelites refuse to look at the brass serpent? What simple things has God asked you to do in order to find peace and joy?

AMULEK SPEAKS OF CHRIST'S ATONEMENT AS THE GREAT AND LAST SACRIFICE

After Alma had spoken to the humbled Zoramites, Amulek added his testimony.

ALMA 34:1, 7–16

And now it came to pass that after Alma
had spoken these words unto them he
sat down upon the ground, and Amulek arose and
began to teach them, saying:
7 My brother has called upon the words of
Zenos, that redemption cometh through the Son
of God, and also upon the words of Zenock; and
also he has appealed unto Moses, to prove that
these things are true.
8 And now, behold, I will testify unto you of
myself that these things are true. Behold, I say
unto you, that I do know that Christ shall come
among the children of men, to take upon him
the transgressions of his people, and that he shall
atone for the sins of the world; for the Lord God
hath spoken it.
9 For it is expedient that an atonement should
be made; for according to the great plan of the
Eternal God there must be an atonement made,
or else all mankind must unavoidably perish; yea,
all are hardened; yea, all are fallen and are lost,
and must perish except it be through the atone-
ment which it is expedient should be made.
10 For it is expedient that there should be a great
and last sacrifice; yea, not a sacrifice of man, nei-
ther of beast, neither of any manner of fowl; for it
shall not be a human sacrifice; but it must be an
infinite and eternal sacrifice.
11 Now there is not any man that can sacrifice
his own blood which will atone for the sins of
another. Now, if a man murdereth, behold will
our law, which is just, take the life of his brother?
I say unto you, Nay.
12 But the law requireth the life of him who hath
murdered; therefore there can be nothing which is
short of an infinite atonement which will suffice
for the sins of the world.
13 Therefore, it is expedient that there should be
a great and last sacrifice, and then shall there be,
or it is expedient there should be, a stop to the
shedding of blood; then shall the law of Moses be
fulfilled; yea, it shall be all fulfilled, every jot and
tittle, and none shall have passed away.
14 And behold, this is the whole meaning of the
law, every whit pointing to that great and last sac-
rifice; and that great and last sacrifice will be the
Son of God, yea, infinite and eternal.
15 And thus he shall bring salvation to all those
who shall believe on his name; this being the in-
tent of this last sacrifice, to bring about the bowels
of mercy, which overpowereth justice, and brin-
geth about means unto men that they may have
faith unto repentance.
16 And thus mercy can satisfy the demands of
justice, and encircles them in the arms of safety,
while he that exercises no faith unto repentance is
exposed to the whole law of the demands of jus-
tice; therefore only unto him that has faith unto
repentance is brought about the great and eternal
plan of redemption.

According to Amulek, what would be the result if Christ did not complete His atoning sacrifice? What did Amulek say was the purpose of Jesus' sacrifice? Why does he call Christ's Atonement the "great and last sacrifice"?

AMULEK TEACHES THE NEED TO BE HUMBLE AND CALL UPON GOD AT ALL TIMES

Amulek continued to teach the humbled Zoramites.

ALMA 34:17–32

Therefore may God grant unto you, my brethren, that ye may begin to exercise your faith unto repentance, that ye begin to call upon his holy name, that he would have mercy upon you;

18 Yea, cry unto him for mercy; for he is mighty to save.

19 Yea, humble yourselves, and continue in prayer unto him.

20 Cry unto him when ye are in your fields, yea, over all your flocks.

21 Cry unto him in your houses, yea, over all your household, both morning, mid-day, and evening.

22 Yea, cry unto him against the power of your enemies.

23 Yea, cry unto him against the devil, who is an enemy to all righteousness.

24 Cry unto him over the crops of your fields, that ye may prosper in them.

25 Cry over the flocks of your fields, that they may increase.

26 But this is not all; ye must pour out your souls in your closets, and your secret places, and in your wilderness.

27 Yea, and when you do not cry unto the Lord, let your hearts be full, drawn out in prayer unto him continually for your welfare, and also for the welfare of those who are around you.

28 And now behold, my beloved brethren, I say unto you, do not suppose that this is all; for after ye have done all these things, if ye turn away the needy, and the naked, and visit not the sick and afflicted, and impart of your substance, if ye have, to those who stand in need—I say unto you, if ye do not any of these things, behold, your prayer is vain, and availeth you nothing, and ye are as hypocrites who do deny the faith.

29 Therefore, if ye do not remember to be charitable, ye are as dross, which the refiners do cast out, (it being of no worth) and is trodden under foot of men.

30 And now, my brethren, I would that, after ye have received so many witnesses, seeing that the holy scriptures testify of these things, ye come forth and bring fruit unto repentance.

31 Yea, I would that ye would come forth and harden not your hearts any longer; for behold, now is the time and the day of your salvation; and therefore, if ye will repent and harden not your hearts, immediately shall the great plan of redemption be brought about unto you.

32 For behold, this life is the time for men to prepare to meet God; yea, behold the day of this life is the day for men to perform their labors.

According to Amulek, in what situations and places should we pray to God? What did Amulek say we must do to ensure our prayers are answered?

AMULEK PLEADS WITH THE PEOPLE NOT TO DELAY THE ACT OF REPENTANCE

Amulek concluded his remarks to the humbled Zoramites.

ALMA 34:33–41

And now, as I said unto you before, as ye have had so many witnesses, therefore, I beseech of you that ye do not procrastinate the day of your repentance until the end; for after this day of life, which is given us to prepare for eternity, behold, if we do not improve our time while in this life, then cometh the night of darkness wherein there can be no labor performed.

34 Ye cannot say, when ye are brought to that awful crisis, that I will repent, that I will return to my God. Nay, ye cannot say this; for that same spirit which doth possess your bodies at the time that ye go out of this life, that same spirit will have power to possess your body in that eternal world.

35 For behold, if ye have procrastinated the day of your repentance even until death, behold, ye have become subjected to the spirit of the devil, and he doth seal you his; therefore, the Spirit of the Lord hath withdrawn from you, and hath no place in you, and the devil hath all power over you; and this is the final state of the wicked.

36 And this I know, because the Lord hath said he dwelleth not in unholy temples, but in the hearts of the righteous doth he dwell; yea, and he has also said that the righteous shall sit down in his kingdom, to go no more out; but their garments should be made white through the blood of the Lamb.

37 And now, my beloved brethren, I desire that ye should remember these things, and that ye should work out your salvation with fear before God, and that ye should no more deny the coming of Christ;

38 That ye contend no more against the Holy Ghost, but that ye receive it, and take upon you the name of Christ; that ye humble yourselves even to the dust, and worship God, in whatsoever place ye may be in, in spirit and in truth; and that ye live in thanksgiving daily, for the many mercies and blessings which he doth bestow upon you.

39 Yea, and I also exhort you, my brethren, that ye be watchful unto prayer continually, that ye may not be led away by the temptations of the devil, that he may not overpower you, that ye may not become his subjects at the last day; for behold, he rewardeth you no good thing.

40 And now my beloved brethren, I would exhort you to have patience, and that ye bear with all manner of afflictions; that ye do not revile against those who do cast you out because of your exceeding poverty, lest ye become sinners like unto them;

41 But that ye have patience, and bear with those afflictions, with a firm hope that ye shall one day rest from all your afflictions.

According to Amulek, why is it wrong to procrastinate your repentance until the end of your life? What will happen if you delay repentance? What does he say you can do to escape the temptations of the devil?

ALMA ADVISES HELAMAN TO REMEMBER THE CAPTIVITY AND DELIVERANCE OF THEIR FATHERS

The majority of the Zoramites rejected the teachings of Alma and his brethren. Those who did believe were cast out of the land and found refuge in the land of Jershon, where they were ministered to by Alma. The wicked Zoramites stirred up the Lamanites in anger against the Nephites and began to make war. Alma grieved over the disobedience and contention among his people. He gathered each of his sons, starting with Helaman, and gave them individual counsel.

Alma 36:1–6

My son, give ear to my words; for I swear unto you, that inasmuch as ye shall keep the commandments of God ye shall prosper in the land.
2 I would that ye should do as I have done, in remembering the captivity of our fathers; for they were in bondage, and none could deliver them except it was the God of Abraham, and the God of Isaac, and the God of Jacob; and he surely did deliver them in their afflictions.
3 And now, O my son Helaman, behold, thou art in thy youth, and therefore, I beseech of thee that thou wilt hear my words and learn of me; for I do know that whosoever shall put their trust in God shall be supported in their trials, and their troubles, and their afflictions, and shall be lifted up at the last day.
4 And I would not that ye think that I know of myself—not of the temporal but of the spiritual, not of the carnal mind but of God.
5 Now, behold, I say unto you, if I had not been born of God I should not have known these things; but God has, by the mouth of his holy angel, made these things known unto me, not of any worthiness of myself;
6 For I went about with the sons of Mosiah, seeking to destroy the church of God; but behold, God sent his holy angel to stop us by the way.

What did Alma promise Helaman would happen if he kept God's commandments? What can you learn from Alma saying that those who put their trust in God "shall be supported *in* their trials, and their troubles, and their afflictions" (emphasis added)? How has God supported you and your family during your trials?

ALMA SHARES HIS PERSONAL EXPERIENCE OF PLEADING TO JESUS CHRIST FOR MERCY

As Alma continued to teach his son Helaman, he spoke of the angel that appeared to him and the sons of Mosiah when they were wicked and seeking to destroy the Church.

ALMA 36:7–19

And behold, he spake unto us, as it were the voice of thunder, and the whole earth did tremble beneath our feet; and we all fell to the earth, for the fear of the Lord came upon us.

8 But behold, the voice said unto me: Arise. And I arose and stood up, and beheld the angel.

9 And he said unto me: If thou wilt of thyself be destroyed, seek no more to destroy the church of God.

10 And it came to pass that I fell to the earth; and it was for the space of three days and three nights that I could not open my mouth, neither had I the use of my limbs.

11 And the angel spake more things unto me, which were heard by my brethren, but I did not hear them; for when I heard the words—If thou wilt be destroyed of thyself, seek no more to destroy the church of God—I was struck with such great fear and amazement lest perhaps I should be destroyed, that I fell to the earth and I did hear no more.

12 But I was racked with eternal torment, for my soul was harrowed up to the greatest degree and racked with all my sins.

13 Yea, I did remember all my sins and iniquities, for which I was tormented with the pains of hell; yea, I saw that I had rebelled against my God, and that I had not kept his holy commandments.

14 Yea, and I had murdered many of his children, or rather led them away unto destruction; yea, and in fine so great had been my iniquities, that the very thought of coming into the presence of my God did rack my soul with inexpressible horror.

15 Oh, thought I, that I could be banished and become extinct both soul and body, that I might not be brought to stand in the presence of my God, to be judged of my deeds.

16 And now, for three days and for three nights was I racked, even with the pains of a damned soul.

17 And it came to pass that as I was thus racked with torment, while I was harrowed up by the memory of my many sins, behold, I remembered also to have heard my father prophesy unto the people concerning the coming of one Jesus Christ, a Son of God, to atone for the sins of the world.

18 Now, as my mind caught hold upon this thought, I cried within my heart: O Jesus, thou Son of God, have mercy on me, who am in the gall of bitterness, and am encircled about by the everlasting chains of death.

19 And now, behold, when I thought this, I could remember my pains no more; yea, I was harrowed up by the memory of my sins no more.

For what sins did Alma feel guilt and torment? What led to Alma being freed from the pains of his sins? What can you learn from Alma about the repentance process?

ALMA SPEAKS OF BEING REPEATEDLY DELIVERED BY THE LORD

As Alma shared his conversion experience with his son Helaman, he spoke of the relief he felt after calling upon Jesus Christ and receiving forgiveness. As you read, look for the different ways the Lord delivered Alma and his fathers.

ALMA 36:20–30

And oh, what joy, and what marvelous light I did behold; yea, my soul was filled with joy as exceeding as was my pain!

21 Yea, I say unto you, my son, that there could be nothing so exquisite and so bitter as were my pains. Yea, and again I say unto you, my son, that on the other hand, there can be nothing so exquisite and sweet as was my joy.

22 Yea, methought I saw, even as our father Lehi saw, God sitting upon his throne, surrounded with numberless concourses of angels, in the attitude of singing and praising their God; yea, and my soul did long to be there.

23 But behold, my limbs did receive their strength again, and I stood upon my feet, and did manifest unto the people that I had been born of God.

24 Yea, and from that time even until now, I have labored without ceasing, that I might bring souls unto repentance; that I might bring them to taste of the exceeding joy of which I did taste; that they might also be born of God, and be filled with the Holy Ghost.

25 Yea, and now behold, O my son, the Lord doth give me exceedingly great joy in the fruit of my labors;

26 For because of the word which he has imparted unto me, behold, many have been born of God, and have tasted as I have tasted, and have seen eye to eye as I have seen; therefore they do know of these things of which I have spoken, as I do know; and the knowledge which I have is of God.

27 And I have been supported under trials and troubles of every kind, yea, and in all manner of afflictions; yea, God has delivered me from prison, and from bonds, and from death; yea, and I do put my trust in him, and he will still deliver me.

28 And I know that he will raise me up at the last day, to dwell with him in glory; yea, and I will praise him forever, for he has brought our fathers out of Egypt, and he has swallowed up the Egyptians in the Red Sea; and he led them by his power into the promised land; yea, and he has delivered them out of bondage and captivity from time to time.

29 Yea, and he has also brought our fathers out of the land of Jerusalem; and he has also, by his everlasting power, delivered them out of bondage and captivity, from time to time even down to the present day; and I have always retained in remembrance their captivity; yea, and ye also ought to retain in remembrance, as I have done, their captivity.

30 But behold, my son, this is not all; for ye ought to know as I do know, that inasmuch as ye shall keep the commandments of God ye shall prosper in the land; and ye ought to know also, that inasmuch as ye will not keep the commandments of God ye shall be cut off from his presence. Now this is according to his word.

Alma spoke of the many ways he and his ancestors had been delivered or saved by the Lord. What were some of those situations? How did Alma describe the pain he felt before his repentance and the joy he felt after his repentance?

ALMA TEACHES HELAMAN THE IMPORTANCE OF SCRIPTURAL RECORDS

Alma continued to counsel his son Helaman. He gave Helaman the plates of brass and the plates of Nephi, commanded him to keep a record of their people, and emphasized the prophetic purpose of scriptures.

ALMA 37:4–12

Behold, it has been prophesied by our
fathers, that they should be kept and
handed down from one generation to another,
and be kept and preserved by the hand of the
Lord until they should go forth unto every na-
tion, kindred, tongue, and people, that they shall
know of the mysteries contained thereon.
5 And now behold, if they are kept they must
retain their brightness; yea, and they will retain
their brightness; yea, and also shall all the plates
which do contain that which is holy writ.
6 Now ye may suppose that this is foolishness in
me; but behold I say unto you, that by small and
simple things are great things brought to pass; and
small means in many instances doth confound the
wise.
7 And the Lord God doth work by means to
bring about his great and eternal purposes; and by
very small means the Lord doth confound the wise
and bringeth about the salvation of many souls.
8 And now, it has hitherto been wisdom in God
that these things should be preserved; for behold,
they have enlarged the memory of this people,
yea, and convinced many of the error of their
ways, and brought them to the knowledge of their
God unto the salvation of their souls.
9 Yea, I say unto you, were it not for these things
that these records do contain, which are on these
plates, Ammon and his brethren could not have
convinced so many thousands of the Lamanites
of the incorrect tradition of their fathers; yea,
these records and their words brought them unto
repentance; that is, they brought them to the
knowledge of the Lord their God, and to rejoice
in Jesus Christ their Redeemer.
10 And who knoweth but what they will be the
means of bringing many thousands of them, yea,
and also many thousands of our stiffnecked breth-
ren, the Nephites, who are now hardening their
hearts in sin and iniquities, to the knowledge of
their Redeemer?
11 Now these mysteries are not yet fully made
known unto me; therefore I shall forbear.
12 And it may suffice if I only say they are pre-
served for a wise purpose, which purpose is
known unto God; for he doth counsel in wisdom
over all his works, and his paths are straight, and
his course is one eternal round.

What did Alma say is the purpose of the scriptures? How has the Book of Mormon fulfilled that purpose in your own life? In what way is the Book of Mormon a "small and simple" thing that has brought to pass "great things"?

ALMA TEACHES HELAMAN THAT GOD WILL FULFILL ALL HIS PROMISES

As Alma taught his son Helaman, he spoke of Helaman's responsibility to care for the scriptural record that had been entrusted to him.

Alma 37:13–20

O remember, remember, my son Helaman,
how strict are the commandments of God.
And he said: If ye will keep my commandments
ye shall prosper in the land—but if ye keep not
his commandments ye shall be cut off from his
presence.
14 And now remember, my son, that God has
entrusted you with these things, which are sacred,
which he has kept sacred, and also which he will
keep and preserve for a wise purpose in him, that
he may show forth his power unto future gener-
ations.
15 And now behold, I tell you by the spirit of
prophecy, that if ye transgress the commandments
of God, behold, these things which are sacred
shall be taken away from you by the power of
God, and ye shall be delivered up unto Satan, that
he may sift you as chaff before the wind.
16 But if ye keep the commandments of God,
and do with these things which are sacred accord-
ing to that which the Lord doth command you,
(for you must appeal unto the Lord for all things
whatsoever ye must do with them) behold, no
power of earth or hell can take them from you, for
God is powerful to the fulfilling of all his words.
17 For he will fulfil all his promises which he
shall make unto you, for he has fulfilled his prom-
ises which he has made unto our fathers.
18 For he promised unto them that he would
preserve these things for a wise purpose in him,
that he might show forth his power unto future
generations.
19 And now behold, one purpose hath he ful-
filled, even to the restoration of many thousands
of the Lamanites to the knowledge of the truth;
and he hath shown forth his power in them, and
he will also still show forth his power in them
unto future generations; therefore they shall be
preserved.
20 Therefore I command you, my son Helaman,
that ye be diligent in fulfilling all my words, and
that ye be diligent in keeping the commandments
of God as they are written.

Helaman was entrusted with the scriptural record, which was sacred. What sacred responsibilities have been given to you? Alma taught that God fulfills all His promises. What promises has God made to you? How have you seen some of those promises fulfilled?

ALMA ENCOURAGES HELAMAN TO COUNSEL WITH THE LORD IN ALL MATTERS

In Alma's counsel to his son Helaman, he spoke of the things Helaman should teach the people.

Alma 37:33–37

Preach unto them repentance, and faith
on the Lord Jesus Christ; teach them to
humble themselves and to be meek and lowly in
heart; teach them to withstand every temptation
of the devil, with their faith on the Lord Jesus
Christ.
34 Teach them to never be weary of good works,
but to be meek and lowly in heart; for such shall
find rest to their souls.
35 O, remember, my son, and learn wisdom in
thy youth; yea, learn in thy youth to keep the
commandments of God.
36 Yea, and cry unto God for all thy support; yea,
let all thy doings be unto the Lord, and whith-
ersoever thou goest let it be in the Lord; yea, let
all thy thoughts be directed unto the Lord; yea,
let the affections of thy heart be placed upon the
Lord forever.
37 Counsel with the Lord in all thy doings, and
he will direct thee for good; yea, when thou liest
down at night lie down unto the Lord, that he
may watch over you in your sleep; and when
thou risest in the morning let thy heart be full of
thanks unto God; and if ye do these things, ye
shall be lifted up at the last day.

According to Alma, in what times and situations should we counsel with the Lord? How is counseling with the Lord different from merely saying your prayers?

ALMA COMPARES THE WORD OF CHRIST TO THE DIRECTIONS OFFERED BY THE LIAHONA

Alma concluded his counsel to his son Helaman.

ALMA 37:38–47

And now, my son, I have somewhat to say
concerning the thing which our fathers
call a ball, or director—or our fathers called it
Liahona, which is, being interpreted, a compass;
and the Lord prepared it.
39 And behold, there cannot any man work after
the manner of so curious a workmanship. And be-
hold, it was prepared to show unto our fathers the
course which they should travel in the wilderness.
40 And it did work for them according to their
faith in God; therefore, if they had faith to be-
lieve that God could cause that those spindles
should point the way they should go, behold, it
was done; therefore they had this miracle, and
also many other miracles wrought by the power of
God, day by day.
41 Nevertheless, because those miracles were
worked by small means it did show unto them
marvelous works. They were slothful, and forgot
to exercise their faith and diligence and then those
marvelous works ceased, and they did not prog-
ress in their journey;
42 Therefore, they tarried in the wilderness, or did
not travel a direct course, and were afflicted with
hunger and thirst, because of their transgressions.
43 And now, my son, I would that ye should
understand that these things are not without a
shadow; for as our fathers were slothful to give
heed to this compass (now these things were
temporal) they did not prosper; even so it is with
things which are spiritual.
44 For behold, it is as easy to give heed to the
word of Christ, which will point to you a straight
course to eternal bliss, as it was for our fathers to
give heed to this compass, which would point
unto them a straight course to the promised land.
45 And now I say, is there not a type in this
thing? For just as surely as this director did bring
our fathers, by following its course, to the prom-
ised land, shall the words of Christ, if we follow
their course, carry us beyond this vale of sorrow
into a far better land of promise.
46 O my son, do not let us be slothful because of
the easiness of the way; for so was it with our fa-
thers; for so was it prepared for them, that if they
would look they might live; even so it is with us.
The way is prepared, and if we will look we may
live forever.
47 And now, my son, see that ye take care of
these sacred things, yea, see that ye look to God
and live. Go unto this people and declare the
word, and be sober. My son, farewell.

To what does Alma compare the Liahona? Alma taught that following the words of Christ would lead us "into a far better land of promise." As you have read the scriptures and tried to follow the words of Christ, where have you been led?

ALMA COMMENDS SHIBLON FOR HIS PATIENCE AND ENCOURAGES HIM TO BE WISE

After counseling Helaman, Alma counseled his son Shiblon.

ALMA 38:1–5, 9–15

My son, give ear to my words, for I say unto you, even as I said unto Helaman, that inasmuch as ye shall keep the commandments of God ye shall prosper in the land; and inasmuch as ye will not keep the commandments of God ye shall be cut off from his presence.

2 And now, my son, I trust that I shall have great joy in you, because of your steadiness and your faithfulness unto God; for as you have commenced in your youth to look to the Lord your God, even so I hope that you will continue in keeping his commandments; for blessed is he that endureth to the end.

3 I say unto you, my son, that I have had great joy in thee already, because of thy faithfulness and thy diligence, and thy patience and thy long-suffering among the people of the Zoramites.

4 For I know that thou wast in bonds; yea, and I also know that thou wast stoned for the word's sake; and thou didst bear all these things with patience because the Lord was with thee; and now thou knowest that the Lord did deliver thee.

5 And now my son, Shiblon, I would that ye should remember, that as much as ye shall put your trust in God even so much ye shall be delivered out of your trials, and your troubles, and your afflictions, and ye shall be lifted up at the last day.

9 And now, my son, I have told you this that ye may learn wisdom, that ye may learn of me that there is no other way or means whereby man can be saved, only in and through Christ. Behold, he is the life and the light of the world. Behold, he is the word of truth and righteousness.

10 And now, as ye have begun to teach the word even so I would that ye should continue to teach; and I would that ye would be diligent and temperate in all things.

11 See that ye are not lifted up unto pride; yea, see that ye do not boast in your own wisdom, nor of your much strength.

12 Use boldness, but not overbearance; and also see that ye bridle all your passions, that ye may be filled with love; see that ye refrain from idleness.

13 Do not pray as the Zoramites do, for ye have seen that they pray to be heard of men, and to be praised for their wisdom.

14 Do not say: O God, I thank thee that we are better than our brethren; but rather say: O Lord, forgive my unworthiness, and remember my brethren in mercy—yea, acknowledge your unworthiness before God at all times.

15 And may the Lord bless your soul, and receive you at the last day into his kingdom, to sit down in peace. Now go, my son, and teach the word unto this people. Be sober. My son, farewell.

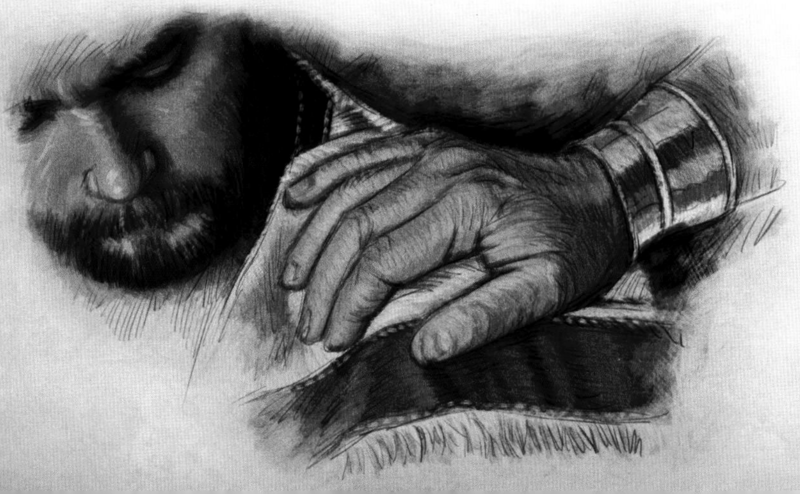

Alma commanded Shiblon to "use boldness, but not overbearance" as he taught the gospel. What do you think that means? How can you use boldness but not overbearance as you share the gospel? What other instruction from Alma to Shiblon can you apply to your own life?

ALMA TEACHES CORIANTON THE SERIOUS NATURE OF SEXUAL SIN

After counseling his son Shiblon, Alma counseled his son Corianton. While Alma had been preaching among the Zoramites with his sons, Corianton had abandoned his missionary duties and committed sexual sin.

ALMA 39:5–13

Know ye not, my son, that these things are an abomination in the sight of the Lord; yea, most abominable above all sins save it be the shedding of innocent blood or denying the Holy Ghost?

6 For behold, if ye deny the Holy Ghost when it once has had place in you, and ye know that ye deny it, behold, this is a sin which is unpardonable; yea, and whosoever murdereth against the light and knowledge of God, it is not easy for him to obtain forgiveness; yea, I say unto you, my son, that it is not easy for him to obtain a forgiveness.

7 And now, my son, I would to God that ye had not been guilty of so great a crime. I would not dwell upon your crimes, to harrow up your soul, if it were not for your good.

8 But behold, ye cannot hide your crimes from God; and except ye repent they will stand as a testimony against you at the last day.

9 Now my son, I would that ye should repent and forsake your sins, and go no more after the lusts of your eyes, but cross yourself in all these things; for except ye do this ye can in nowise inherit the kingdom of God. Oh, remember, and take it upon you, and cross yourself in these things.

10 And I command you to take it upon you to counsel with your elder brothers in your undertakings; for behold, thou art in thy youth, and ye stand in need to be nourished by your brothers. And give heed to their counsel.

11 Suffer not yourself to be led away by any vain or foolish thing; suffer not the devil to lead away your heart again after those wicked harlots. Behold, O my son, how great iniquity ye brought upon the Zoramites; for when they saw your conduct they would not believe in my words.

12 And now the Spirit of the Lord doth say unto me: Command thy children to do good, lest they lead away the hearts of many people to destruction; therefore I command you, my son, in the fear of God, that ye refrain from your iniquities;

13 That ye turn to the Lord with all your mind, might, and strength; that ye lead away the hearts of no more to do wickedly; but rather return unto them, and acknowledge your faults and that wrong which ye have done.

According to Alma, what are the only sins that are more serious than sexual sin? What were some of the negative consequences of Corianton's sin? What guidance have you been given to help you obey the law of chastity, or not commit sexual sin?

ALMA TEACHES CORIANTON OF THE RESURRECTION BROUGHT ABOUT BY JESUS CHRIST

Alma continued teaching his son Corianton, who had boasted in his own strength and had committed sexual sin. As you read, look for Alma's description of death and resurrection.

ALMA 40:1–3, 11–14, 23, 25–26

Now my son, here is somewhat more I
would say unto thee; for I perceive that
thy mind is worried concerning the resurrection
of the dead.
2 Behold, I say unto you, that there is no
resurrection—or, I would say, in other words, that
this mortal does not put on immortality, this cor-
ruption does not put on incorruption—until after
the coming of Christ.
3 Behold, he bringeth to pass the resurrection of
the dead. But behold, my son, the resurrection is
not yet. Now, I unfold unto you a mystery; never-
theless, there are many mysteries which are kept,
that no one knoweth them save God himself. But
I show unto you one thing which I have inquired
diligently of God that I might know—that is con-
cerning the resurrection.
11 Now, concerning the state of the soul between
death and the resurrection—Behold, it has been
made known unto me by an angel, that the spirits
of all men, as soon as they are departed from this
mortal body, yea, the spirits of all men, whether
they be good or evil, are taken home to that God
who gave them life.
12 And then shall it come to pass, that the spirits
of those who are righteous are received into a state
of happiness, which is called paradise, a state of
rest, a state of peace, where they shall rest from all
their troubles and from all care, and sorrow.
13 And then shall it come to pass, that the spirits
of the wicked, yea, who are evil—for behold, they
have no part nor portion of the Spirit of the Lord;
for behold, they chose evil works rather than
good; therefore the spirit of the devil did enter
into them, and take possession of their house—
and these shall be cast out into outer darkness;
there shall be weeping, and wailing, and gnashing
of teeth, and this because of their own iniquity,
being led captive by the will of the devil.
14 Now this is the state of the souls of the
wicked, yea, in darkness, and a state of awful, fear-
ful looking for the fiery indignation of the wrath
of God upon them; thus they remain in this state,
as well as the righteous in paradise, until the time
of their resurrection.
23 The soul shall be restored to the body, and the
body to the soul; yea, and every limb and joint
shall be restored to its body; yea, even a hair of
the head shall not be lost; but all things shall be
restored to their proper and perfect frame.
25 And then shall the righteous shine forth in the
kingdom of God.
26 But behold, an awful death cometh upon
the wicked; for they die as to things pertaining
to things of righteousness; for they are unclean,
and no unclean thing can inherit the kingdom of
God; but they are cast out, and consigned to par-
take of the fruits of their labors or their works,
which have been evil; and they drink the dregs of
a bitter cup.

According to Alma, what happens to the spirits of all people as soon as they die? What then happens to the spirits of the righteous and of the wicked? What happens to a person's body and spirit during the Resurrection?

ALMA SPEAKS OF GOD'S JUSTICE RESTORING GOOD FOR GOOD AND EVIL FOR EVIL

Alma continued to counsel his son Corianton.

Alma 41:2–7, 10, 14–15

I say unto thee, my son, that the plan of restoration is requisite with the justice of God; for it is requisite that all things should be restored to their proper order. Behold, it is requisite and just, according to the power and resurrection of Christ, that the soul of man should be restored to its body, and that every part of the body should be restored to itself.

3 And it is requisite with the justice of God that men should be judged according to their works; and if their works were good in this life, and the desires of their hearts were good, that they should also, at the last day, be restored unto that which is good.

4 And if their works are evil they shall be restored unto them for evil. Therefore, all things shall be restored to their proper order, every thing to its natural frame—mortality raised to immortality, corruption to incorruption—raised to endless happiness to inherit the kingdom of God, or to endless misery to inherit the kingdom of the devil, the one on one hand, the other on the other—

5 The one raised to happiness according to his desires of happiness, or good according to his desires of good; and the other to evil according to his desires of evil; for as he has desired to do evil all the day long even so shall he have his reward of evil when the night cometh.

6 And so it is on the other hand. If he hath repented of his sins, and desired righteousness until the end of his days, even so he shall be rewarded unto righteousness.

7 These are they that are redeemed of the Lord; yea, these are they that are taken out, that are delivered from that endless night of darkness; and thus they stand or fall; for behold, they are their own judges, whether to do good or do evil.

10 Do not suppose, because it has been spoken concerning restoration, that ye shall be restored from sin to happiness. Behold, I say unto you, wickedness never was happiness.

14 Therefore, my son, see that you are merciful unto your brethren; deal justly, judge righteously, and do good continually; and if ye do all these things then shall ye receive your reward; yea, ye shall have mercy restored unto you again; ye shall have justice restored unto you again; ye shall have a righteous judgment restored unto you again; and ye shall have good rewarded unto you again.

15 For that which ye do send out shall return unto you again, and be restored; therefore, the word restoration more fully condemneth the sinner, and justifieth him not at all.

What kind of people did Alma say "are they that are redeemed of the Lord"? Alma taught that "wickedness never was happiness." What examples have you seen of this principle?

ALMA SPEAKS OF THE ATONEMENT OF JESUS CHRIST SATISFYING THE DEMANDS OF JUSTICE

As Alma counseled his son Corianton, he sensed Corianton's opinion that it was unjust for God to punish the wicked.

ALMA 42:2, 4, 7, 10, 12–15

Now behold, my son, I will explain this thing unto thee. For behold, after the Lord God sent our first parents forth from the garden of Eden, to till the ground, from whence they were taken—yea, he drew out the man, and he placed at the east end of the garden of Eden, cherubim, and a flaming sword which turned every way, to keep the tree of life—

4 And thus we see, that there was a time granted unto man to repent, yea, a probationary time, a time to repent and serve God.

7 And now, ye see by this that our first parents were cut off both temporally and spiritually from the presence of the Lord; and thus we see they became subjects to follow after their own will.

10 Therefore, as they had become carnal, sensual, and devilish, by nature, this probationary state became a state for them to prepare; it became a preparatory state.

12 And now, there was no means to reclaim men from this fallen state, which man had brought upon himself because of his own disobedience;

13 Therefore, according to justice, the plan of redemption could not be brought about, only on conditions of repentance of men in this probationary state, yea, this preparatory state; for except it were for these conditions, mercy could not take effect except it should destroy the work of justice. Now the work of justice could not be destroyed; if so, God would cease to be God.

14 And thus we see that all mankind were fallen, and they were in the grasp of justice; yea, the justice of God, which consigned them forever to be cut off from his presence.

15 And now, the plan of mercy could not be brought about except an atonement should be made; therefore God himself atoneth for the sins of the world, to bring about the plan of mercy, to appease the demands of justice, that God might be a perfect, just God, and a merciful God also.

Alma described the effects of the Fall of Adam and Jesus Christ's Atonement. What were the results of those two events? What qualities did the Fall bring to mankind, making Christ's Atonement necessary?

ALMA TEACHES THAT IN GOD'S PLAN BOTH MERCY AND JUSTICE WILL BE SATISFIED

Alma concluded his personal counsel to his son Corianton.

ALMA 42:23–30

But God ceaseth not to be God, and mercy claimeth the penitent, and mercy cometh because of the atonement; and the atonement bringeth to pass the resurrection of the dead; and the resurrection of the dead bringeth back men into the presence of God; and thus they are restored into his presence, to be judged according to their works, according to the law and justice.

24 For behold, justice exerciseth all his demands, and also mercy claimeth all which is her own; and thus, none but the truly penitent are saved.

25 What, do ye suppose that mercy can rob justice? I say unto you, Nay; not one whit. If so, God would cease to be God.

26 And thus God bringeth about his great and eternal purposes, which were prepared from the foundation of the world. And thus cometh about the salvation and the redemption of men, and also their destruction and misery.

27 Therefore, O my son, whosoever will come may come and partake of the waters of life freely; and whosoever will not come the same is not compelled to come; but in the last day it shall be restored unto him according to his deeds.

28 If he has desired to do evil, and has not repented in his days, behold, evil shall be done unto him, according to the restoration of God.

29 And now, my son, I desire that ye should let these things trouble you no more, and only let your sins trouble you, with that trouble which shall bring you down unto repentance.

30 O my son, I desire that ye should deny the justice of God no more. Do not endeavor to excuse yourself in the least point because of your sins, by denying the justice of God; but do you let the justice of God, and his mercy, and his long-suffering have full sway in your heart; and let it bring you down to the dust in humility.

According to Alma, who can partake of the "waters of life" offered through Christ's redemption? Alma spoke of the need to be "truly penitent" and to be brought "down to the dust in humility." What does penitent mean? (You may want to use a dictionary.) What examples have you seen of people with that level of humility? What choices can you make to become more humble?

MORONI RAISES THE TITLE OF LIBERTY AMONG THE NEPHITES

It was now about seventy-four years before the birth of Jesus Christ. After Alma counseled each of his sons, he led them among the people to preach the gospel. Meanwhile, the Lamanites were again stirred up in anger toward the Nephites and began to prepare for war. A righteous man named Moroni was appointed captain over all the Nephite armies. He was twenty-five years old. He prepared his army with many weapons, shields, and armor. He used spies and strategic movements and asked Alma to pray to know the plans of the Lamanite army. The Lord told Alma the Lamanite's plans, and the Nephites defended themselves in a great battle, forcing the Lamanites to retreat. Many Nephites were killed, but the people thanked God for delivering them. Alma prophesied to Helaman that four generations after the appearance of Jesus Christ, the Nephites would dwindle in unbelief and be destroyed by the Lamanites. Alma blessed his sons and the Church and was assumed by the people to have been taken up into heaven without dying, as Moses had been. Helaman and his brothers preached among the people, who were becoming proud and wicked. A cunning and wicked man named Amalickiah began a movement to make himself king over the people. Many—including Church members—sided with Amalickiah, and a division arose among the people.

ALMA 46:11–13, 18, 21–22

And now it came to pass that when Moroni, who was the chief commander of the armies of the Nephites, had heard of these dissensions, he was angry with Amalickiah.

12 And it came to pass that he rent his coat; and he took a piece thereof, and wrote upon it—In memory of our God, our religion, and freedom, and our peace, our wives, and our children—and he fastened it upon the end of a pole.

13 And he fastened on his head-plate, and his breastplate, and his shields, and girded on his armor about his loins; and he took the pole, which had on the end thereof his rent coat, (and he called it the title of liberty) and he bowed himself to the earth, and he prayed mightily unto his God for the blessings of liberty to rest upon his brethren, so long as there should a band of Christians remain to possess the land—

18 And he said: Surely God shall not suffer that we, who are despised because we take upon us the name of Christ, shall be trodden down and destroyed, until we bring it upon us by our own transgressions.

21 And it came to pass that when Moroni had proclaimed these words, behold, the people came running together with their armor girded about their loins, rending their garments in token, or as a covenant, that they would not forsake the Lord their God; or, in other words, if they should transgress the commandments of God, or fall into transgression, and be ashamed to take upon them the name of Christ, the Lord should rend them even as they had rent their garments.

22 Now this was the covenant which they made, and they cast their garments at the feet of Moroni, saying: We covenant with our God, that we shall be destroyed, even as our brethren in the land northward, if we shall fall into transgression; yea, he may cast us at the feet of our enemies, even as we have cast our garments at thy feet to be trodden under foot, if we shall fall into transgression.

What did the righteous Nephites covenant to do in response to Moroni's proclamation of the title of liberty? What does *liberty* mean? How can you help strengthen and protect political and religious liberty where you live?

CAPTAIN MORONI IS DESCRIBED AS A MAN OF PERFECT UNDERSTANDING

After Amalickiah's forces were driven out of the land by Moroni's forces, Amalickiah journeyed to the land of the Lamanites. There he employed a cunning plan of treachery and murder that placed him first at the head of the Lamanite army and then as the king over all the Lamanites. He stirred up the Lamanites to anger against the Nephites. He intended to destroy the Nephite army and rule over both the Lamanites and Nephites. As you read, look for descriptions of Moroni's character and behavior.

ALMA 48:7, 10–13, 17–18

Now it came to pass that while
Amalickiah had thus been obtaining
power by fraud and deceit, Moroni, on the other
hand, had been preparing the minds of the people
to be faithful unto the Lord their God.
10 And thus he was preparing to support their
liberty, their lands, their wives, and their children,
and their peace, and that they might live unto the
Lord their God, and that they might maintain
that which was called by their enemies the cause
of Christians.
11 And Moroni was a strong and a mighty man;
he was a man of a perfect understanding; yea, a
man that did not delight in bloodshed; a man
whose soul did joy in the liberty and the freedom
of his country, and his brethren from bondage
and slavery;
12 Yea, a man whose heart did swell with thanks-
giving to his God, for the many privileges and
blessings which he bestowed upon his people; a
man who did labor exceedingly for the welfare
and safety of his people.
13 Yea, and he was a man who was firm in the
faith of Christ, and he had sworn with an oath to
defend his people, his rights, and his country, and
his religion, even to the loss of his blood.
17 Yea, verily, verily I say unto you, if all men
had been, and were, and ever would be, like unto
Moroni, behold, the very powers of hell would
have been shaken forever; yea, the devil would
never have power over the hearts of the children
of men.
18 Behold, he was a man like unto Ammon, the
son of Mosiah, yea, and even the other sons of
Mosiah, yea, and also Alma and his sons, for they
were all men of God.

What was Moroni like? Review the qualities of Moroni described in this passage, and select one or more that you would like to develop more fully. What actions can you take to strengthen that quality in yourself?

THE NEPHITES ARE BLESSED WITH PROSPERITY AND HAPPINESS IN THE MIDST OF WAR

Amalickiah's Lamanite forces began to attack the Nephites in their cities but found that the Nephite armies were prepared for them. Throughout the land, Moroni had strategically prepared defensive positions behind pickets of timber and atop high banks of earth. Amalickiah was enraged at the Lamanites' inability to destroy the Nephites. He cursed God and swore that he would drink the blood of Moroni. The Lamanites attempted various attacks upon the Nephites. The Nephites were preserved and over a thousand Lamanites were slaughtered.

ALMA 50:17–23

And in these prosperous circumstances were the people of Nephi in the commencement of the twenty and first year of the reign of the judges over the people of Nephi.

18 And they did prosper exceedingly, and they became exceedingly rich; yea, and they did multiply and wax strong in the land.

19 And thus we see how merciful and just are all the dealings of the Lord, to the fulfilling of all his words unto the children of men; yea, we can behold that his words are verified, even at this time, which he spake unto Lehi, saying:

20 Blessed art thou and thy children; and they shall be blessed, inasmuch as they shall keep my commandments they shall prosper in the land. But remember, inasmuch as they will not keep my commandments they shall be cut off from the presence of the Lord.

21 And we see that these promises have been verified to the people of Nephi; for it has been their quarrelings and their contentions, yea, their murderings, and their plunderings, their idolatry, their whoredoms, and their abominations, which were among themselves, which brought upon them their wars and their destructions.

22 And those who were faithful in keeping the commandments of the Lord were delivered at all times, whilst thousands of their wicked brethren have been consigned to bondage, or to perish by the sword, or to dwindle in unbelief, and mingle with the Lamanites.

23 But behold there never was a happier time among the people of Nephi, since the days of Nephi, than in the days of Moroni, yea, even at this time, in the twenty and first year of the reign of the judges.

What promise did the Lord give to Lehi that was later fulfilled as Moroni led the Nephites? Despite the Nephites involvement in an ongoing war, the scriptures say that "there never was a happier time among the people of Nephi." How do you think the Nephites found happiness amid such difficult circumstances? How can you find joy in the midst of trial?

2,000 SONS OF THE PEOPLE OF AMMON JOIN THE NEPHITES IN BATTLING THE LAMANITES

After a time of peace and prosperity, contention arose among the Nephites. Some people wanted to do away with the system of judges and instead have a king rule over them. A vote was held, and the system of judges remained the governing body of the people. Meanwhile, Amalickiah had again been preparing the Lamanite army for battle. Many who had voted for a king to rule over them refused to defend their fellow Nephites against the approaching Lamanites. Moroni was granted authority to put such Nephites to death. Being distracted by internal contention, many Nephite cities were overtaken by the Lamanites and many Nephites were killed. Teancum, a leader in the Nephite army, battled Amalickiah's forces and later killed Amalickiah as he slept in his tent. Amalickiah's brother Ammoron assumed the role of king of the Lamanites and retreated his forces. Moroni and Teancum used strategic movements to lure the Lamanites from their strongholds, killed many, and took others prisoner. As the fighting continued, the people of Ammon—who had previously made a covenant to never again take up weapons of war—felt compelled to join the Nephites in battling the Lamanites. Helaman, another leader in the Nephite army, counseled the people of Ammon against going to battle.

ALMA 53:15–22

And Helaman feared lest by so doing they should lose their souls; therefore all those who had entered into this covenant were compelled to behold their brethren wade through their afflictions, in their dangerous circumstances at this time.

16 But behold, it came to pass they had many sons, who had not entered into a covenant that they would not take their weapons of war to defend themselves against their enemies; therefore they did assemble themselves together at this time, as many as were able to take up arms, and they called themselves Nephites.

17 And they entered into a covenant to fight for the liberty of the Nephites, yea, to protect the land unto the laying down of their lives; yea, even they covenanted that they never would give up their liberty, but they would fight in all cases to protect the Nephites and themselves from bondage.

18 Now behold, there were two thousand of those young men, who entered into this covenant and took their weapons of war to defend their country.

19 And now behold, as they never had hitherto been a disadvantage to the Nephites, they became now at this period of time also a great support; for they took their weapons of war, and they would that Helaman should be their leader.

20 And they were all young men, and they were exceedingly valiant for courage, and also for strength and activity; but behold, this was not all—they were men who were true at all times in whatsoever thing they were entrusted.

21 Yea, they were men of truth and soberness, for they had been taught to keep the commandments of God and to walk uprightly before him.

22 And now it came to pass that Helaman did march at the head of his two thousand stripling soldiers, to the support of the people in the borders of the land on the south by the west sea.

Why did Helaman counsel the people of Ammon not to go to battle? How were the sons of the people of Ammon described? How can you be valiant and strong even in your youth?

HELAMAN'S 2,000 YOUNG WARRIORS FIGHT VALIANTLY AND ARE SPARED FROM DEATH

Moroni received a letter from Helaman detailing the actions of the 2,000 young warriors who had joined the Nephite cause. The 2,000 warriors, led by Helaman, had come to the aid of another Nephite commander, named Antipus, whose forces were being defeated by Lamanites. In his letter to Moroni, Helaman recounted the words he had spoken to the young warriors.

ALMA 56:44–49, 54–56

Therefore what say ye, my sons, will ye go
against them to battle?
45 And now I say unto you, my beloved brother
Moroni, that never had I seen so great courage,
nay, not amongst all the Nephites.
46 For as I had ever called them my sons (for
they were all of them very young) even so they
said unto me: Father, behold our God is with us,
and he will not suffer that we should fall; then
let us go forth; we would not slay our brethren if
they would let us alone; therefore let us go, lest
they should overpower the army of Antipus.
47 Now they never had fought, yet they did not
fear death; and they did think more upon the lib-
erty of their fathers than they did upon their lives;
yea, they had been taught by their mothers, that
if they did not doubt, God would deliver them.
48 And they rehearsed unto me the words of
their mothers, saying: We do not doubt our
mothers knew it.
49 And it came to pass that I did return with
my two thousand against these Lamanites who
had pursued us. And now behold, the armies of
Antipus had overtaken them, and a terrible battle
had commenced.
54 And now it came to pass that we, the people
of Nephi, the people of Antipus, and I with my
two thousand, did surround the Lamanites, and
did slay them; yea, insomuch that they were com-
pelled to deliver up their weapons of war and also
themselves as prisoners of war.
55 And now it came to pass that when they had
surrendered themselves up unto us, behold, I
numbered those young men who had fought with
me, fearing lest there were many of them slain.
56 But behold, to my great joy, there had not
one soul of them fallen to the earth; yea, and
they had fought as if with the strength of God;
yea, never were men known to have fought with
such miraculous strength; and with such mighty
power did they fall upon the Lamanites, that
they did frighten them; and for this cause did the
Lamanites deliver themselves up as prisoners of
war.

What reasons did the 2,000 young warriors give for their willingness to go to battle? How had they learned to have great faith in God's willingness to protect them? What have you learned from your mother?

THE 2,000 YOUNG WARRIORS ARE EXACTLY OBEDIENT AND ARE AGAIN SPARED IN BATTLE

After being defeated in several battles by the Nephites, the Lamanite army returned in force against Helaman's army. As his letter to Moroni continued, Helaman described the actions of his 2,000 young warriors as the Nephites faced the possibility of defeat.

ALMA 57:19–27

But behold, my little band of two thou-
sand and sixty fought most desperately;
yea, they were firm before the Lamanites, and
did administer death unto all those who opposed
them.
20 And as the remainder of our army were about
to give way before the Lamanites, behold, those
two thousand and sixty were firm and undaunted.
21 Yea, and they did obey and observe to per-
form every word of command with exactness; yea,
and even according to their faith it was done unto
them; and I did remember the words which they
said unto me that their mothers had taught them.
22 And now behold, it was these my sons, and
those men who had been selected to convey the
prisoners, to whom we owe this great victory; for
it was they who did beat the Lamanites; therefore
they were driven back to the city of Manti.
23 And we retained our city Cumeni, and were
not all destroyed by the sword; nevertheless, we
had suffered great loss.
24 And it came to pass that after the Lamanites
had fled, I immediately gave orders that my men
who had been wounded should be taken from
among the dead, and caused that their wounds
should be dressed.
25 And it came to pass that there were two hun-
dred, out of my two thousand and sixty, who had
fainted because of the loss of blood; nevertheless,
according to the goodness of God, and to our
great astonishment, and also the joy of our whole
army, there was not one soul of them who did
perish; yea, and neither was there one soul among
them who had not received many wounds.
26 And now, their preservation was astonishing
to our whole army, yea, that they should be spared
while there was a thousand of our brethren who
were slain. And we do justly ascribe it to the mi-
raculous power of God, because of their exceed-
ing faith in that which they had been taught to
believe—that there was a just God, and whoso-
ever did not doubt, that they should be preserved
by his marvelous power.
27 Now this was the faith of these of whom I have
spoken; they are young, and their minds are firm,
and they do put their trust in God continually.

Helaman's young warriors fought in another dangerous battle—and none of them died. What did Helaman say was the reason for the preservation of their lives? Helaman described his young warriors as young men who "did obey and observe to perform every word of command with exactness." What does it mean to obey "with exactness"? How have you been blessed when you have obeyed in this way?

MORMON SPEAKS OF THE GATES OF HEAVEN BEING OPEN TO ALL BELIEVERS IN CHRIST

As the Lamanite and Nephite armies continued to battle, a rebellion began among the Nephites in Zarahemla. Moroni brought order to the internal strife, defeated the Lamanites, and appointed his son Moronihah leader of the Nephite army. Later, a wicked man named Gadianton attempted to dethrone the chief judge and led a group of followers into the wilderness. It was now about thirty-nine years before the birth of Jesus Christ. Peace was again established. Mormon, abridging Helaman's record, summarized the state of the Church in the land.

HELAMAN 3:24–30, 37

And it came to pass that in this same year there was exceedingly great prosperity in the church, insomuch that there were thousands who did join themselves unto the church and were baptized unto repentance.
25 And so great was the prosperity of the church, and so many the blessings which were poured out upon the people, that even the high priests and the teachers were themselves astonished beyond measure.
26 And it came to pass that the work of the Lord did prosper unto the baptizing and uniting to the church of God, many souls, yea, even tens of thousands.
27 Thus we may see that the Lord is merciful unto all who will, in the sincerity of their hearts, call upon his holy name.
28 Yea, thus we see that the gate of heaven is open unto all, even to those who will believe on the name of Jesus Christ, who is the Son of God.
29 Yea, we see that whosoever will may lay hold upon the word of God, which is quick and powerful, which shall divide asunder all the cunning and the snares and the wiles of the devil, and lead the man of Christ in a strait and narrow course across that everlasting gulf of misery which is prepared to engulf the wicked—
30 And land their souls, yea, their immortal souls, at the right hand of God in the kingdom of heaven, to sit down with Abraham, and Isaac, and with Jacob, and with all our holy fathers, to go no more out.
37 And it came to pass in the fifty and third year of the reign of the judges, Helaman died, and his eldest son Nephi began to reign in his stead. And it came to pass that he did fill the judgment-seat with justice and equity; yea, he did keep the commandments of God, and did walk in the ways of his father.

According to Mormon, to whom is the gate of heaven opened? What does the word of God have the power to do? What do we have to do to access this power?

THE NEPHITES BECOME WICKED AND CEASE TO BE PRESERVED BY THE LORD

After a period of peace, internal contention arose among the Nephites. Some dissented and joined the Lamanites, who made war upon the Nephites and drove them from many of their cities, including Zarahemla. Moronihah led the Nephite army in reclaiming some of their lands.

HELAMAN 4:11–13, 21–25

Now this great loss of the Nephites, and the great slaughter which was among them, would not have happened had it not been for their wickedness and their abomination which was among them; yea, and it was among those also who professed to belong to the church of God.

12 And it was because of the pride of their hearts, because of their exceeding riches, yea, it was because of their oppression to the poor, withholding their food from the hungry, withholding their clothing from the naked, and smiting their humble brethren upon the cheek, making a mock of that which was sacred, denying the spirit of prophecy and of revelation, murdering, plundering, lying, stealing, committing adultery, rising up in great contentions, and deserting away into the land of Nephi, among the Lamanites—

13 And because of this their great wickedness, and their boastings in their own strength, they were left in their own strength; therefore they did not prosper, but were afflicted and smitten, and driven before the Lamanites, until they had lost possession of almost all their lands.

21 Yea, they began to remember the prophecies of Alma, and also the words of Mosiah; and they saw that they had been a stiffnecked people, and that they had set at naught the commandments of God;

22 And that they had altered and trampled under their feet the laws of Mosiah, or that which the Lord commanded him to give unto the people; and they saw that their laws had become corrupted, and that they had become a wicked people, insomuch that they were wicked even like unto the Lamanites.

23 And because of their iniquity the church had begun to dwindle; and they began to disbelieve in the spirit of prophecy and in the spirit of revelation; and the judgments of God did stare them in the face.

24 And they saw that they had become weak, like unto their brethren, the Lamanites, and that the Spirit of the Lord did no more preserve them; yea, it had withdrawn from them because the Spirit of the Lord doth not dwell in unholy temples—

25 Therefore the Lord did cease to preserve them by his miraculous and matchless power, for they had fallen into a state of unbelief and awful wickedness; and they saw that the Lamanites were exceedingly more numerous than they, and except they should cleave unto the Lord their God they must unavoidably perish.

What did the Nephites do that caused them to lose the Spirit and the protection of the Lord? What modern-day examples have you seen of similar sins? How can you remain humble while you seek to develop your strengths and talents?

HELAMAN COUNSELS HIS SONS TO BUILD THEIR LIVES UPON THE FOUNDATION OF CHRIST

Seeing the great wickedness among the Nephites, Nephi resigned his position as chief judge and began journeying through the land with his brother Lehi, preaching the word of God. Helaman, their father, had named his sons Nephi and Lehi as a reminder of their ancestors' righteous examples. Look for the things Helaman invited his sons to "remember."

Helaman 5:7–12

Therefore, my sons, I would that ye should do that which is good, that it may be said of you, and also written, even as it has been said and written of them.

8 And now my sons, behold I have somewhat more to desire of you, which desire is, that ye may not do these things that ye may boast, but that ye may do these things to lay up for yourselves a treasure in heaven, yea, which is eternal, and which fadeth not away; yea, that ye may have that precious gift of eternal life, which we have reason to suppose hath been given to our fathers.

9 O remember, remember, my sons, the words which king Benjamin spake unto his people; yea, remember that there is no other way nor means whereby man can be saved, only through the atoning blood of Jesus Christ, who shall come; yea, remember that he cometh to redeem the world.

10 And remember also the words which Amulek spake unto Zeezrom, in the city of Ammonihah; for he said unto him that the Lord surely should come to redeem his people, but that he should not come to redeem them in their sins, but to redeem them from their sins.

11 And he hath power given unto him from the Father to redeem them from their sins because of repentance; therefore he hath sent his angels to declare the tidings of the conditions of repentance, which bringeth unto the power of the Redeemer, unto the salvation of their souls.

12 And now, my sons, remember, remember that it is upon the rock of our Redeemer, who is Christ, the Son of God, that ye must build your foundation; that when the devil shall send forth his mighty winds, yea, his shafts in the whirlwind, yea, when all his hail and his mighty storm shall beat upon you, it shall have no power over you to drag you down to the gulf of misery and endless wo, because of the rock upon which ye are built, which is a sure foundation, a foundation whereon if men build they cannot fall.

How many times did Helaman use the word "remember" in this passage? What did Helaman invite his sons to remember? What do you think it means to "build your foundation" upon the rock of Jesus Christ?

NEPHI AND LEHI ARE PROTECTED BY HEAVENLY FIRE AND HEAR A PIERCING VOICE

Nephi and Lehi journeyed throughout all the land and preached the word of God with such power and authority that many wicked Nephites repented and 8,000 Lamanites were baptized. An army of Lamanites then took Nephi and Lehi and cast them into prison.

HELAMAN 5:22–24, 29–34

And after they had been cast into prison
many days without food, behold, they
went forth into the prison to take them that they
might slay them.
23 And it came to pass that Nephi and Lehi
were encircled about as if by fire, even insomuch
that they durst not lay their hands upon them
for fear lest they should be burned. Nevertheless,
Nephi and Lehi were not burned; and they were
as standing in the midst of fire and were not
burned.
24 And when they saw that they were encircled
about with a pillar of fire, and that it burned them
not, their hearts did take courage.
29 And it came to pass that there came a voice
as if it were above the cloud of darkness, saying:
Repent ye, repent ye, and seek no more to destroy
my servants whom I have sent unto you to declare
good tidings.
30 And it came to pass when they heard this
voice, and beheld that it was not a voice of thun-
der, neither was it a voice of a great tumultuous
noise, but behold, it was a still voice of perfect
mildness, as if it had been a whisper, and it did
pierce even to the very soul—
31 And notwithstanding the mildness of the
voice, behold the earth shook exceedingly, and
the walls of the prison trembled again, as if it
were about to tumble to the earth; and behold
the cloud of darkness, which had overshadowed
them, did not disperse—
32 And behold the voice came again, saying:
Repent ye, repent ye, for the kingdom of heaven
is at hand; and seek no more to destroy my ser-
vants. And it came to pass that the earth shook
again, and the walls trembled.
33 And also again the third time the voice came,
and did speak unto them marvelous words which
cannot be uttered by man; and the walls did trem-
ble again, and the earth shook as if it were about
to divide asunder.
34 And it came to pass that the Lamanites could
not flee because of the cloud of darkness which
did overshadow them; yea, and also they were im-
movable because of the fear which did come upon
them.

How do the scriptures describe the voice that spoke to the Lamanites? How would you describe your own experiences in hearing the promptings and influence of the Spirit?

THE HOLY SPIRIT OF GOD ENTERS INTO THE HEARTS OF REPENTANT LAMANITES

While Nephi and Lehi were encircled in a protective pillar of fire, a repentant Nephite named Aminadab spoke to the wicked Lamanites who were overpowered by a cloud of darkness.

Helaman 5:41–51

And Aminadab said unto them: You must repent, and cry unto the voice, even until ye shall have faith in Christ, who was taught unto you by Alma, and Amulek, and Zeezrom; and when ye shall do this, the cloud of darkness shall be removed from overshadowing you.

42 And it came to pass that they all did begin to cry unto the voice of him who had shaken the earth; yea, they did cry even until the cloud of darkness was dispersed.

43 And it came to pass that when they cast their eyes about, and saw that the cloud of darkness was dispersed from overshadowing them, behold, they saw that they were encircled about, yea every soul, by a pillar of fire.

44 And Nephi and Lehi were in the midst of them; yea, they were encircled about; yea, they were as if in the midst of a flaming fire, yet it did harm them not, neither did it take hold upon the walls of the prison; and they were filled with that joy which is unspeakable and full of glory.

45 And behold, the Holy Spirit of God did come down from heaven, and did enter into their hearts, and they were filled as if with fire, and they could speak forth marvelous words.

46 And it came to pass that there came a voice unto them, yea, a pleasant voice, as if it were a whisper, saying:

47 Peace, peace be unto you, because of your faith in my Well Beloved, who was from the foundation of the world.

48 And now, when they heard this they cast up their eyes as if to behold from whence the voice came; and behold, they saw the heavens open; and angels came down out of heaven and ministered unto them.

49 And there were about three hundred souls who saw and heard these things; and they were bidden to go forth and marvel not, neither should they doubt.

50 And it came to pass that they did go forth, and did minister unto the people, declaring throughout all the regions round about all the things which they had heard and seen, insomuch that the more part of the Lamanites were convinced of them, because of the greatness of the evidences which they had received.

51 And as many as were convinced did lay down their weapons of war, and also their hatred and the tradition of their fathers.

What did the Lamanites do that allowed them to hear the voice of God? What did they do after receiving a witness from the Spirit? When you want to feel the comfort or guidance of the Holy Ghost, what can you do?

NEPHI CONDEMNS WICKEDNESS AND PROPHESIES OF THE NEPHITES' DESTRUCTION

Following their conversion, the righteous Lamanites began to preach the gospel among the Nephites. Both peoples enjoyed a period of peace and friendly association. After a time, Gadianton and his band of robbers resumed their secret works of murder and wickedness. The Lamanites hunted down the robbers in their land and converted many to righteousness. The Nephites embraced the robbers, descended into wickedness, and overtook the government. In a short period of time, Satan had laid great hold upon the hearts of the Nephites, and the Spirit of the Lord withdrew from them. Nephi went to a garden tower in his home, bowed himself in prayer, and cried aloud for the wickedness he had seen. People heard him praying, and a crowd gathered on the street below.

HELAMAN 7:12–22, 25, 28

And now, when Nephi arose he beheld the multitudes of people who had gathered together.

13 And it came to pass that he opened his mouth and said unto them: Behold, why have ye gathered yourselves together? That I may tell you of your iniquities?

14 Yea, because I have got upon my tower that I might pour out my soul unto my God, because of the exceeding sorrow of my heart, which is because of your iniquities!

15 And because of my mourning and lamentation ye have gathered yourselves together, and do marvel; yea, and ye have great need to marvel; yea, ye ought to marvel because ye are given away that the devil has got so great hold upon your hearts.

16 Yea, how could you have given way to the enticing of him who is seeking to hurl away your souls down to everlasting misery and endless wo?

17 O repent ye, repent ye! Why will ye die? Turn ye, turn ye unto the Lord your God. Why has he forsaken you?

18 It is because you have hardened your hearts; yea, ye will not hearken unto the voice of the good shepherd; yea, ye have provoked him to anger against you.

19 And behold, instead of gathering you, except ye will repent, behold, he shall scatter you forth that ye shall become meat for dogs and wild beasts.

20 O, how could you have forgotten your God in the very day that he has delivered you?

21 But behold, it is to get gain, to be praised of men, yea, and that ye might get gold and silver. And ye have set your hearts upon the riches and the vain things of this world, for the which ye do murder, and plunder, and steal, and bear false witness against your neighbor, and do all manner of iniquity.

22 And for this cause wo shall come unto you except ye shall repent. For if ye will not repent, behold, this great city, and also all those great cities which are round about, which are in the land of our possession, shall be taken away that ye shall have no place in them; for behold, the Lord will not grant unto you strength, as he has hitherto done, to withstand against your enemies.

25 Yea, wo be unto you because of that great abomination which has come among you; and ye have united yourselves unto it, yea, to that secret band which was established by Gadianton!

28 And except ye repent ye shall perish; yea, even your lands shall be taken from you, and ye shall be destroyed from off the face of the earth.

Nephi spoke of Satan as one who was "seeking to hurl away your souls down to everlasting misery and endless wo." How did the Nephites give in to Satan's enticing? What is Satan doing to try to cause you everlasting misery?

NEPHI SPEAKS OF THE ROLE OF PROPHETS THROUGHOUT HISTORY

After Nephi spoke boldly to the Nephites of their need to repent, the people's opinions were divided. The wicked followers of Gadianton wanted to silence Nephi. Others felt Nephi was correct in calling them to repentance. Nephi resumed speaking, taught of the role of prophets, and made a bold prophecy.

HELAMAN 8:11–13, 19–20, 24–28

Therefore he was constrained to speak more
unto them saying: Behold, my brethren,
have ye not read that God gave power unto one
man, even Moses, to smite upon the waters of the
Red Sea, and they parted hither and thither, in-
somuch that the Israelites, who were our fathers,
came through upon dry ground, and the waters
closed upon the armies of the Egyptians and swal-
lowed them up?
12 And now behold, if God gave unto this man
such power, then why should ye dispute among
yourselves, and say that he hath given unto me no
power whereby I may know concerning the judg-
ments that shall come upon you except ye repent?
13 But, behold, ye not only deny my words,
but ye also deny all the words which have been
spoken by our fathers, and also the words which
were spoken by this man, Moses, who had such
great power given unto him, yea, the words which
he hath spoken concerning the coming of the
Messiah.
19 And now I would that ye should know, that
even since the days of Abraham there have been
many prophets that have testified these things;
yea, behold, the prophet Zenos did testify boldly;
for the which he was slain.
20 And behold, also Zenock, and also Ezias, and
also Isaiah, and Jeremiah, (Jeremiah being that
same prophet who testified of the destruction of
Jerusalem) and now we know that Jerusalem was
destroyed according to the words of Jeremiah. O
then why not the Son of God come, according to
his prophecy?
24 And now, seeing ye know these things and
cannot deny them except ye shall lie, therefore
in this ye have sinned, for ye have rejected all
these things, notwithstanding so many evidences
which ye have received; yea, even ye have received
all things, both things in heaven, and all things
which are in the earth, as a witness that they are
true.
25 But behold, ye have rejected the truth, and
rebelled against your holy God; and even at this
time, instead of laying up for yourselves trea-
sures in heaven, where nothing doth corrupt, and
where nothing can come which is unclean, ye are
heaping up for yourselves wrath against the day of
judgment.
26 Yea, even at this time ye are ripening, because
of your murders and your fornication and wick-
edness, for everlasting destruction; yea, and except
ye repent it will come unto you soon.
27 Yea, behold it is now even at your doors; yea,
go ye in unto the judgment-seat, and search; and
behold, your judge is murdered, and he lieth in
his blood; and he hath been murdered by his
brother, who seeketh to sit in the judgment-seat.
28 And behold, they both belong to your secret
band, whose author is Gadianton and the evil one
who seeketh to destroy the souls of men.

Nephi identified some ancient prophets who had testified of things to come. What common events have ancient and modern prophets testified of? What commandments have ancient and modern prophets taught to people throughout history?

NEPHI CONTINUES TO PROPHESY AGAINST THE FOLLOWERS OF GADIANTON

After Nephi prophesied to the crowd that Seezoram, the chief judge, had been murdered, five men ran to the judgment seat and found that the prophecy was true—the chief judge had been stabbed to death and lay in his own blood. The wicked judges accused Nephi of conspiring with someone to commit the murder in an attempt to convince people he had the gift of prophecy. Nephi responded.

HELAMAN 9:21–22, 25–41

But Nephi said unto them: O ye fools, ye uncircumcised of heart, ye blind, and ye stiffnecked people, do ye know how long the Lord your God will suffer you that ye shall go on in this your way of sin?

22 O ye ought to begin to howl and mourn, because of the great destruction which at this time doth await you, except ye shall repent.

25 And now behold, I will show unto you another sign, and see if ye will in this thing seek to destroy me.

26 Behold I say unto you: Go to the house of Seantum, who is the brother of Seezoram, and say unto him—

27 Has Nephi, the pretended prophet, who doth prophesy so much evil concerning this people, agreed with thee, in the which ye have murdered Seezoram, who is your brother?

28 And behold, he shall say unto you, Nay.

29 And ye shall say unto him: Have ye murdered your brother?

30 And he shall stand with fear, and wist not what to say. And behold, he shall deny unto you; and he shall make as if he were astonished; nevertheless, he shall declare unto you that he is innocent.

31 But behold, ye shall examine him, and ye shall find blood upon the skirts of his cloak.

32 And when ye have seen this, ye shall say: From whence cometh this blood? Do we not know that it is the blood of your brother?

33 And then shall he tremble, and shall look pale, even as if death had come upon him.

34 And then shall ye say: Because of this fear and this paleness which has come upon your face, behold, we know that thou art guilty.

35 And then shall greater fear come upon him; and then shall he confess unto you, and deny no more that he has done this murder.

36 And then shall he say unto you, that I, Nephi, know nothing concerning the matter save it were given unto me by the power of God. And then shall ye know that I am an honest man, and that I am sent unto you from God.

37 And it came to pass that they went and did, even according as Nephi had said unto them. And behold, the words which he had said were true; for according to the words he did deny; and also according to the words he did confess.

38 And he was brought to prove that he himself was the very murderer, insomuch that the five were set at liberty, and also was Nephi.

39 And there were some of the Nephites who believed on the words of Nephi; and there were some also, who believed because of the testimony of the five, for they had been converted while they were in prison.

40 And now there were some among the people, who said that Nephi was a prophet.

41 And there were others who said: Behold, he is a god, for except he was a god he could not know of all things. For behold, he has told us the thoughts of our hearts, and also has told us things; and even he has brought unto our knowledge the true murderer of our chief judge.

Nephi declared that he knew only what was "given unto [him] by the power of God." What does this teach you about the words of the prophets today? How can you know if someone is a prophet of God?

GOD GIVES NEPHI THE SEALING POWER

After correctly prophesying of the murder of the chief judge, Nephi pondered the things God had shown him. God then told Nephi he would "bless [him] forever." As you read, look for the reasons God said He would bless Nephi and the specific blessings God promised.

HELAMAN 10:3–12

And it came to pass as he was thus pondering—being much cast down because of the wickedness of the people of the Nephites, their secret works of darkness, and their murderings, and their plunderings, and all manner of iniquities—and it came to pass as he was thus pondering in his heart, behold, a voice came unto him saying:

4 Blessed art thou, Nephi, for those things which thou hast done; for I have beheld how thou hast with unwearyingness declared the word, which I have given unto thee, unto this people. And thou hast not feared them, and hast not sought thine own life, but hast sought my will, and to keep my commandments.

5 And now, because thou hast done this with such unwearyingness, behold, I will bless thee forever; and I will make thee mighty in word and in deed, in faith and in works; yea, even that all things shall be done unto thee according to thy word, for thou shalt not ask that which is contrary to my will.

6 Behold, thou art Nephi, and I am God. Behold, I declare it unto thee in the presence of mine angels, that ye shall have power over this people, and shall smite the earth with famine, and with pestilence, and destruction, according to the wickedness of this people.

7 Behold, I give unto you power, that whatsoever ye shall seal on earth shall be sealed in heaven; and whatsoever ye shall loose on earth shall be loosed in heaven; and thus shall ye have power among this people.

8 And thus, if ye shall say unto this temple it shall be rent in twain, it shall be done.

9 And if ye shall say unto this mountain, Be thou cast down and become smooth, it shall be done.

10 And behold, if ye shall say that God shall smite this people, it shall come to pass.

11 And now behold, I command you, that ye shall go and declare unto this people, that thus saith the Lord God, who is the Almighty: Except ye repent ye shall be smitten, even unto destruction.

12 And behold, now it came to pass that when the Lord had spoken these words unto Nephi, he did stop and did not go unto his own house, but did return unto the multitudes who were scattered about upon the face of the land, and began to declare unto them the word of the Lord which had been spoken unto him, concerning their destruction if they did not repent.

What reasons did God give for blessing Nephi forever? What did He promise to give Nephi? What do you learn about God's sealing power from verse 7? Discuss how the sealing power of God is used today.

NEPHI PRAYS FOR A FAMINE THAT STIRS THE NEPHITES TO REPENTANCE

After receiving the sealing power from God, Nephi commanded the Nephites to repent or be destroyed. The people refused to repent and, led by the Gadianton robbers, engaged in battle with one another. Nephi asked the Lord for a famine to be brought upon the land to stir the people up in remembrance of God. After two years of famine, thousands of people died, and those who survived asked Nephi to stop the famine. Nephi prayed to God on behalf of the repentant Nephites.

HELAMAN 11:10–13, 15–18

O Lord, behold this people repenteth; and they have swept away the band of Gadianton from amongst them insomuch that they have become extinct, and they have concealed their secret plans in the earth.

11 Now, O Lord, because of this their humility wilt thou turn away thine anger, and let thine anger be appeased in the destruction of those wicked men whom thou hast already destroyed.

12 O Lord, wilt thou turn away thine anger, yea, thy fierce anger, and cause that this famine may cease in this land.

13 O Lord, wilt thou hearken unto me, and cause that it may be done according to my words, and send forth rain upon the face of the earth, that she may bring forth her fruit, and her grain in the season of grain.

15 Yea, O Lord, and thou seest that they have repented, because of the famine and the pestilence and destruction which has come unto them.

16 And now, O Lord, wilt thou turn away thine anger, and try again if they will serve thee? And if so, O Lord, thou canst bless them according to thy words which thou hast said.

17 And it came to pass that in the seventy and sixth year the Lord did turn away his anger from the people, and caused that rain should fall upon the earth, insomuch that it did bring forth her fruit in the season of her fruit. And it came to pass that it did bring forth her grain in the season of her grain.

18 And behold, the people did rejoice and glorify God, and the whole face of the land was filled with rejoicing; and they did no more seek to destroy Nephi, but they did esteem him as a great prophet, and a man of God, having great power and authority given unto him from God.

What did the wicked Nephites have to do before God would take the famine away? Though Nephi was initially rejected by the wicked Nephites, he hoped they would eventually repent, and he sacrificed much to help them find God's blessings. How can you show compassion and patience to those who may reject or make fun of your beliefs?

MORMON SPEAKS OF MAN'S SPEEDY EMBRACE OF VANITY AND PRIDE

After the famine had passed, the Nephites enjoyed a few years of righteousness and peace and then fell back into wickedness. Nephite dissenters joined with wicked Lamanites, embraced the secret workings of the Gadianton robbers, and committed murder, plunder, and havoc. Armies were sent to destroy the robbers, but the robbers increased in number, repelled the armies, and hid in the wilderness. The Nephites became increasingly wicked and forgot God. As Mormon organized the scriptural record about 400 years later, he commented on the Nephites' fall from righteousness. Consider the things Mormon says man is "quick" to do and the things man is "slow" to do.

HELAMAN 12:1–6

And thus we can behold how false, and
also the unsteadiness of the hearts of the
children of men; yea, we can see that the Lord in
his great infinite goodness doth bless and prosper
those who put their trust in him.
2 Yea, and we may see at the very time when he
doth prosper his people, yea, in the increase of
their fields, their flocks and their herds, and in
gold, and in silver, and in all manner of precious
things of every kind and art; sparing their lives,
and delivering them out of the hands of their en-
emies; softening the hearts of their enemies that
they should not declare wars against them; yea,
and in fine, doing all things for the welfare and
happiness of his people; yea, then is the time
that they do harden their hearts, and do forget
the Lord their God, and do trample under their
feet the Holy One—yea, and this because of their
ease, and their exceedingly great prosperity.
3 And thus we see that except the Lord doth
chasten his people with many afflictions, yea,
except he doth visit them with death and with
terror, and with famine and with all manner of
pestilence, they will not remember him.
4 O how foolish, and how vain, and how evil,
and devilish, and how quick to do iniquity, and
how slow to do good, are the children of men;
yea, how quick to hearken unto the words of the
evil one, and to set their hearts upon the vain
things of the world!
5 Yea, how quick to be lifted up in pride; yea,
how quick to boast, and do all manner of that
which is iniquity; and how slow are they to re-
member the Lord their God, and to give ear unto
his counsels, yea, how slow to walk in wisdom's
paths!
6 Behold, they do not desire that the Lord their
God, who hath created them, should rule and
reign over them; notwithstanding his great good-
ness and his mercy towards them, they do set at
naught his counsels, and they will not that he
should be their guide.

What things did Mormon say we are "quick" to do and what things are we "slow" to do? What things can you do every day to make sure you remember God? How will you know if God, and not the world, is your "guide"?

MORMON SPEAKS OF THE NOTHINGNESS OF MAN

As he continued to comment on the wicked state of the Nephites, Mormon spoke of man's nothingness.

HELAMAN 12:7–11, 20–26

O how great is the nothingness of the chil-
dren of men; yea, even they are less than
the dust of the earth.
8 For behold, the dust of the earth moveth hither
and thither, to the dividing asunder, at the com-
mand of our great and everlasting God.
9 Yea, behold at his voice do the hills and the
mountains tremble and quake.
10 And by the power of his voice they are bro-
ken up, and become smooth, yea, even like unto
a valley.
11 Yea, by the power of his voice doth the whole
earth shake;
20 And behold, if the Lord shall say unto a
man—Because of thine iniquities, thou shalt be
accursed forever—it shall be done.
21 And if the Lord shall say—Because of thine in-
iquities thou shalt be cut off from my presence—
he will cause that it shall be so.
22 And wo unto him to whom he shall say this,
for it shall be unto him that will do iniquity, and
he cannot be saved; therefore, for this cause, that
men might be saved, hath repentance been de-
clared.
23 Therefore, blessed are they who will repent
and hearken unto the voice of the Lord their God;
for these are they that shall be saved.
24 And may God grant, in his great fulness, that
men might be brought unto repentance and good
works, that they might be restored unto grace for
grace, according to their works.
25 And I would that all men might be saved. But
we read that in the great and last day there are
some who shall be cast out, yea, who shall be cast
off from the presence of the Lord;
26 Yea, who shall be consigned to a state of end-
less misery, fulfilling the words which say: They
that have done good shall have everlasting life;
and they that have done evil shall have everlasting
damnation. And thus it is. Amen.

According to Mormon, how does the Lord's power show our own nothingness? How do you have both "nothingness" and a divine heritage?

SAMUEL THE LAMANITE PREACHES REPENTANCE FROM ATOP THE WALL OF ZARAHEMLA

It was now about six years before the birth of Jesus Christ. The Nephites remained in wickedness, while the Lamanites remained strictly obedient to the law of Moses. A Lamanite named Samuel began preaching repentance in the city of Zarahemla, was cast out by the wicked Nephites, and considered returning home.

HELAMAN 13:3–8, 11

But behold, the voice of the Lord came unto him, that he should return again, and prophesy unto the people whatsoever things should come into his heart.

4 And it came to pass that they would not suffer that he should enter into the city; therefore he went and got upon the wall thereof, and stretched forth his hand and cried with a loud voice, and prophesied unto the people whatsoever things the Lord put into his heart.

5 And he said unto them: Behold, I, Samuel, a Lamanite, do speak the words of the Lord which he doth put into my heart; and behold he hath put it into my heart to say unto this people that the sword of justice hangeth over this people; and four hundred years pass not away save the sword of justice falleth upon this people.

6 Yea, heavy destruction awaiteth this people, and it surely cometh unto this people, and nothing can save this people save it be repentance and faith on the Lord Jesus Christ, who surely shall come into the world, and shall suffer many things and shall be slain for his people.

7 And behold, an angel of the Lord hath declared it unto me, and he did bring glad tidings to my soul. And behold, I was sent unto you to declare it unto you also, that ye might have glad tidings; but behold ye would not receive me.

8 Therefore, thus saith the Lord: Because of the hardness of the hearts of the people of the Nephites, except they repent I will take away my word from them, and I will withdraw my Spirit from them, and I will suffer them no longer, and I will turn the hearts of their brethren against them.

11 But if ye will repent and return unto the Lord your God I will turn away mine anger, saith the Lord; yea, thus saith the Lord, blessed are they who will repent and turn unto me, but wo unto him that repenteth not.

What did Samuel tell the Nephites was the only thing that could save them from destruction? What other consequences would the people face if they remained hard-hearted? How would they feel if they received the word of the Lord?

SAMUEL CHASTISES THE NEPHITES FOR BEING FLATTERED BY BLIND GUIDES

Samuel continued to preach repentance to the wicked Nephites from atop the city wall of Zarahemla.

Helaman 13:21–22, 27–30, 39

Behold ye, the people of this great city, and hearken unto my words; yea, hearken unto the words which the Lord saith; for behold, he saith that ye are cursed because of your riches, and also are your riches cursed because ye have set your hearts upon them, and have not hearkened unto the words of him who gave them unto you.

22 Ye do not remember the Lord your God in the things with which he hath blessed you, but ye do always remember your riches, not to thank the Lord your God for them; yea, your hearts are not drawn out unto the Lord, but they do swell with great pride, unto boasting, and unto great swelling, envyings, strifes, malice, persecutions, and murders, and all manner of iniquities.

27 But behold, if a man shall come among you and shall say: Do this, and there is no iniquity; do that and ye shall not suffer; yea, he will say: Walk after the pride of your own hearts; yea, walk after the pride of your eyes, and do whatsoever your heart desireth—and if a man shall come among you and say this, ye will receive him, and say that he is a prophet.

28 Yea, ye will lift him up, and ye will give unto him of your substance; ye will give unto him of your gold, and of your silver, and ye will clothe him with costly apparel; and because he speaketh flattering words unto you, and he saith that all is well, then ye will not find fault with him.

29 O ye wicked and ye perverse generation; ye hardened and ye stiffnecked people, how long will ye suppose that the Lord will suffer you? Yea, how long will ye suffer yourselves to be led by foolish and blind guides? Yea, how long will ye choose darkness rather than light?

30 Yea, behold, the anger of the Lord is already kindled against you; behold, he hath cursed the land because of your iniquity.

39 O ye people of the land, that ye would hear my words! And I pray that the anger of the Lord be turned away from you, and that ye would repent and be saved.

What modern-day examples have you seen of people who say, "Do this, and there is no iniquity" and "do whatsoever your heart desireth"? How can you recognize "blind guides" who would try to lead you astray? How can you know who to trust for spiritual and ethical guidance?

SAMUEL PROPHESIES OF HEAVENLY SIGNS ACCOMPANYING THE BIRTH OF JESUS CHRIST

As he continued to call the Nephites to repentance from atop the city wall, Samuel prophesied of unmistakable signs that would soon appear.

Helaman 14:2–5, 8–13

And behold, he said unto them: Behold, I give unto you a sign; for five years more cometh, and behold, then cometh the Son of God to redeem all those who shall believe on his name.

3 And behold, this will I give unto you for a sign at the time of his coming; for behold, there shall be great lights in heaven, insomuch that in the night before he cometh there shall be no darkness, insomuch that it shall appear unto man as if it was day.

4 Therefore, there shall be one day and a night and a day, as if it were one day and there were no night; and this shall be unto you for a sign; for ye shall know of the rising of the sun and also of its setting; therefore they shall know of a surety that there shall be two days and a night; nevertheless the night shall not be darkened; and it shall be the night before he is born.

5 And behold, there shall a new star arise, such an one as ye never have beheld; and this also shall be a sign unto you.

8 And it shall come to pass that whosoever shall believe on the Son of God, the same shall have everlasting life.

9 And behold, thus hath the Lord commanded me, by his angel, that I should come and tell this thing unto you; yea, he hath commanded that I should prophesy these things unto you; yea, he hath said unto me: Cry unto this people, repent and prepare the way of the Lord.

10 And now, because I am a Lamanite, and have spoken unto you the words which the Lord hath commanded me, and because it was hard against you, ye are angry with me and do seek to destroy me, and have cast me out from among you.

11 And ye shall hear my words, for, for this intent have I come up upon the walls of this city, that ye might hear and know of the judgments of God which do await you because of your iniquities, and also that ye might know the conditions of repentance;

12 And also that ye might know of the coming of Jesus Christ, the Son of God, the Father of heaven and of earth, the Creator of all things from the beginning; and that ye might know of the signs of his coming, to the intent that ye might believe on his name.

13 And if ye believe on his name ye will repent of all your sins, that thereby ye may have a remission of them through his merits.

What signs did Samuel say would occur at the time of Christ's birth? Samuel said he wanted the people to "know the conditions of repentance." What have you learned about the repentance process? What steps should a person take to truly repent?

SAMUEL PROPHESIES OF SIGNS ACCOMPANYING THE DEATH OF JESUS CHRIST

After prophesying of signs that would occur at the birth of Jesus Christ, Samuel spoke of signs that would accompany the Savior's death.

HELAMAN 14:15–21, 30–31

For behold, he surely must die that salvation may come; yea, it behooveth him and becometh expedient that he dieth, to bring to pass the resurrection of the dead, that thereby men may be brought into the presence of the Lord.

16 Yea, behold, this death bringeth to pass the resurrection, and redeemeth all mankind from the first death—that spiritual death; for all mankind, by the fall of Adam being cut off from the presence of the Lord, are considered as dead, both as to things temporal and to things spiritual.

17 But behold, the resurrection of Christ redeemeth mankind, yea, even all mankind, and bringeth them back into the presence of the Lord.

18 Yea, and it bringeth to pass the condition of repentance, that whosoever repenteth the same is not hewn down and cast into the fire; but whosoever repenteth not is hewn down and cast into the fire; and there cometh upon them again a spiritual death, yea, a second death, for they are cut off again as to things pertaining to righteousness.

19 Therefore repent ye, repent ye, lest by knowing these things and not doing them ye shall suffer yourselves to come under condemnation, and ye are brought down unto this second death.

20 But behold, as I said unto you concerning another sign, a sign of his death, behold, in that day that he shall suffer death the sun shall be darkened and refuse to give his light unto you; and also the moon and the stars; and there shall be no light upon the face of this land, even from the time that he shall suffer death, for the space of three days, to the time that he shall rise again from the dead.

21 Yea, at the time that he shall yield up the ghost there shall be thunderings and lightnings for the space of many hours, and the earth shall shake and tremble; and the rocks which are upon the face of this earth, which are both above the earth and beneath, which ye know at this time are solid, or the more part of it is one solid mass, shall be broken up;

30 And now remember, remember, my brethren, that whosoever perisheth, perisheth unto himself; and whosoever doeth iniquity, doeth it unto himself; for behold, ye are free; ye are permitted to act for yourselves; for behold, God hath given unto you a knowledge and he hath made you free.

31 He hath given unto you that ye might know good from evil, and he hath given unto you that ye might choose life or death; and ye can do good and be restored unto that which is good, or have that which is good restored unto you; or ye can do evil, and have that which is evil restored unto you.

What signs did Samuel say would occur at the time of Jesus Christ's death? What are the two types of death that Samuel teaches about? Samuel taught that "God hath given unto you a knowledge and he hath made you free." What knowledge has God given you? How does that knowledge make you free?

SAMUEL'S LIFE IS MIRACULOUSLY PRESERVED AS HE PROPHESIES TO THE WICKED NEPHITES

Standing atop the city wall, Samuel continued to preach to the wicked Nephites. He spoke of the Lord's love for the Nephites, which was the reason for his chastening them and calling them to repentance. He also prophesied of the preservation of the Lamanite people and their latter-day embrace of the gospel. Some Nephites believed Samuel's words. Others were angry and threw stones and shot arrows at him, but the Spirit of the Lord was with Samuel and no stones or arrows could hit him.

HELAMAN 16:6–7, 14–22

But the more part of them did not believe
in the words of Samuel; therefore when
they saw that they could not hit him with their
stones and their arrows, they cried unto their cap-
tains, saying: Take this fellow and bind him, for
behold he hath a devil; and because of the power
of the devil which is in him we cannot hit him
with our stones and our arrows; therefore take
him and bind him, and away with him.
7 And as they went forth to lay their hands on
him, behold, he did cast himself down from the
wall, and did flee out of their lands, yea, even
unto his own country, and began to preach and to
prophesy among his own people.
14 And angels did appear unto men, wise men,
and did declare unto them glad tidings of great joy;
thus in this year the scriptures began to be fulfilled.
15 Nevertheless, the people began to harden
their hearts, all save it were the most believing
part of them, both of the Nephites and also of the
Lamanites, and began to depend upon their own
strength and upon their own wisdom, saying:
16 Some things they may have guessed right,
among so many; but behold, we know that all
these great and marvelous works cannot come to
pass, of which has been spoken.
17 And they began to reason and to contend
among themselves, saying:
18 That it is not reasonable that such a being as
a Christ shall come; if so, and he be the Son of
God, the Father of heaven and of earth, as it has
been spoken, why will he not show himself unto
us as well as unto them who shall be at Jerusalem?
19 Yea, why will he not show himself in this land
as well as in the land of Jerusalem?
20 But behold, we know that this is a wicked tradi-
tion, which has been handed down unto us by our
fathers, to cause us that we should believe in some
great and marvelous thing which should come to
pass, but not among us, but in a land which is far
distant, a land which we know not; therefore they
can keep us in ignorance, for we cannot witness
with our own eyes that they are true.
21 And they will, by the cunning and the myste-
rious arts of the evil one, work some great mystery
which we cannot understand, which will keep us
down to be servants to their words, and also ser-
vants unto them, for we depend upon them to
teach us the word; and thus will they keep us in
ignorance if we will yield ourselves unto them, all
the days of our lives.
22 And many more things did the people imagine
up in their hearts, which were foolish and vain;
and they were much disturbed, for Satan did stir
them up to do iniquity continually; yea, he did
go about spreading rumors and contentions upon
all the face of the land, that he might harden the
hearts of the people against that which was good
and against that which should come.

What examples have you seen of people depending "upon their own wisdom" instead of being led by God? In what ways do people today deny signs of God's existence and His works? How can you both think for yourself and stay open to God's inspiration?

JESUS CHRIST'S BIRTH IS CONFIRMED AS THE NEPHITES EXPERIENCE A NIGHT WITHOUT DARKNESS

Six hundred years had passed since Lehi and his family left Jerusalem. Nephi, who had been prophesying among the wicked Nephites, entrusted the scriptural record to his son Nephi and departed the land. Though prophecies and signs of Christ's birth began to be fulfilled, many wicked people refused to believe and mocked those who did believe.

3 Nephi 1:6–15, 19–21

And they began to rejoice over their
brethren, saying: Behold the time is
past, and the words of Samuel are not fulfilled;
therefore, your joy and your faith concerning this
thing hath been vain.
7 And it came to pass that they did make a great
uproar throughout the land; and the people who
believed began to be very sorrowful, lest by any
means those things which had been spoken might
not come to pass.
8 But behold, they did watch steadfastly for that
day and that night and that day which should
be as one day as if there were no night, that they
might know that their faith had not been vain.
9 Now it came to pass that there was a day set
apart by the unbelievers, that all those who be-
lieved in those traditions should be put to death
except the sign should come to pass, which had
been given by Samuel the prophet.
10 Now it came to pass that when Nephi, the son
of Nephi, saw this wickedness of his people, his
heart was exceedingly sorrowful.
11 And it came to pass that he went out and
bowed himself down upon the earth, and cried
mightily to his God in behalf of his people, yea,
those who were about to be destroyed because of
their faith in the tradition of their fathers.
12 And it came to pass that he cried mightily
unto the Lord all that day; and behold, the voice
of the Lord came unto him, saying:
13 Lift up your head and be of good cheer; for
behold, the time is at hand, and on this night
shall the sign be given, and on the morrow come I
into the world, to show unto the world that I will
fulfil all that which I have caused to be spoken by
the mouth of my holy prophets.
14 Behold, I come unto my own, to fulfil all
things which I have made known unto the chil-
dren of men from the foundation of the world,
and to do the will, both of the Father and of the
Son—of the Father because of me, and of the Son
because of my flesh. And behold, the time is at
hand, and this night shall the sign be given.
15 And it came to pass that the words which
came unto Nephi were fulfilled, according as they
had been spoken; for behold, at the going down
of the sun there was no darkness; and the people
began to be astonished because there was no dark-
ness when the night came.
19 And it came to pass that there was no dark-
ness in all that night, but it was as light as though
it was mid-day. And it came to pass that the sun
did rise in the morning again, according to its
proper order; and they knew that it was the day
that the Lord should be born, because of the sign
which had been given.
20 And it had come to pass, yea, all things, every
whit, according to the words of the prophets.
21 And it came to pass also that a new star did
appear, according to the word.

Jesus Christ told Nephi that He would be born into the world to "fulfil all things which [He had] made known unto the children of men." What was Jesus Christ going to "fulfill," or accomplish, during His life on earth?

NEPHI RAISES HIS BROTHER FROM THE DEAD AND TESTIFIES OF JESUS CHRIST

Despite the fulfillment of signs and prophecies of Christ's birth, many people increased in wickedness. The Nephites and Lamanites joined forces in the land of Zarahemla to defend themselves against the Gadianton robbers. Following many battles and an unsuccessful siege of Zarahemla, the majority of the Gadianton robbers were killed, their leaders executed, and the remainder imprisoned. The Nephites and Lamanites rejoiced in their deliverance and enjoyed temporary peace and righteousness before turning again to wickedness, political upheaval, murder, and secret combinations. It was now about AD 32. Nephi was counted among a small minority of righteous people in the land. As you read, consider the similarities between Nephi's actions and experiences and those of Jesus Christ—who was ministering to the people at Jerusalem at the same time.

3 Nephi 7:15–22

And it came to pass that Nephi—having
been visited by angels and also the voice
of the Lord, therefore having seen angels, and
being eye-witness, and having had power given
unto him that he might know concerning the
ministry of Christ, and also being eye-witness to
their quick return from righteousness unto their
wickedness and abominations;
16 Therefore, being grieved for the hardness of
their hearts and the blindness of their minds—
went forth among them in that same year, and
began to testify, boldly, repentance and remission
of sins through faith on the Lord Jesus Christ.
17 And he did minister many things unto them;
and all of them cannot be written, and a part of
them would not suffice, therefore they are not
written in this book. And Nephi did minister
with power and with great authority.
18 And it came to pass that they were angry with
him, even because he had greater power than they,
for it were not possible that they could disbelieve
his words, for so great was his faith on the Lord
Jesus Christ that angels did minister unto him
daily.
19 And in the name of Jesus did he cast out dev-
ils and unclean spirits; and even his brother did he
raise from the dead, after he had been stoned and
suffered death by the people.
20 And the people saw it, and did witness of it,
and were angry with him because of his power;
and he did also do many more miracles, in the
sight of the people, in the name of Jesus.
21 And it came to pass that the thirty and first year
did pass away, and there were but few who were
converted unto the Lord; but as many as were con-
verted did truly signify unto the people that they
had been visited by the power and Spirit of God,
which was in Jesus Christ, in whom they believed.
22 And as many as had devils cast out from them,
and were healed of their sicknesses and their infir-
mities, did truly manifest unto the people that they
had been wrought upon by the Spirit of God, and
had been healed; and they did show forth signs also
and did do some miracles among the people.

What are some similarities between the actions and experiences of Nephi and Jesus Christ as they each ministered in different parts of the world? What did Nephi do in response to the wickedness of the Nephites? How can you follow his example when you see others making bad choices?

DESTRUCTION AND DARKNESS SIGNAL THE DEATH OF JESUS CHRIST, WHOSE VOICE IS THEN HEARD

Thirty-three years had passed since the signs of Christ's birth. In the first month of the thirty-fourth year, Samuel the Lamanite's prophecy of darkness, indicating the death of the Savior, was fulfilled as a great storm arose throughout the land. For three hours, thunder, lightning, whirlwinds, and massive earthquakes permanently altered the face of the land. Zarahemla was destroyed by fire. Other cities were buried by water or mountains. A vapor of darkness—so thick it could be felt—descended, and no light could be seen on earth or in the sky. Those who survived mourned the dead and acknowledged their own wickedness.

3 Nephi 9:1–2, 13–22

And it came to pass that there was a voice
heard among all the inhabitants of the
earth, upon all the face of this land, crying:
2 Wo, wo, wo unto this people; wo unto the in-
habitants of the whole earth except they shall re-
pent; for the devil laugheth, and his angels rejoice,
because of the slain of the fair sons and daughters
of my people; and it is because of their iniquity
and abominations that they are fallen!
13 O all ye that are spared because ye were more
righteous than they, will ye not now return unto
me, and repent of your sins, and be converted,
that I may heal you?
14 Yea, verily I say unto you, if ye will come unto
me ye shall have eternal life. Behold, mine arm
of mercy is extended towards you, and whosoever
will come, him will I receive; and blessed are those
who come unto me.
15 Behold, I am Jesus Christ the Son of God. I
created the heavens and the earth, and all things
that in them are. I was with the Father from the
beginning. I am in the Father, and the Father in
me; and in me hath the Father glorified his name.
16 I came unto my own, and my own received
me not. And the scriptures concerning my com-
ing are fulfilled.
17 And as many as have received me, to them
have I given to become the sons of God; and even
so will I to as many as shall believe on my name,
for behold, by me redemption cometh, and in me
is the law of Moses fulfilled.
18 I am the light and the life of the world. I am
Alpha and Omega, the beginning and the end.
19 And ye shall offer up unto me no more the
shedding of blood; yea, your sacrifices and your
burnt offerings shall be done away, for I will ac-
cept none of your sacrifices and your burnt offer-
ings.
20 And ye shall offer for a sacrifice unto me a
broken heart and a contrite spirit. And whoso
cometh unto me with a broken heart and a con-
trite spirit, him will I baptize with fire and with
the Holy Ghost, even as the Lamanites, because of
their faith in me at the time of their conversion,
were baptized with fire and with the Holy Ghost,
and they knew it not.
21 Behold, I have come unto the world to bring
redemption unto the world, to save the world
from sin.
22 Therefore, whoso repenteth and cometh unto
me as a little child, him will I receive, for of such
is the kingdom of God. Behold, for such I have
laid down my life, and have taken it up again;
therefore repent, and come unto me ye ends of
the earth, and be saved.

Jesus Christ proclaimed that animal sacrifices were no longer acceptable. What were the people commanded to offer as a sacrifice instead? How can you give these things to the Lord? What blessings did Jesus Christ promise would be given to those who obeyed?

THE VOICE OF JESUS CHRIST IS HEARD, INVITING THE PEOPLE TO REPENT

After the great destruction throughout the land and upon hearing the voice of Jesus Christ, the people ceased their cries of despair and there was silence.

3 Nephi 10:3–10

And it came to pass that there came a
voice again unto the people, and all the
people did hear, and did witness of it, saying:
4 O ye people of these great cities which have
fallen, who are descendants of Jacob, yea, who are
of the house of Israel, how oft have I gathered you
as a hen gathereth her chickens under her wings,
and have nourished you.
5 And again, how oft would I have gathered you
as a hen gathereth her chickens under her wings,
yea, O ye people of the house of Israel, who have
fallen; yea, O ye people of the house of Israel, ye
that dwell at Jerusalem, as ye that have fallen; yea,
how oft would I have gathered you as a hen gath-
ereth her chickens, and ye would not.
6 O ye house of Israel whom I have spared, how
oft will I gather you as a hen gathereth her chick-
ens under her wings, if ye will repent and return
unto me with full purpose of heart.
7 But if not, O house of Israel, the places of
your dwellings shall become desolate until the
time of the fulfilling of the covenant to your
fathers.
8 And now it came to pass that after the people
had heard these words, behold, they began to
weep and howl again because of the loss of their
kindred and friends.
9 And it came to pass that thus did the three
days pass away. And it was in the morning, and
the darkness dispersed from off the face of the
land, and the earth did cease to tremble, and the
rocks did cease to rend, and the dreadful groan-
ings did cease, and all the tumultuous noises did
pass away.
10 And the earth did cleave together again, that
it stood; and the mourning, and the weeping, and
the wailing of the people who were spared alive
did cease; and their mourning was turned into
joy, and their lamentations into the praise and
thanksgiving unto the Lord Jesus Christ, their
Redeemer.

Jesus Christ spoke of gathering and nourishing His people. What image did He use to illustrate this? What qualities about the Savior does that symbol teach you? In what ways has He gathered and nourished you and your family?

GOD THE FATHER INTRODUCES HIS SON JESUS CHRIST, WHO APPEARS TO THE MULTITUDE

After the people heard the voice of Jesus Christ speaking to them, the thick darkness dispersed and the earth was still.

3 Nephi 11:1–12

And now it came to pass that there were a great multitude gathered together, of the people of Nephi, round about the temple which was in the land Bountiful; and they were marveling and wondering one with another, and were showing one to another the great and marvelous change which had taken place.
2 And they were also conversing about this Jesus Christ, of whom the sign had been given concerning his death.
3 And it came to pass that while they were thus conversing one with another, they heard a voice as if it came out of heaven; and they cast their eyes round about, for they understood not the voice which they heard; and it was not a harsh voice, neither was it a loud voice; nevertheless, and notwithstanding it being a small voice it did pierce them that did hear to the center, insomuch that there was no part of their frame that it did not cause to quake; yea, it did pierce them to the very soul, and did cause their hearts to burn.
4 And it came to pass that again they heard the voice, and they understood it not.
5 And again the third time they did hear the voice, and did open their ears to hear it; and their eyes were towards the sound thereof; and they did look steadfastly towards heaven, from whence the sound came.
6 And behold, the third time they did understand the voice which they heard; and it said unto them:
7 Behold my Beloved Son, in whom I am well pleased, in whom I have glorified my name—hear ye him.
8 And it came to pass, as they understood they cast their eyes up again towards heaven; and behold, they saw a Man descending out of heaven; and he was clothed in a white robe; and he came down and stood in the midst of them; and the eyes of the whole multitude were turned upon him, and they durst not open their mouths, even one to another, and wist not what it meant, for they thought it was an angel that had appeared unto them.
9 And it came to pass that he stretched forth his hand and spake unto the people, saying:
10 Behold, I am Jesus Christ, whom the prophets testified shall come into the world.
11 And behold, I am the light and the life of the world; and I have drunk out of that bitter cup which the Father hath given me, and have glorified the Father in taking upon me the sins of the world, in the which I have suffered the will of the Father in all things from the beginning.
12 And it came to pass that when Jesus had spoken these words the whole multitude fell to the earth; for they remembered that it had been prophesied among them that Christ should show himself unto them after his ascension into heaven.

How was Heavenly Father's voice described? What did Heavenly Father say about His Son? How did Jesus Christ describe Himself as He appeared to the people? What do you learn about the nature of God the Father and Jesus Christ from this passage?

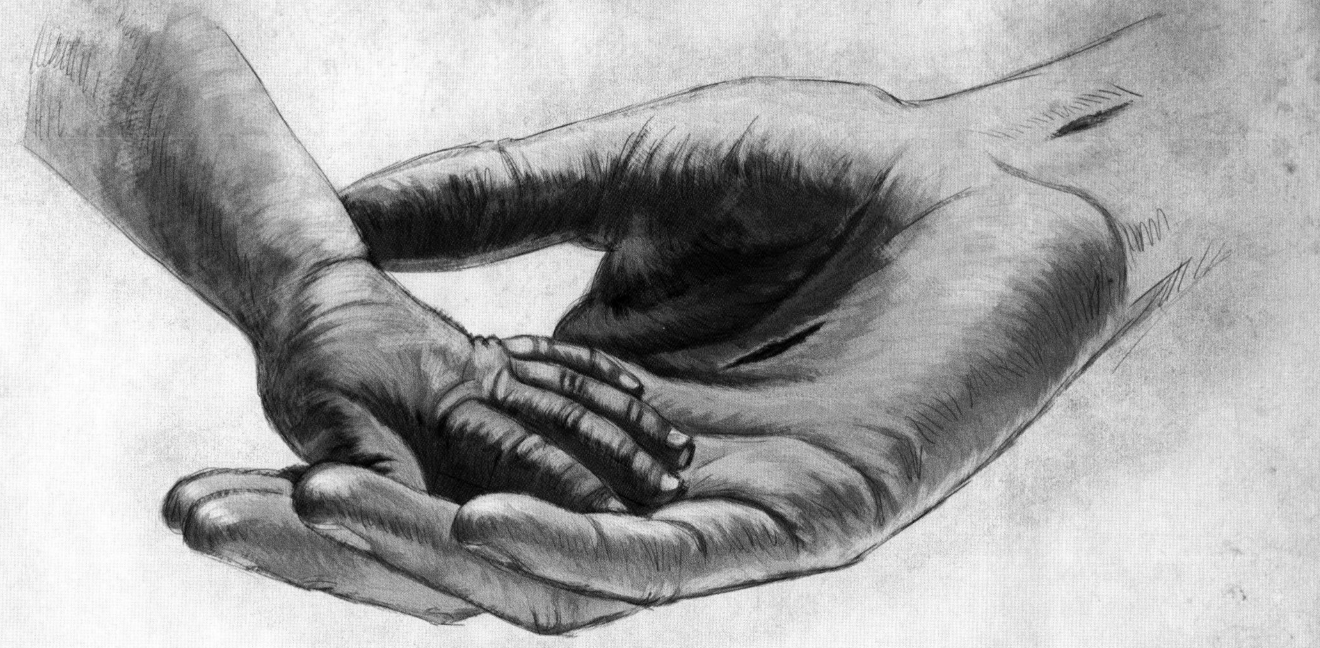

JESUS CHRIST INVITES THE MULTITUDE TO FEEL THE WOUNDS IN HIS HANDS AND FEET

After Jesus Christ descended from heaven and identified Himself as the Savior of the world, He continued to speak to the people.

3 Nephi 11:13–19

And it came to pass that the Lord spake
unto them saying:
14 Arise and come forth unto me, that ye may
thrust your hands into my side, and also that ye
may feel the prints of the nails in my hands and in
my feet, that ye may know that I am the God of
Israel, and the God of the whole earth, and have
been slain for the sins of the world.
15 And it came to pass that the multitude went
forth, and thrust their hands into his side, and
did feel the prints of the nails in his hands and in
his feet; and this they did do, going forth one by
one until they had all gone forth, and did see with
their eyes and did feel with their hands, and did
know of a surety and did bear record, that it was
he, of whom it was written by the prophets, that
should come.
16 And when they had all gone forth and had
witnessed for themselves, they did cry out with
one accord, saying:
17 Hosanna! Blessed be the name of the Most
High God! And they did fall down at the feet of
Jesus, and did worship him.
18 And it came to pass that he spake unto Nephi
(for Nephi was among the multitude) and he
commanded him that he should come forth.
19 And Nephi arose and went forth, and bowed
himself before the Lord and did kiss his feet.

Why did Jesus Christ want the people to feel the nail prints in His hands and feet? Jesus invited the people "one by one" to come to Him. How has Jesus Christ invited you personally to come unto Him?

JESUS CHRIST INSTRUCTS THE NEPHITES ON THE CORRECT MODE OF BAPTISM

After Nephi had bowed himself before Jesus Christ and kissed his feet, the Lord spoke to him.

3 Nephi 11:20–27

And the Lord commanded him that he should arise. And he arose and stood before him.
21 And the Lord said unto him: I give unto you power that ye shall baptize this people when I am again ascended into heaven.
22 And again the Lord called others, and said unto them likewise; and he gave unto them power to baptize. And he said unto them: On this wise shall ye baptize; and there shall be no disputations among you.
23 Verily I say unto you, that whoso repenteth of his sins through your words, and desireth to be baptized in my name, on this wise shall ye baptize them—Behold, ye shall go down and stand in the water, and in my name shall ye baptize them.
24 And now behold, these are the words which ye shall say, calling them by name, saying:
25 Having authority given me of Jesus Christ, I baptize you in the name of the Father, and of the Son, and of the Holy Ghost. Amen.
26 And then shall ye immerse them in the water, and come forth again out of the water.
27 And after this manner shall ye baptize in my name; for behold, verily I say unto you, that the Father, and the Son, and the Holy Ghost are one; and I am in the Father, and the Father in me, and the Father and I are one.

What specific instructions did Jesus Christ give the people about the ordinance of baptism? What were the first commandments Christ gave to the Nephites? How is that similar to the order of principles and ordinances today?

JESUS CHRIST COMMANDS THE PEOPLE TO BECOME AS LITTLE CHILDREN

After teaching the mode of baptism, Jesus Christ continued to teach the Nephites.

3 Nephi 11:28–41

And according as I have commanded you
thus shall ye baptize. And there shall be
no disputations among you, as there have hitherto
been; neither shall there be disputations among
you concerning the points of my doctrine, as
there have hitherto been.
29 For verily, verily I say unto you, he that hath
the spirit of contention is not of me, but is of the
devil, who is the father of contention, and he stir-
reth up the hearts of men to contend with anger,
one with another.
30 Behold, this is not my doctrine, to stir up the
hearts of men with anger, one against another;
but this is my doctrine, that such things should
be done away.
31 Behold, verily, verily, I say unto you, I will
declare unto you my doctrine.
32 And this is my doctrine, and it is the doctrine
which the Father hath given unto me; and I bear
record of the Father, and the Father beareth re-
cord of me, and the Holy Ghost beareth record
of the Father and me; and I bear record that the
Father commandeth all men, everywhere, to re-
pent and believe in me.
33 And whoso believeth in me, and is baptized,
the same shall be saved; and they are they who
shall inherit the kingdom of God.
34 And whoso believeth not in me, and is not
baptized, shall be damned.
35 Verily, verily, I say unto you, that this is my
doctrine, and I bear record of it from the Father;
and whoso believeth in me believeth in the Father
also; and unto him will the Father bear record of
me, for he will visit him with fire and with the
Holy Ghost.
36 And thus will the Father bear record of me,
and the Holy Ghost will bear record unto him of
the Father and me; for the Father, and I, and the
Holy Ghost are one.
37 And again I say unto you, ye must repent,
and become as a little child, and be baptized
in my name, or ye can in nowise receive these
things.
38 And again I say unto you, ye must repent, and
be baptized in my name, and become as a little
child, or ye can in nowise inherit the kingdom of
God.
39 Verily, verily, I say unto you, that this is my
doctrine, and whoso buildeth upon this buildeth
upon my rock, and the gates of hell shall not pre-
vail against them.
40 And whoso shall declare more or less than
this, and establish it for my doctrine, the same
cometh of evil, and is not built upon my rock;
but he buildeth upon a sandy foundation, and the
gates of hell stand open to receive such when the
floods come and the winds beat upon them.
41 Therefore, go forth unto this people, and de-
clare the words which I have spoken, unto the
ends of the earth.

What is contention? Who did Christ say was the father of contention? Who did Christ say would inherit the kingdom of God? Jesus Christ commanded the people to "become as a little child." What do you think that means? How can you follow that commandment?

JESUS CHRIST DESCRIBES THE BLESSINGS THAT AWAIT THE MEEK AND MERCIFUL

Jesus Christ continued to teach the Nephites gathered at the temple.

3 Nephi 12:1–9

And it came to pass that when Jesus had spoken these words unto Nephi, and to those who had been called, (now the number of them who had been called, and received power and authority to baptize, was twelve) and behold, he stretched forth his hand unto the multitude, and cried unto them, saying: Blessed are ye if ye shall give heed unto the words of these twelve whom I have chosen from among you to minister unto you, and to be your servants; and unto them I have given power that they may baptize you with water; and after that ye are baptized with water, behold, I will baptize you with fire and with the Holy Ghost; therefore blessed are ye if ye shall believe in me and be baptized, after that ye have seen me and know that I am.
2 And again, more blessed are they who shall believe in your words because that ye shall testify that ye have seen me, and that ye know that I am. Yea, blessed are they who shall believe in your words, and come down into the depths of humility and be baptized, for they shall be visited with fire and with the Holy Ghost, and shall receive a remission of their sins.
3 Yea, blessed are the poor in spirit who come unto me, for theirs is the kingdom of heaven.
4 And again, blessed are all they that mourn, for they shall be comforted.
5 And blessed are the meek, for they shall inherit the earth.
6 And blessed are all they who do hunger and thirst after righteousness, for they shall be filled with the Holy Ghost.
7 And blessed are the merciful, for they shall obtain mercy.
8 And blessed are all the pure in heart, for they shall see God.
9 And blessed are all the peacemakers, for they shall be called the children of God.

Review the list of types of people that Jesus Christ said will be blessed. What does each of these attributes mean? What blessings will each receive? How do the qualities described by Jesus Christ differ from the attitudes and actions often celebrated in popular culture today?

JESUS CHRIST COMMANDS THE PEOPLE TO LET THEIR LIGHT SHINE BEFORE MEN

Jesus Christ continued to teach the Nephite multitude of the blessings that await the righteous.

3 Nephi 12:10–16

And blessed are all they who are persecuted for my name's sake, for theirs is the kingdom of heaven.
11 And blessed are ye when men shall revile you and persecute, and shall say all manner of evil against you falsely, for my sake;
12 For ye shall have great joy and be exceedingly glad, for great shall be your reward in heaven; for so persecuted they the prophets who were before you.
13 Verily, verily, I say unto you, I give unto you to be the salt of the earth; but if the salt shall lose its savor wherewith shall the earth be salted? The salt shall be thenceforth good for nothing, but to be cast out and to be trodden under foot of men.
14 Verily, verily, I say unto you, I give unto you to be the light of this people. A city that is set on a hill cannot be hid.
15 Behold, do men light a candle and put it under a bushel? Nay, but on a candlestick, and it giveth light to all that are in the house;
16 Therefore let your light so shine before this people, that they may see your good works and glorify your Father who is in heaven.

What blessings did Jesus Christ promise to those who are persecuted for following Him? What can you do to "let your light so shine" before others? Share examples of people who are letting their light shine.

JESUS CHRIST COMMANDS THE PEOPLE TO TURN AWAY FROM ANGER AND LUST

As Jesus Christ continued to teach the multitude, He spoke of new commandments that replaced the old laws originally given to Moses and the children of Israel.

3 Nephi 12:21–25, 27–30

Ye have heard that it hath been said by them of old time, and it is also written before you, that thou shalt not kill, and whosoever shall kill shall be in danger of the judgment of God;
22 But I say unto you, that whosoever is angry with his brother shall be in danger of his judgment. And whosoever shall say to his brother, Raca, shall be in danger of the council; and whosoever shall say, Thou fool, shall be in danger of hell fire.
23 Therefore, if ye shall come unto me, or shall desire to come unto me, and rememberest that thy brother hath aught against thee—
24 Go thy way unto thy brother, and first be reconciled to thy brother, and then come unto me with full purpose of heart, and I will receive you.
25 Agree with thine adversary quickly while thou art in the way with him, lest at any time he shall get thee, and thou shalt be cast into prison.
27 Behold, it is written by them of old time, that thou shalt not commit adultery;
28 But I say unto you, that whosoever looketh on a woman, to lust after her, hath committed adultery already in his heart.
29 Behold, I give unto you a commandment, that ye suffer none of these things to enter into your heart;
30 For it is better that ye should deny yourselves of these things, wherein ye will take up your cross, than that ye should be cast into hell.

What counsel does the Savior give to help you resolve anger? How does He clarify the law against committing adultery? What can you do to overcome angry or sinful thoughts that enter your mind?

JESUS CHRIST INVITES THE NEPHITES TO PATIENTLY ENDURE AFFLICTION AND LOVE THEIR ENEMIES

Jesus Christ continued to teach of new commandments that replaced the old laws.

3 Nephi 12:38–48

And behold, it is written, an eye for an eye, and a tooth for a tooth;
39 But I say unto you, that ye shall not resist evil,
but whosoever shall smite thee on thy right cheek,
turn to him the other also;
40 And if any man will sue thee at the law and
take away thy coat, let him have thy cloak also;
41 And whosoever shall compel thee to go a mile,
go with him twain.
42 Give to him that asketh thee, and from him
that would borrow of thee turn thou not away.
43 And behold it is written also, that thou shalt
love thy neighbor and hate thine enemy;
44 But behold I say unto you, love your enemies,
bless them that curse you, do good to them that
hate you, and pray for them who despitefully use
you and persecute you;
45 That ye may be the children of your Father
who is in heaven; for he maketh his sun to rise on
the evil and on the good.
46 Therefore those things which were of old time,
which were under the law, in me are all fulfilled.
47 Old things are done away, and all things have
become new.
48 Therefore I would that ye should be perfect
even as I, or your Father who is in heaven is perfect.

Jesus Christ commanded the people to respond peacefully to violence. He taught that if someone asks for your help, you should offer twice the help they have requested. How can you follow those commandments today? How did Jesus Christ show love to His enemies?

JESUS CHRIST TEACHES THE NEED FOR HUMBLE SERVICE AND SINCERE PRAYER

The Savior continued to teach the Nephites gathered at the temple.

3 NEPHI 13:1–13

Verily, verily, I say that I would that ye should do alms unto the poor; but take heed that ye do not your alms before men to be seen of them; otherwise ye have no reward of your Father who is in heaven.

2 Therefore, when ye shall do your alms do not sound a trumpet before you, as will hypocrites do in the synagogues and in the streets, that they may have glory of men. Verily I say unto you, they have their reward.

3 But when thou doest alms let not thy left hand know what thy right hand doeth;

4 That thine alms may be in secret; and thy Father who seeth in secret, himself shall reward thee openly.

5 And when thou prayest thou shalt not do as the hypocrites, for they love to pray, standing in the synagogues and in the corners of the streets, that they may be seen of men. Verily I say unto you, they have their reward.

6 But thou, when thou prayest, enter into thy closet, and when thou hast shut thy door, pray to thy Father who is in secret; and thy Father, who seeth in secret, shall reward thee openly.

7 But when ye pray, use not vain repetitions, as the heathen, for they think that they shall be heard for their much speaking.

8 Be not ye therefore like unto them, for your Father knoweth what things ye have need of before ye ask him.

9 After this manner therefore pray ye: Our Father who art in heaven, hallowed be thy name.

10 Thy will be done on earth as it is in heaven.

11 And forgive us our debts, as we forgive our debtors.

12 And lead us not into temptation, but deliver us from evil.

13 For thine is the kingdom, and the power, and the glory, forever. Amen.

The Savior taught that people should avoid "vain repetitions" in prayer. What do you think "vain repetitions" are? How can you avoid using them? Jesus offered an example of how we should pray. Discuss the meaning of the words He used and the things He prayed for. What do they teach you about how to pray?

JESUS CHRIST COMMANDS THE PEOPLE TO FORGIVE ONE ANOTHER AND FOCUS ON HEAVENLY REWARDS

The Savior continued to teach the Nephites gathered at the temple.

3 NEPHI 13:14–24

For, if ye forgive men their trespasses your
heavenly Father will also forgive you;
15 But if ye forgive not men their trespasses nei-
ther will your Father forgive your trespasses.
16 Moreover, when ye fast be not as the hyp-
ocrites, of a sad countenance, for they disfigure
their faces that they may appear unto men to fast.
Verily I say unto you, they have their reward.
17 But thou, when thou fastest, anoint thy head,
and wash thy face;
18 That thou appear not unto men to fast, but
unto thy Father, who is in secret; and thy Father,
who seeth in secret, shall reward thee openly.
19 Lay not up for yourselves treasures upon
earth, where moth and rust doth corrupt, and
thieves break through and steal;
20 But lay up for yourselves treasures in heaven,
where neither moth nor rust doth corrupt, and
where thieves do not break through nor steal.
21 For where your treasure is, there will your
heart be also.
22 The light of the body is the eye; if, therefore,
thine eye be single, thy whole body shall be full
of light.
23 But if thine eye be evil, thy whole body shall
be full of darkness. If, therefore, the light that is in
thee be darkness, how great is that darkness!
24 No man can serve two masters; for either he
will hate the one and love the other, or else he will
hold to the one and despise the other. Ye cannot
serve God and Mammon.

What blessings do we receive if we forgive others? What consequences do we face if we do not forgive others? What earthly treasures can you turn your attention away from? What heavenly treasures can you turn your attention to?

JESUS CHRIST COMMANDS THE NEPHITE APOSTLES TO FOCUS ON THEIR SPIRITUAL MINISTRY

After teaching the entire multitude, Jesus Christ turned His attention to the Apostles he had chosen from among the Nephites.

3 Nephi 13:25–34

And now it came to pass that when Jesus had spoken these words he looked upon the twelve whom he had chosen, and said unto them: Remember the words which I have spoken. For behold, ye are they whom I have chosen to minister unto this people. Therefore I say unto you, take no thought for your life, what ye shall eat, or what ye shall drink; nor yet for your body, what ye shall put on. Is not the life more than meat, and the body than raiment?

26 Behold the fowls of the air, for they sow not, neither do they reap nor gather into barns; yet your heavenly Father feedeth them. Are ye not much better than they?

27 Which of you by taking thought can add one cubit unto his stature?

28 And why take ye thought for raiment? Consider the lilies of the field how they grow; they toil not, neither do they spin;

29 And yet I say unto you, that even Solomon, in all his glory, was not arrayed like one of these.

30 Wherefore, if God so clothe the grass of the field, which today is, and tomorrow is cast into the oven, even so will he clothe you, if ye are not of little faith.

31 Therefore take no thought, saying, What shall we eat? or, What shall we drink? or, Wherewithal shall we be clothed?

32 For your heavenly Father knoweth that ye have need of all these things.

33 But seek ye first the kingdom of God and his righteousness, and all these things shall be added unto you.

34 Take therefore no thought for the morrow, for the morrow shall take thought for the things of itself. Sufficient is the day unto the evil thereof.

What do you think it means to "seek ye first the kingdom of God"? How will you be blessed if you seek the things of God first?

JESUS CHRIST WARNS AGAINST HYPOCRITICAL JUDGMENT AND COMMANDS THE PEOPLE TO SEEK THE GIFTS OF HEAVENLY FATHER

After instructing the twelve Nephite Apostles, Jesus spoke again to the multitude gathered at the temple.

3 Nephi 14:1–12

And now it came to pass that when Jesus had spoken these words he turned again to the multitude, and did open his mouth unto them again, saying: Verily, verily, I say unto you, Judge not, that ye be not judged.
2 For with what judgment ye judge, ye shall be judged; and with what measure ye mete, it shall be measured to you again.
3 And why beholdest thou the mote that is in thy brother's eye, but considerest not the beam that is in thine own eye?
4 Or how wilt thou say to thy brother: Let me pull the mote out of thine eye—and behold, a beam is in thine own eye?
5 Thou hypocrite, first cast the beam out of thine own eye; and then shalt thou see clearly to cast the mote out of thy brother's eye.
6 Give not that which is holy unto the dogs, neither cast ye your pearls before swine, lest they trample them under their feet, and turn again and rend you.
7 Ask, and it shall be given unto you; seek, and ye shall find; knock, and it shall be opened unto you.
8 For every one that asketh, receiveth; and he that seeketh, findeth; and to him that knocketh, it shall be opened.
9 Or what man is there of you, who, if his son ask bread, will give him a stone?
10 Or if he ask a fish, will he give him a serpent?
11 If ye then, being evil, know how to give good gifts unto your children, how much more shall your Father who is in heaven give good things to them that ask him?
12 Therefore, all things whatsoever ye would that men should do to you, do ye even so to them, for this is the law and the prophets.

What does it mean to be a hypocrite? How can you avoid being a hypocrite? The Savior commanded, "Ask, and it shall be given unto you; seek, and ye shall find." What answers or blessings do you hope to receive from Heavenly Father? What can you do to actively ask and seek for those answers?

JESUS CHRIST TEACHES OF THE STRAIGHT GATE, FALSE PROPHETS, AND BUILDING A HOUSE UPON A ROCK

The Savior continued to teach the Nephites gathered at the temple.

3 NEPHI 14:13–27

Enter ye in at the strait gate; for wide is the
gate, and broad is the way, which leadeth to
destruction, and many there be who go in thereat;
14 Because strait is the gate, and narrow is the
way, which leadeth unto life, and few there be
that find it.
15 Beware of false prophets, who come to you in
sheep's clothing, but inwardly they are ravening
wolves.
16 Ye shall know them by their fruits. Do men
gather grapes of thorns, or figs of thistles?
17 Even so every good tree bringeth forth good
fruit; but a corrupt tree bringeth forth evil fruit.
18 A good tree cannot bring forth evil fruit, nei-
ther a corrupt tree bring forth good fruit.
19 Every tree that bringeth not forth good fruit is
hewn down, and cast into the fire.
20 Wherefore, by their fruits ye shall know them.
21 Not every one that saith unto me, Lord, Lord,
shall enter into the kingdom of heaven; but he
that doeth the will of my Father who is in heaven.
22 Many will say to me in that day: Lord, Lord,
have we not prophesied in thy name, and in thy
name have cast out devils, and in thy name done
many wonderful works?
23 And then will I profess unto them: I never
knew you; depart from me, ye that work iniq-
uity.
24 Therefore, whoso heareth these sayings of
mine and doeth them, I will liken him unto a
wise man, who built his house upon a rock—
25 And the rain descended, and the floods came,
and the winds blew, and beat upon that house;
and it fell not, for it was founded upon a rock.
26 And every one that heareth these sayings of
mine and doeth them not shall be likened unto
a foolish man, who built his house upon the
sand—
27 And the rain descended, and the floods came,
and the winds blew, and beat upon that house;
and it fell, and great was the fall of it.

According to this passage, how can you recognize false prophets? Jesus said that wise people both hear *and* obey His commandments. If you do this, what will happen to you when trials come? What commandments do you feel you can more fully "do" and not merely "hear"?

JESUS CHRIST DECLARES THAT THE LAW OF MOSES IS FULFILLED IN HIM

The Savior continued to teach the Nephites gathered at the temple.

3 Nephi 15:1–10

And now it came to pass that when Jesus had ended these sayings he cast his eyes round about on the multitude, and said unto them: Behold, ye have heard the things which I taught before I ascended to my Father; therefore, whoso remembereth these sayings of mine and doeth them, him will I raise up at the last day.

2 And it came to pass that when Jesus had said these words he perceived that there were some among them who marveled, and wondered what he would concerning the law of Moses; for they understood not the saying that old things had passed away, and that all things had become new.

3 And he said unto them: Marvel not that I said unto you that old things had passed away, and that all things had become new.

4 Behold, I say unto you that the law is fulfilled that was given unto Moses.

5 Behold, I am he that gave the law, and I am he who covenanted with my people Israel; therefore, the law in me is fulfilled, for I have come to fulfil the law; therefore it hath an end.

6 Behold, I do not destroy the prophets, for as many as have not been fulfilled in me, verily I say unto you, shall all be fulfilled.

7 And because I said unto you that old things have passed away, I do not destroy that which hath been spoken concerning things which are to come.

8 For behold, the covenant which I have made with my people is not all fulfilled; but the law which was given unto Moses hath an end in me.

9 Behold, I am the law, and the light. Look unto me, and endure to the end, and ye shall live; for unto him that endureth to the end will I give eternal life.

10 Behold, I have given unto you the commandments; therefore keep my commandments. And this is the law and the prophets, for they truly testified of me.

What did Jesus teach about the relationship He had with Moses and the house of Israel long before His birth? What do you know about Jesus Christ's roles before, during, and after His mortal life?

JESUS CHRIST SPEAKS OF THE LATTER-DAY GATHERING OF ISRAEL

Jesus Christ told the Nephites that they were the "other sheep" spoken of during His mortal ministry in Jerusalem. He then spoke of other people in other lands to whom He would also minister and of the fulfilling of covenants in the latter days that would make membership in the house of Israel available to all people.

3 Nephi 16:1–3, 5–7, 9, 12–13

And verily, verily, I say unto you that I have other sheep, which are not of this land, neither of the land of Jerusalem, neither in any parts of that land round about whither I have been to minister.
2 For they of whom I speak are they who have not as yet heard my voice; neither have I at any time manifested myself unto them.
3 But I have received a commandment of the Father that I shall go unto them, and that they shall hear my voice, and shall be numbered among my sheep, that there may be one fold and one shepherd; therefore I go to show myself unto them.
5 And then will I gather them in from the four quarters of the earth; and then will I fulfil the covenant which the Father hath made unto all the people of the house of Israel.
6 And blessed are the Gentiles, because of their belief in me, in and of the Holy Ghost, which witnesses unto them of me and of the Father.
7 Behold, because of their belief in me, saith the Father, and because of the unbelief of you, O house of Israel, in the latter day shall the truth come unto the Gentiles, that the fulness of these things shall be made known unto them.
9 And because of the mercies of the Father unto the Gentiles, and also the judgments of the Father upon my people who are of the house of Israel, verily, verily, I say unto you, that after all this, and I have caused my people who are of the house of Israel to be smitten, and to be afflicted, and to be slain, and to be cast out from among them, and to become hated by them, and to become a hiss and a byword among them—
12 And I will show unto thee, O house of Israel, that the Gentiles shall not have power over you; but I will remember my covenant unto you, O house of Israel, and ye shall come unto the knowledge of the fulness of my gospel.
13 But if the Gentiles will repent and return unto me, saith the Father, behold they shall be numbered among my people, O house of Israel.

What is required for someone to become a part of the house of Israel? Are you a member of the house of Israel? What role do you play in the gathering of Israel?

JESUS CHRIST HEALS ALL THE SICK AMONG THE NEPHITE MULTITUDE

After teaching of the gathering of the house of Israel, the Savior continued speaking to the people.

3 Nephi 17:1–10

Behold, now it came to pass that when
Jesus had spoken these words he looked
round about again on the multitude, and he said
unto them: Behold, my time is at hand.
2 I perceive that ye are weak, that ye cannot un-
derstand all my words which I am commanded of
the Father to speak unto you at this time.
3 Therefore, go ye unto your homes, and ponder
upon the things which I have said, and ask of the
Father, in my name, that ye may understand, and
prepare your minds for the morrow, and I come
unto you again.
4 But now I go unto the Father, and also to show
myself unto the lost tribes of Israel, for they are
not lost unto the Father, for he knoweth whither
he hath taken them.
5 And it came to pass that when Jesus had thus
spoken, he cast his eyes round about again on the
multitude, and beheld they were in tears, and did
look steadfastly upon him as if they would ask
him to tarry a little longer with them.
6 And he said unto them: Behold, my bowels are
filled with compassion towards you.
7 Have ye any that are sick among you? Bring
them hither. Have ye any that are lame, or blind,
or halt, or maimed, or leprous, or that are with-
ered, or that are deaf, or that are afflicted in any
manner? Bring them hither and I will heal them,
for I have compassion upon you; my bowels are
filled with mercy.
8 For I perceive that ye desire that I should show
unto you what I have done unto your brethren
at Jerusalem, for I see that your faith is sufficient
that I should heal you.
9 And it came to pass that when he had thus spo-
ken, all the multitude, with one accord, did go
forth with their sick and their afflicted, and their
lame, and with their blind, and with their dumb,
and with all them that were afflicted in any man-
ner; and he did heal them every one as they were
brought forth unto him.
10 And they did all, both they who had been
healed and they who were whole, bow down at his
feet, and did worship him; and as many as could
come for the multitude did kiss his feet, insomuch
that they did bathe his feet with their tears.

What does it mean to ponder upon the teachings of Jesus Christ? Why do you think the people were unable to immediately understand all of Christ's teachings? What do you learn about the nature of Jesus Christ from this account of His blessing the sick and the afflicted?

ANGELS JOIN JESUS CHRIST IN PERSONALLY MINISTERING TO THE NEPHITES

After healing all the sick among the Nephite multitude, the Savior continued to minister to the people. As you read, look for the different emotions Jesus felt as He prayed to Heavenly Father and blessed the people.

3 Nephi 17:11–25

And it came to pass that he commanded that their little children should be brought.

12 So they brought their little children and set them down upon the ground round about him, and Jesus stood in the midst; and the multitude gave way till they had all been brought unto him.

13 And it came to pass that when they had all been brought, and Jesus stood in the midst, he commanded the multitude that they should kneel down upon the ground.

14 And it came to pass that when they had knelt upon the ground, Jesus groaned within himself, and said: Father, I am troubled because of the wickedness of the people of the house of Israel.

15 And when he had said these words, he himself also knelt upon the earth; and behold he prayed unto the Father, and the things which he prayed cannot be written, and the multitude did bear record who heard him.

16 And after this manner do they bear record: The eye hath never seen, neither hath the ear heard, before, so great and marvelous things as we saw and heard Jesus speak unto the Father;

17 And no tongue can speak, neither can there be written by any man, neither can the hearts of men conceive so great and marvelous things as we both saw and heard Jesus speak; and no one can conceive of the joy which filled our souls at the time we heard him pray for us unto the Father.

18 And it came to pass that when Jesus had made an end of praying unto the Father, he arose; but so great was the joy of the multitude that they were overcome.

19 And it came to pass that Jesus spake unto them, and bade them arise.

20 And they arose from the earth, and he said unto them: Blessed are ye because of your faith. And now behold, my joy is full.

21 And when he had said these words, he wept, and the multitude bare record of it, and he took their little children, one by one, and blessed them, and prayed unto the Father for them.

22 And when he had done this he wept again;

23 And he spake unto the multitude, and said unto them: Behold your little ones.

24 And as they looked to behold they cast their eyes towards heaven, and they saw the heavens open, and they saw angels descending out of heaven as it were in the midst of fire; and they came down and encircled those little ones about, and they were encircled about with fire; and the angels did minister unto them.

25 And the multitude did see and hear and bear record; and they know that their record is true for they all of them did see and hear, every man for himself; and they were in number about two thousand and five hundred souls; and they did consist of men, women, and children.

What different emotions did Jesus feel as He ministered among the people? What do these emotions tell you about Jesus Christ's character? What does it mean to "minister" to someone? What opportunities do you have to minister to those around you?

JESUS CHRIST OFFERS THE SACRAMENT TO THE NEPHITE MULTITUDE

After individually blessing each of the Nephite children, Jesus Christ continued to instruct the people.

3 Nephi 18:1–11

And it came to pass that Jesus com-
manded his disciples that they should
bring forth some bread and wine unto him.
2 And while they were gone for bread and wine,
he commanded the multitude that they should sit
themselves down upon the earth.
3 And when the disciples had come with bread
and wine, he took of the bread and brake and
blessed it; and he gave unto the disciples and
commanded that they should eat.
4 And when they had eaten and were filled, he
commanded that they should give unto the mul-
titude.
5 And when the multitude had eaten and were
filled, he said unto the disciples: Behold there shall
one be ordained among you, and to him will I give
power that he shall break bread and bless it and
give it unto the people of my church, unto all those
who shall believe and be baptized in my name.
6 And this shall ye always observe to do, even
as I have done, even as I have broken bread and
blessed it and given it unto you.
7 And this shall ye do in remembrance of my
body, which I have shown unto you. And it shall
be a testimony unto the Father that ye do always
remember me. And if ye do always remember me
ye shall have my Spirit to be with you.
8 And it came to pass that when he said these
words, he commanded his disciples that they
should take of the wine of the cup and drink of it,
and that they should also give unto the multitude
that they might drink of it.
9 And it came to pass that they did so, and did
drink of it and were filled; and they gave unto
the multitude, and they did drink, and they were
filled.
10 And when the disciples had done this, Jesus
said unto them: Blessed are ye for this thing which
ye have done, for this is fulfilling my command-
ments, and this doth witness unto the Father that
ye are willing to do that which I have commanded
you.
11 And this shall ye always do to those who re-
pent and are baptized in my name; and ye shall do
it in remembrance of my blood, which I have shed
for you, that ye may witness unto the Father that
ye do always remember me. And if ye do always re-
member me ye shall have my Spirit to be with you.

What did Jesus Christ say was the purpose of the sacrament? What should you think about as you take the sacrament? How has partaking of the sacrament made a difference in your life? How do you feel during that ordinance?

JESUS CHRIST COMMANDS THE PEOPLE TO PRAY ALWAYS

After Jesus Christ had explained the purpose of the sacrament, He gave the multitude additional instructions.

3 Nephi 18:12–21

And I give unto you a commandment
that ye shall do these things. And if ye
shall always do these things blessed are ye, for ye
are built upon my rock.
13 But whoso among you shall do more or less
than these are not built upon my rock, but are
built upon a sandy foundation; and when the rain
descends, and the floods come, and the winds
blow, and beat upon them, they shall fall, and the
gates of hell are ready open to receive them.
14 Therefore blessed are ye if ye shall keep my
commandments, which the Father hath com-
manded me that I should give unto you.
15 Verily, verily, I say unto you, ye must watch
and pray always, lest ye be tempted by the devil,
and ye be led away captive by him.
16 And as I have prayed among you even so shall
ye pray in my church, among my people who do
repent and are baptized in my name. Behold I am
the light; I have set an example for you.
17 And it came to pass that when Jesus had spo-
ken these words unto his disciples, he turned
again unto the multitude and said unto them:
18 Behold, verily, verily, I say unto you, ye must
watch and pray always lest ye enter into tempta-
tion; for Satan desireth to have you, that he may
sift you as wheat.
19 Therefore ye must always pray unto the Father
in my name;
20 And whatsoever ye shall ask the Father in my
name, which is right, believing that ye shall re-
ceive, behold it shall be given unto you.
21 Pray in your families unto the Father, always
in my name, that your wives and your children
may be blessed.

What did Jesus Christ say was the reason to "pray always"? How can you make it a habit to pray always without using vain repetitions or letting your prayers become insincere?

JESUS CHRIST COMMANDS THE PEOPLE TO BE INCLUSIVE AND MEET TOGETHER OFTEN

After commanding the Nephite multitude to pray always, Jesus Christ continued to teach them.

3 Nephi 18:22–25, 35–39

And behold, ye shall meet together oft;
and ye shall not forbid any man from
coming unto you when ye shall meet together, but
suffer them that they may come unto you and for-
bid them not;
23 But ye shall pray for them, and shall not cast
them out; and if it so be that they come unto you
oft ye shall pray for them unto the Father, in my
name.
24 Therefore, hold up your light that it may
shine unto the world. Behold I am the light which
ye shall hold up—that which ye have seen me do.
Behold ye see that I have prayed unto the Father,
and ye all have witnessed.
25 And ye see that I have commanded that none
of you should go away, but rather have com-
manded that ye should come unto me, that ye
might feel and see; even so shall ye do unto the
world; and whosoever breaketh this command-
ment suffereth himself to be led into temptation.
35 And now I go unto the Father, because it is
expedient that I should go unto the Father for
your sakes.
36 And it came to pass that when Jesus had made
an end of these sayings, he touched with his hand
the disciples whom he had chosen, one by one,
even until he had touched them all, and spake
unto them as he touched them.
37 And the multitude heard not the words which
he spake, therefore they did not bear record; but
the disciples bare record that he gave them power
to give the Holy Ghost. And I will show unto you
hereafter that this record is true.
38 And it came to pass that when Jesus had
touched them all, there came a cloud and overshad-
owed the multitude that they could not see Jesus.
39 And while they were overshadowed he de-
parted from them, and ascended into heaven.
And the disciples saw and did bear record that he
ascended again into heaven.

How does Jesus say we should treat all those who want to attend Church meetings? Jesus said, "Hold up your light that it may shine unto the world. I am the light which ye shall hold up—that which ye have seen me do." What things has Christ done that you can do as well?

THE NEPHITES AGAIN WITNESS JESUS CHRIST AND RECEIVE AN OUTPOURING OF THE HOLY GHOST

After Jesus Christ had departed from the Nephites and ascended into heaven, word traveled throughout the land that He would again appear to the people the following day. Throughout the night a great number of people made the journey to witness the Savior for themselves. When they arrived, Nephi and his fellow Apostles taught and prayed among the people. Nephi was baptized and then baptized each of the other Apostles Jesus had chosen. As you read, consider how the three members of the Godhead—Heavenly Father, Jesus Christ, and the Holy Ghost—helped bless the Nephites.

3 Nephi 19:13–23

And it came to pass when they were all
baptized and had come up out of the
water, the Holy Ghost did fall upon them, and
they were filled with the Holy Ghost and with fire.
14 And behold, they were encircled about as if it
were by fire; and it came down from heaven, and
the multitude did witness it, and did bear record;
and angels did come down out of heaven and did
minister unto them.
15 And it came to pass that while the angels were
ministering unto the disciples, behold, Jesus came
and stood in the midst and ministered unto them.
16 And it came to pass that he spake unto the
multitude, and commanded them that they should
kneel down again upon the earth, and also that his
disciples should kneel down upon the earth.
17 And it came to pass that when they had all
knelt down upon the earth, he commanded his
disciples that they should pray.
18 And behold, they began to pray; and they did
pray unto Jesus, calling him their Lord and their
God.
19 And it came to pass that Jesus departed out of
the midst of them, and went a little way off from
them and bowed himself to the earth, and he said:
20 Father, I thank thee that thou hast given the
Holy Ghost unto these whom I have chosen; and
it is because of their belief in me that I have cho-
sen them out of the world.
21 Father, I pray thee that thou wilt give the
Holy Ghost unto all them that shall believe in
their words.
22 Father, thou hast given them the Holy Ghost
because they believe in me; and thou seest that
they believe in me because thou hearest them, and
they pray unto me; and they pray unto me be-
cause I am with them.
23 And now Father, I pray unto thee for them,
and also for all those who shall believe on their
words, that they may believe in me, that I may be
in them as thou, Father, art in me, that we may
be one.

In what ways did the three members of the Godhead help bless the Nephites? What caused the Father to give the Holy Ghost to the Nephites? How does it make you feel to know that Jesus Christ prays to His Father for you?

JESUS CHRIST PRAYS FOR THE MULTITUDE USING WORDS THAT CANNOT BE WRITTEN

After privately praying to Heavenly Father on behalf of the Nephites, Jesus Christ returned to find the multitude continuing in prayer unto the Father.

3 Nephi 19:25–36

And it came to pass that Jesus blessed
them as they did pray unto him; and his
countenance did smile upon them, and the light
of his countenance did shine upon them, and be-
hold they were as white as the countenance and
also the garments of Jesus; and behold the white-
ness thereof did exceed all the whiteness, yea, even
there could be nothing upon earth so white as the
whiteness thereof.
26 And Jesus said unto them: Pray on; neverthe-
less they did not cease to pray.
27 And he turned from them again, and went a
little way off and bowed himself to the earth; and
he prayed again unto the Father, saying:
28 Father, I thank thee that thou hast purified
those whom I have chosen, because of their faith,
and I pray for them, and also for them who shall
believe on their words, that they may be purified
in me, through faith on their words, even as they
are purified in me.
29 Father, I pray not for the world, but for those
whom thou hast given me out of the world, be-
cause of their faith, that they may be purified in
me, that I may be in them as thou, Father, art in
me, that we may be one, that I may be glorified
in them.
30 And when Jesus had spoken these words he
came again unto his disciples; and behold they
did pray steadfastly, without ceasing, unto him;
and he did smile upon them again; and behold
they were white, even as Jesus.
31 And it came to pass that he went again a little
way off and prayed unto the Father;
32 And tongue cannot speak the words which he
prayed, neither can be written by man the words
which he prayed.
33 And the multitude did hear and do bear re-
cord; and their hearts were open and they did un-
derstand in their hearts the words which he prayed.
34 Nevertheless, so great and marvelous were the
words which he prayed that they cannot be writ-
ten, neither can they be uttered by man.
35 And it came to pass that when Jesus had made
an end of praying he came again to the disciples,
and said unto them: So great faith have I never
seen among all the Jews; wherefore I could not
show unto them so great miracles, because of their
unbelief.
36 Verily I say unto you, there are none of them
that have seen so great things as ye have seen; nei-
ther have they heard so great things as ye have
heard.

What things did Jesus thank and ask His Father for in behalf of the people? What do you think it means to "be one" with Heavenly Father and Jesus Christ? How can you become one with your family, Jesus Christ, and Heavenly Father?

JESUS CHRIST PROPHESIES OF THE COMING FORTH OF THE BOOK OF MORMON

After praying on behalf of the Nephites, Jesus Christ again administered the sacrament, using bread and wine miraculously provided for that purpose. He then spoke of the latter-day gathering of Israel, which would be dependent upon a free nation of Gentiles, through which the Book of Mormon would come to the latter-day descendants of the Nephites and Lamanites. As you read Christ's prophecies, consider which ones have already been fulfilled.

3 Nephi 20:29; 21:1–4, 7, 9

And I will remember the covenant which I have made with my people; and I have covenanted with them that I would gather them together in mine own due time, that I would give unto them again the land of their fathers for their inheritance, which is the land of Jerusalem, which is the promised land unto them forever, saith the Father.

3 Nephi 21

1 And verily I say unto you, I give unto you a sign, that ye may know the time when these things shall be about to take place—that I shall gather in, from their long dispersion, my people, O house of Israel, and shall establish again among them my Zion;

2 And behold, this is the thing which I will give unto you for a sign—for verily I say unto you that when these things which I declare unto you, and which I shall declare unto you hereafter of myself, and by the power of the Holy Ghost which shall be given unto you of the Father, shall be made known unto the Gentiles that they may know concerning this people who are a remnant of the house of Jacob, and concerning this my people who shall be scattered by them;

3 Verily, verily, I say unto you, when these things shall be made known unto them of the Father, and shall come forth of the Father, from them unto you;

4 For it is wisdom in the Father that they should be established in this land, and be set up as a free people by the power of the Father, that these things might come forth from them unto a remnant of your seed, that the covenant of the Father may be fulfilled which he hath covenanted with his people, O house of Israel;

7 And when these things come to pass that thy seed shall begin to know these things—it shall be a sign unto them, that they may know that the work of the Father hath already commenced unto the fulfilling of the covenant which he hath made unto the people who are of the house of Israel.

9 For in that day, for my sake shall the Father work a work, which shall be a great and a marvelous work among them; and there shall be among them those who will not believe it, although a man shall declare it unto them.

What did Jesus Christ prophesy would happen in the latter days? In what ways have these prophecies of Jesus Christ been fulfilled? How are they still being fulfilled?

JESUS CHRIST TEACHES THAT MEMBERSHIP IN THE HOUSE OF ISRAEL IS AVAILABLE TO ALL

After prophesying to the Nephites of the coming forth of the Book of Mormon, Jesus prophesied of the latter-day opportunity for all people to become members of the house of Israel.

3 Nephi 21:11, 19–20, 22–25

Therefore it shall come to pass that whosoever will not believe in my words, who am Jesus Christ, which the Father shall cause him to bring forth unto the Gentiles, and shall give unto him power that he shall bring them forth unto the Gentiles, (it shall be done even as Moses said) they shall be cut off from among my people who are of the covenant.

19 And it shall come to pass that all lyings, and deceivings, and envyings, and strifes, and priestcrafts, and whoredoms, shall be done away.

20 For it shall come to pass, saith the Father, that at that day whosoever will not repent and come unto my Beloved Son, them will I cut off from among my people, O house of Israel;

22 But if they will repent and hearken unto my words, and harden not their hearts, I will establish my church among them, and they shall come in unto the covenant and be numbered among this the remnant of Jacob, unto whom I have given this land for their inheritance;

23 And they shall assist my people, the remnant of Jacob, and also as many of the house of Israel as shall come, that they may build a city, which shall be called the New Jerusalem.

24 And then shall they assist my people that they may be gathered in, who are scattered upon all the face of the land, in unto the New Jerusalem.

25 And then shall the power of heaven come down among them; and I also will be in the midst.

What kind of people did Jesus Christ say would be "cut off"—or excluded—from the house of Israel? What kind of people did Jesus Christ say would become part of the house of Israel? Why should we desire to be part of the house of Israel?

JESUS CHRIST COMMANDS THE PEOPLE TO DILIGENTLY SEARCH THE WORDS OF ISAIAH

After prophesying of the opportunity extended to all people to join the house of Israel, Jesus Christ quoted from the prophecies of Isaiah. Isaiah lived about 700 years before the birth of Christ. His original writings are contained in the Old Testament and were also quoted by Lehi's son Nephi.

3 Nephi 23:1–5

And now, behold, I say unto you, that ye
ought to search these things. Yea, a com-
mandment I give unto you that ye search these
things diligently; for great are the words of Isaiah.
2 For surely he spake as touching all things con-
cerning my people which are of the house of
Israel; therefore it must needs be that he must
speak also to the Gentiles.
3 And all things that he spake have been and shall
be, even according to the words which he spake.
4 Therefore give heed to my words; write the
things which I have told you; and according to
the time and the will of the Father they shall go
forth unto the Gentiles.
5 And whosoever will hearken unto my words
and repenteth and is baptized, the same shall be
saved. Search the prophets, for many there be that
testify of these things.

What word does Jesus use to describe how we should search the scriptures? The scriptures—including the prophecies of Isaiah—often use unique language that can be difficult to understand. What are some ways you can understand the scriptures and diligently search them?

JESUS CHRIST EXAMINES THE NEPHITE SCRIPTURAL RECORD AND COMMANDS THAT ADDITIONAL EVENTS BE RECORDED

After commanding the people to diligently search the words of Isaiah, Jesus Christ gave additional direction about the scriptural record kept by the Nephites.

3 Nephi 23:6–14

And now it came to pass that when Jesus
had said these words he said unto them
again, after he had expounded all the scriptures
unto them which they had received, he said unto
them: Behold, other scriptures I would that ye
should write, that ye have not.
7 And it came to pass that he said unto Nephi:
Bring forth the record which ye have kept.
8 And when Nephi had brought forth the re-
cords, and laid them before him, he cast his eyes
upon them and said:
9 Verily I say unto you, I commanded my servant
Samuel, the Lamanite, that he should testify unto
this people, that at the day that the Father should
glorify his name in me that there were many saints
who should arise from the dead, and should ap-
pear unto many, and should minister unto them.
And he said unto them: Was it not so?
10 And his disciples answered him and said:
Yea, Lord, Samuel did prophesy according to thy
words, and they were all fulfilled.
11 And Jesus said unto them: How be it that ye
have not written this thing, that many saints did
arise and appear unto many and did minister unto
them?
12 And it came to pass that Nephi remembered
that this thing had not been written.
13 And it came to pass that Jesus commanded
that it should be written; therefore it was written
according as he commanded.
14 And now it came to pass that when Jesus
had expounded all the scriptures in one, which
they had written, he commanded them that they
should teach the things which he had expounded
unto them.

What kind of experience did the Savior command the people to record? Why do you think the Savior commanded that those specific events be recorded in the scriptures? What does this teach you about the kinds of things you should record in a journal? What goal can you set to record important experiences?

JESUS CHRIST TEACHES THE LAW OF TITHING BY QUOTING MALACHI'S PROPHECY

After examining the Nephite's scriptural record, Jesus Christ commanded that the words of the prophet Malachi should also be recorded. Malachi prophesied in the land near Jerusalem about 400 years before the birth of Christ. His prophecies were originally recorded in what became the Old Testament. As you read, consider the blessings the Lord promises to those who pay tithing.

3 Nephi 24:1–2, 5, 8–12

And it came to pass that he commanded
them that they should write the words
which the Father had given unto Malachi, which
he should tell unto them. And it came to pass that
after they were written he expounded them. And
these are the words which he did tell unto them,
saying: Thus said the Father unto Malachi—
Behold, I will send my messenger, and he shall
prepare the way before me, and the Lord whom
ye seek shall suddenly come to his temple, even
the messenger of the covenant, whom ye delight
in; behold, he shall come, saith the Lord of Hosts.
2 But who may abide the day of his coming, and
who shall stand when he appeareth? For he is like
a refiner's fire, and like fuller's soap.
5 And I will come near to you to judgment; and
I will be a swift witness against the sorcerers, and
against the adulterers, and against false swearers,
and against those that oppress the hireling in his
wages, the widow and the fatherless, and that turn
aside the stranger, and fear not me, saith the Lord
of Hosts.
8 Will a man rob God? Yet ye have robbed me.
But ye say: Wherein have we robbed thee? In
tithes and offerings.
9 Ye are cursed with a curse, for ye have robbed
me, even this whole nation.
10 Bring ye all the tithes into the storehouse, that
there may be meat in my house; and prove me
now herewith, saith the Lord of Hosts, if I will
not open you the windows of heaven, and pour
you out a blessing that there shall not be room
enough to receive it.
11 And I will rebuke the devourer for your sakes,
and he shall not destroy the fruits of your ground;
neither shall your vine cast her fruit before the
time in the fields, saith the Lord of Hosts.
12 And all nations shall call you blessed, for ye
shall be a delightsome land, saith the Lord of
Hosts.

What does the Lord promise those who pay tithing? What blessings have you received from paying tithing?

JESUS CHRIST SPEAKS OF ELIJAH'S INFLUENCE ON FAMILIES IN THE LATTER DAYS

As He taught the Nephite multitude, Jesus Christ continued to quote the prophecies of Malachi, which spoke of events leading up to Christ's Second Coming in the latter days.

3 Nephi 25:1–6

For behold, the day cometh that shall burn
as an oven; and all the proud, yea, and
all that do wickedly, shall be stubble; and the day
that cometh shall burn them up, saith the Lord
of Hosts, that it shall leave them neither root nor
branch.
2 But unto you that fear my name, shall the Son of
Righteousness arise with healing in his wings; and
ye shall go forth and grow up as calves in the stall.
3 And ye shall tread down the wicked; for they
shall be ashes under the soles of your feet in the
day that I shall do this, saith the Lord of Hosts.
4 Remember ye the law of Moses, my servant,
which I commanded unto him in Horeb for all
Israel, with the statutes and judgments.
5 Behold, I will send you Elijah the prophet be-
fore the coming of the great and dreadful day of
the Lord;
6 And he shall turn the heart of the fathers to the
children, and the heart of the children to their
fathers, lest I come and smite the earth with a
curse.

On April 3, 1836, in the Kirtland Temple, the prophet Elijah appeared to Joseph Smith and Oliver Cowdery. This event was a fulfillment of Malachi's prophecy that Jesus Christ "will send you Elijah the prophet before the coming . . . of the Lord." Elijah gave Joseph Smith the sealing power, the power by which temple ordinances are performed for the living and the dead, allowing families to be united for eternity. How can you participate in family history and temple work? How have you felt your heart turned to your ancestors as you have done so?

JESUS CHRIST COMMANDS THAT HIS CHURCH BE CALLED IN HIS NAME

After quoting the prophecies of Malachi, Jesus Christ explained all things from the beginning until the time of His Second Coming. He continued to administer the sacrament and ministered to the children, who themselves spoke great prophecies. The Savior then ascended into heaven for the second time. The Nephites obeyed His commandments, shared their possessions, and ministered to one another.

3 Nephi 27:1–9

And it came to pass that as the disciples of Jesus were journeying and were preaching the things which they had both heard and seen, and were baptizing in the name of Jesus, it came to pass that the disciples were gathered together and were united in mighty prayer and fasting.

2 And Jesus again showed himself unto them, for they were praying unto the Father in his name; and Jesus came and stood in the midst of them, and said unto them: What will ye that I shall give unto you?

3 And they said unto him: Lord, we will that thou wouldst tell us the name whereby we shall call this church; for there are disputations among the people concerning this matter.

4 And the Lord said unto them: Verily, verily, I say unto you, why is it that the people should murmur and dispute because of this thing?

5 Have they not read the scriptures, which say ye must take upon you the name of Christ, which is my name? For by this name shall ye be called at the last day;

6 And whoso taketh upon him my name, and endureth to the end, the same shall be saved at the last day.

7 Therefore, whatsoever ye shall do, ye shall do it in my name; therefore ye shall call the church in my name; and ye shall call upon the Father in my name that he will bless the church for my sake.

8 And how be it my church save it be called in my name? For if a church be called in Moses' name then it be Moses' church; or if it be called in the name of a man then it be the church of a man; but if it be called in my name then it is my church, if it so be that they are built upon my gospel.

9 Verily I say unto you, that ye are built upon my gospel; therefore ye shall call whatsoever things ye do call, in my name; therefore if ye call upon the Father, for the church, if it be in my name the Father will hear you;

What did Jesus Christ promise to those who take His name upon them and endure to the end? What have you been commanded to do in the name of Christ? In what ways can you take the name of Christ upon you?

JESUS CHRIST COMMANDS ALL PEOPLE TO REPENT AND BE BAPTIZED IN HIS NAME

After Jesus Christ taught the Nephites that His Church would bear His name, He continued to teach the people.

3 Nephi 27:13–22

Behold I have given unto you my gospel,
and this is the gospel which I have given
unto you—that I came into the world to do the
will of my Father, because my Father sent me.
14 And my Father sent me that I might be lifted
up upon the cross; and after that I had been lifted
up upon the cross, that I might draw all men unto
me, that as I have been lifted up by men even so
should men be lifted up by the Father, to stand
before me, to be judged of their works, whether
they be good or whether they be evil—
15 And for this cause have I been lifted up; there-
fore, according to the power of the Father I will
draw all men unto me, that they may be judged
according to their works.
16 And it shall come to pass, that whoso repen-
teth and is baptized in my name shall be filled;
and if he endureth to the end, behold, him will I
hold guiltless before my Father at that day when I
shall stand to judge the world.
17 And he that endureth not unto the end, the
same is he that is also hewn down and cast into
the fire, from whence they can no more return,
because of the justice of the Father.
18 And this is the word which he hath given
unto the children of men. And for this cause he
fulfilleth the words which he hath given, and he
lieth not, but fulfilleth all his words.
19 And no unclean thing can enter into his king-
dom; therefore nothing entereth into his rest save
it be those who have washed their garments in my
blood, because of their faith, and the repentance
of all their sins, and their faithfulness unto the
end.
20 Now this is the commandment: Repent, all
ye ends of the earth, and come unto me and be
baptized in my name, that ye may be sanctified
by the reception of the Holy Ghost, that ye may
stand spotless before me at the last day.
21 Verily, verily, I say unto you, this is my gospel;
and ye know the things that ye must do in my
church; for the works which ye have seen me do
that shall ye also do; for that which ye have seen
me do even that shall ye do;
22 Therefore, if ye do these things blessed are ye,
for ye shall be lifted up at the last day.

Before, during, and after His earthly life, Jesus Christ repeatedly commanded all people to repent, be baptized, and endure to the end. Why do you think He placed such emphasis on those commandments? What blessings did the Savior say will come to those who follow them?

MORMON WARNS THOSE WHO DENY CHRIST AND HIS WORKS

Before ascending to the Father, Jesus Christ asked the Nephite Apostles what each of them he desired. Nine of the Apostles requested that at the end of their mortal lives they would speedily enter Christ's kingdom. The remaining three requested that they remain alive to witness the unfolding of God's work upon the earth until Christ's Second Coming. Christ promised all the Apostles that their requests would be granted. Mormon, speaking hundreds of years later, confirmed that three of the Nephite Apostles were spared from death, pain, and imprisonment as they preached Christ's gospel and ministered to people throughout the land, including to Mormon himself. Speaking to latter-day readers, Mormon then gave a prophecy and warning about the coming forth of the Book of Mormon.

3 Nephi 29:1–6

And now behold, I say unto you that when the Lord shall see fit, in his wisdom, that these sayings shall come unto the Gentiles according to his word, then ye may know that the covenant which the Father hath made with the children of Israel, concerning their restoration to the lands of their inheritance, is already beginning to be fulfilled.

2 And ye may know that the words of the Lord, which have been spoken by the holy prophets, shall all be fulfilled; and ye need not say that the Lord delays his coming unto the children of Israel.

3 And ye need not imagine in your hearts that the words which have been spoken are vain, for behold, the Lord will remember his covenant which he hath made unto his people of the house of Israel.

4 And when ye shall see these sayings coming forth among you, then ye need not any longer spurn at the doings of the Lord, for the sword of his justice is in his right hand; and behold, at that day, if ye shall spurn at his doings he will cause that it shall soon overtake you.

5 Wo unto him that spurneth at the doings of the Lord; yea, wo unto him that shall deny the Christ and his works!

6 Yea, wo unto him that shall deny the revelations of the Lord, and that shall say the Lord no longer worketh by revelation, or by prophecy, or by gifts, or by tongues, or by healings, or by the power of the Holy Ghost!

According to Mormon, what is the coming forth of the Book of Mormon a sign of? What evidence have you seen of revelations, miracles, prophecies, gifts, or healings?

The Book of Fourth Nephi

THE NEPHITES ENJOY MANY DECADES OF PEACE AND RIGHTEOUSNESS

After Jesus Christ again ascended into heaven, the Nephite Apostles organized Christ's Church throughout the land.

4 Nephi 1:2–3, 5, 10–13, 15–18

And it came to pass in the thirty and sixth year, the people were all converted unto the Lord, upon all the face of the land, both Nephites and Lamanites, and there were no contentions and disputations among them, and every man did deal justly one with another.

3 And they had all things common among them; therefore there were not rich and poor, bond and free, but they were all made free, and partakers of the heavenly gift.

5 And there were great and marvelous works wrought by the disciples of Jesus, insomuch that they did heal the sick, and raise the dead, and cause the lame to walk, and the blind to receive their sight, and the deaf to hear; and all manner of miracles did they work among the children of men; and in nothing did they work miracles save it were in the name of Jesus.

10 And now, behold, it came to pass that the people of Nephi did wax strong, and did multiply exceedingly fast, and became an exceedingly fair and delightsome people.

11 And they were married, and given in marriage, and were blessed according to the multitude of the promises which the Lord had made unto them.

12 And they did not walk any more after the performances and ordinances of the law of Moses; but they did walk after the commandments which they had received from their Lord and their God, continuing in fasting and prayer, and in meeting together oft both to pray and to hear the word of the Lord.

13 And it came to pass that there was no contention among all the people, in all the land; but there were mighty miracles wrought among the disciples of Jesus.

15 And it came to pass that there was no contention in the land, because of the love of God which did dwell in the hearts of the people.

16 And there were no envyings, nor strifes, nor tumults, nor whoredoms, nor lyings, nor murders, nor any manner of lasciviousness; and surely there could not be a happier people among all the people who had been created by the hand of God.

17 There were no robbers, nor murderers, neither were there Lamanites, nor any manner of -ites; but they were in one, the children of Christ, and heirs to the kingdom of God.

18 And how blessed were they! For the Lord did bless them in all their doings; yea, even they were blessed and prospered until an hundred and ten years had passed away; and the first generation from Christ had passed away, and there was no contention in all the land.

What was the cause of there being "no contention in the land" among all people? What do you think it means that there was not "any manner of -ites"? How can you increase unity in the world today?

The Book of Mormon

MORMON LEADS THE NEPHITES IN BATTLE AS WAR AND WICKEDNESS CONSUME THE PEOPLE

After all people in every land were converted to Jesus Christ and became Nephites, they enjoyed many decades of peace and righteousness. Nephi and the other nine Apostles passed away, leaving the three Nephite Apostles who would live until Christ's Second Coming to witness the events unfolding among the people. Over the next two centuries, pride, wickedness, witchcraft, and persecution arose, and the people divided into tribes of Lamanites and Nephites and engaged in war. The three remaining Apostles were taken out of the land—as were the presence of the Holy Ghost, miracles, and healings. About 293 years had passed since Christ had appeared among the Nephites. The scriptural record was passed down to Nephi's descendants and entrusted to Mormon, one of a few righteous Nephites left in the land. At age sixteen, Mormon was appointed to lead the unrepentant Nephite armies in battle and kept a record of his efforts to bring the people to repentance.

MORMON 2:9–15

And now, the Lamanites had a king, and his name was Aaron; and he came against us with an army of forty and four thousand. And behold, I withstood him with forty and two thousand. And it came to pass that I beat him with my army that he fled before me. And behold, all this was done, and three hundred and thirty years had passed away.

10 And it came to pass that the Nephites began to repent of their iniquity, and began to cry even as had been prophesied by Samuel the prophet; for behold no man could keep that which was his own, for the thieves, and the robbers, and the murderers, and the magic art, and the witchcraft which was in the land.

11 Thus there began to be a mourning and a lamentation in all the land because of these things, and more especially among the people of Nephi.

12 And it came to pass that when I, Mormon, saw their lamentation and their mourning and their sorrow before the Lord, my heart did begin to rejoice within me, knowing the mercies and the long-suffering of the Lord, therefore supposing that he would be merciful unto them that they would again become a righteous people.

13 But behold this my joy was vain, for their sorrowing was not unto repentance, because of the goodness of God; but it was rather the sorrowing of the damned, because the Lord would not always suffer them to take happiness in sin.

14 And they did not come unto Jesus with broken hearts and contrite spirits, but they did curse God, and wish to die. Nevertheless they would struggle with the sword for their lives.

15 And it came to pass that my sorrow did return unto me again, and I saw that the day of grace was passed with them, both temporally and spiritually; for I saw thousands of them hewn down in open rebellion against their God, and heaped up as dung upon the face of the land. And thus three hundred and forty and four years had passed away.

Why do you think Mormon would initially rejoice over the mourning and sorrow of the Nephites? Why did his rejoicing change when he learned the reason for their sorrow? What does this teach you about the difference between sorrowing "unto repentance" and worldly sorrow?

MORMON PLEADS WITH ALL MEN TO BELIEVE IN CHRIST AND PREPARE FOR HIS JUDGMENT

Mormon preached repentance among the Nephites, but the people remained hard-hearted. For the next ten years, Mormon led the Nephites in various battles. After a surprising victory over a large number of Lamanites, the Nephites began to brag of their own strength and swore that they would avenge their dead brethren. Mormon was repulsed by their behavior. Frustrated with his own people, Mormon turned his attention to latter-day readers of the Book of Mormon.

Mormon 3:11–12, 17–22

And it came to pass that I, Mormon, did utterly refuse from this time forth to be a commander and a leader of this people, because of their wickedness and abomination.
12 Behold, I had led them, notwithstanding their wickedness I had led them many times to battle, and had loved them, according to the love of God which was in me, with all my heart; and my soul had been poured out in prayer unto my God all the day long for them; nevertheless, it was without faith, because of the hardness of their hearts.
17 Therefore I write unto you, Gentiles, and also unto you, house of Israel, when the work shall commence, that ye shall be about to prepare to return to the land of your inheritance;
18 Yea, behold, I write unto all the ends of the earth; yea, unto you, twelve tribes of Israel, who shall be judged according to your works by the twelve whom Jesus chose to be his disciples in the land of Jerusalem.
19 And I write also unto the remnant of this people, who shall also be judged by the twelve whom Jesus chose in this land; and they shall be judged by the other twelve whom Jesus chose in the land of Jerusalem.
20 And these things doth the Spirit manifest unto me; therefore I write unto you all. And for this cause I write unto you, that ye may know that ye must all stand before the judgment-seat of Christ, yea, every soul who belongs to the whole human family of Adam; and ye must stand to be judged of your works, whether they be good or evil;
21 And also that ye may believe the gospel of Jesus Christ, which ye shall have among you; and also that the Jews, the covenant people of the Lord, shall have other witness besides him whom they saw and heard, that Jesus, whom they slew, was the very Christ and the very God.
22 And I would that I could persuade all ye ends of the earth to repent and prepare to stand before the judgment-seat of Christ.

What impressions come to your mind as you consider Mormon writing directly to you? What is he commanding you to do?

MORMON DESCRIBES THE TIMING AND PURPOSE OF THE COMING FORTH OF THE BOOK OF MORMON

It was now about 375 years since the birth of Jesus Christ. War continued throughout the land. The Nephites and Lamanites had become more wicked than any other descendants of the House of Israel. The Nephite population declined as the Lamanites slaughtered thousands and sacrificed women and children to idols. Mormon agreed to again lead the Nephite army in battle, but he knew their cause was hopeless. Speaking to latter-day readers, Mormon prophesied of the Book of Mormon coming forth in the latter days.

MORMON 5:8, 13–19

And now behold, I, Mormon, do not desire to harrow up the souls of men in casting before them such an awful scene of blood and carnage as was laid before mine eyes; but I, knowing that these things must surely be made known, and that all things which are hid must be revealed upon the house-tops—
13 And this is the commandment which I have received; and behold, they shall come forth according to the commandment of the Lord, when he shall see fit, in his wisdom.
14 And behold, they shall go unto the unbelieving of the Jews; and for this intent shall they go—that they may be persuaded that Jesus is the Christ, the Son of the living God; that the Father may bring about, through his most Beloved, his great and eternal purpose, in restoring the Jews, or all the house of Israel, to the land of their inheritance, which the Lord their God hath given them, unto the fulfilling of his covenant;
15 And also that the seed of this people may more fully believe his gospel, which shall go forth unto them from the Gentiles; for this people shall be scattered, and shall become a dark, a filthy, and a loathsome people, beyond the description of that which ever hath been amongst us, yea, even that which hath been among the Lamanites, and this because of their unbelief and idolatry.
16 For behold, the Spirit of the Lord hath already ceased to strive with their fathers; and they are without Christ and God in the world; and they are driven about as chaff before the wind.
17 They were once a delightsome people, and they had Christ for their shepherd; yea, they were led even by God the Father.
18 But now, behold, they are led about by Satan, even as chaff is driven before the wind, or as a vessel is tossed about upon the waves, without sail or anchor, or without anything wherewith to steer her; and even as she is, so are they.
19 And behold, the Lord hath reserved their blessings, which they might have received in the land, for the Gentiles who shall possess the land.

What did Mormon say was the purpose of the Book of Mormon? What effect has the Book of Mormon had on you? How does it influence your life and your knowledge of and relationship with Jesus Christ?

MORMON LAMENTS THE FINAL DESTRUCTION OF THE NEPHITE NATION

About ten years after he resumed command of the Nephite army, Mormon hid all the scriptural records that had been passed down to him—except for the plates that would become the Book of Mormon—in the Hill Cumorah. The Nephites and Lamanites then met in a great and final battle. The Lamanites were victorious as hundreds of thousands were slain, including the group of ten thousand who were led personally by Mormon.

Mormon 6:11, 16–22

And when they had gone through and hewn down all my people save it were twenty and four of us, (among whom was my son Moroni) and we having survived the dead of our people, did behold on the morrow, when the Lamanites had returned unto their camps, from the top of the hill Cumorah, the ten thousand of my people who were hewn down, being led in the front by me.

16 And my soul was rent with anguish, because of the slain of my people, and I cried:

17 O ye fair ones, how could ye have departed from the ways of the Lord! O ye fair ones, how could ye have rejected that Jesus, who stood with open arms to receive you!

18 Behold, if ye had not done this, ye would not have fallen. But behold, ye are fallen, and I mourn your loss.

19 O ye fair sons and daughters, ye fathers and mothers, ye husbands and wives, ye fair ones, how is it that ye could have fallen!

20 But behold, ye are gone, and my sorrows cannot bring your return.

21 And the day soon cometh that your mortal must put on immortality, and these bodies which are now moldering in corruption must soon become incorruptible bodies; and then ye must stand before the judgment-seat of Christ, to be judged according to your works; and if it so be that ye are righteous, then are ye blessed with your fathers who have gone before you.

22 O that ye had repented before this great destruction had come upon you. But behold, ye are gone, and the Father, yea, the Eternal Father of heaven, knoweth your state; and he doeth with you according to his justice and mercy.

How did Mormon describe Jesus' invitation to the Nephites? Considering all the sin that the Nephites had committed, what does this image teach you about the nature of Christ? How do you feel knowing the Savior stands with open arms to receive you?

MORMON PLEADS WITH THE LATTER-DAY LAMANITES TO LAY HOLD UPON THE GOSPEL OF CHRIST

After the destruction of the Nephites, Mormon spoke to the latter-day Lamanites. As you read, look for the specific things Mormon wanted the latter-day Lamanites to know and to do.

Mormon 7:1–10

And now, behold, I would speak some-
what unto the remnant of this people
who are spared, if it so be that God may give unto
them my words, that they may know of the things
of their fathers; yea, I speak unto you, ye remnant
of the house of Israel; and these are the words
which I speak:
2 Know ye that ye are of the house of Israel.
3 Know ye that ye must come unto repentance,
or ye cannot be saved.
4 Know ye that ye must lay down your weapons
of war, and delight no more in the shedding of
blood, and take them not again, save it be that
God shall command you.
5 Know ye that ye must come to the knowledge
of your fathers, and repent of all your sins and
iniquities, and believe in Jesus Christ, that he
is the Son of God, and that he was slain by the
Jews, and by the power of the Father he hath risen
again, whereby he hath gained the victory over
the grave; and also in him is the sting of death
swallowed up.
6 And he bringeth to pass the resurrection of the
dead, whereby man must be raised to stand before
his judgment-seat.
7 And he hath brought to pass the redemption
of the world, whereby he that is found guiltless
before him at the judgment day hath it given
unto him to dwell in the presence of God in his
kingdom, to sing ceaseless praises with the choirs
above, unto the Father, and unto the Son, and
unto the Holy Ghost, which are one God, in a
state of happiness which hath no end.
8 Therefore repent, and be baptized in the name
of Jesus, and lay hold upon the gospel of Christ,
which shall be set before you, not only in this re-
cord but also in the record which shall come unto
the Gentiles from the Jews, which record shall
come from the Gentiles unto you.
9 For behold, this is written for the intent that
ye may believe that; and if ye believe that ye will
believe this also; and if ye believe this ye will know
concerning your fathers, and also the marvelous
works which were wrought by the power of God
among them.
10 And ye will also know that ye are a remnant
of the seed of Jacob; therefore ye are numbered
among the people of the first covenant; and if it
so be that ye believe in Christ, and are baptized,
first with water, then with fire and with the Holy
Ghost, following the example of our Savior, ac-
cording to that which he hath commanded us,
it shall be well with you in the day of judgment.
Amen.

What things did Mormon want the latter-day Lamanites to know and to do? Even though the Lamanites had destroyed his people, Mormon spoke lovingly and hopefully to their latter-day descendants. What do you think enabled Mormon to have such charity? What can you learn from his example?

MORONI SPEAKS OF THE BOOK OF MORMON SHINING FORTH OUT OF DARKNESS BY THE POWER OF GOD

It was now 400 years since the birth of Jesus Christ. The Lamanites hunted and killed Mormon and the last of Moroni's fellow Nephites, leaving Moroni as the only Nephite left in all the land. Moroni spent the remainder of his life hiding from the Lamanites, protecting the scriptural record, and recording instructions for latter-day readers.

MORMON 8:12, 14–17, 21–22

And whoso receiveth this record, and shall not condemn it because of the imperfections which are in it, the same shall know of greater things than these. Behold, I am Moroni; and were it possible, I would make all things known unto you.

14 And I am the same who hideth up this record unto the Lord; the plates thereof are of no worth, because of the commandment of the Lord. For he truly saith that no one shall have them to get gain; but the record thereof is of great worth; and whoso shall bring it to light, him will the Lord bless.

15 For none can have power to bring it to light save it be given him of God; for God wills that it shall be done with an eye single to his glory, or the welfare of the ancient and long dispersed covenant people of the Lord.

16 And blessed be he that shall bring this thing to light; for it shall be brought out of darkness unto light, according to the word of God; yea, it shall be brought out of the earth, and it shall shine forth out of darkness, and come unto the knowledge of the people; and it shall be done by the power of God.

17 And if there be faults they be the faults of a man. But behold, we know no fault; nevertheless God knoweth all things; therefore, he that condemneth, let him be aware lest he shall be in danger of hell fire.

21 And he that shall breathe out wrath and strifes against the work of the Lord, and against the covenant people of the Lord who are the house of Israel, and shall say: We will destroy the work of the Lord, and the Lord will not remember his covenant which he hath made unto the house of Israel—the same is in danger to be hewn down and cast into the fire;

22 For the eternal purposes of the Lord shall roll on, until all his promises shall be fulfilled.

What are some things that Moroni says about the Book of Mormon in bearing his testimony of that record? How can your testimony be strengthened knowing that "if there be faults they be the faults of a man"? Moroni spoke of the power of God bringing the Book of Mormon to light in the last days. If possible, discuss the process of the Book of Mormon being translated, published, and shared throughout the world—and how the power of God has been shown in that process.

MORONI CONDEMNS THE WICKEDNESS FOUND IN THE LATTER DAYS

Writing to latter-day readers, Moroni prophesied of the conditions that would be on earth when the Book of Mormon would come forth. As you read, look for the different signs and sins that would be present in the last days.

MORMON 8:28–33, 36–41

Yea, it shall come in a day when the power
of God shall be denied, and churches be-
come defiled and be lifted up in the pride of their
hearts; yea, even in a day when leaders of churches
and teachers shall rise in the pride of their hearts,
even to the envying of them who belong to their
churches.
29 Yea, it shall come in a day when there shall be
heard of fires, and tempests, and vapors of smoke
in foreign lands;
30 And there shall also be heard of wars, rumors
of wars, and earthquakes in divers places.
31 Yea, it shall come in a day when there shall
be great pollutions upon the face of the earth;
there shall be murders, and robbing, and lying,
and deceivings, and whoredoms, and all manner
of abominations; when there shall be many who
will say, Do this, or do that, and it mattereth not,
for the Lord will uphold such at the last day. But
wo unto such, for they are in the gall of bitterness
and in the bonds of iniquity.
32 Yea, it shall come in a day when there shall be
churches built up that shall say: Come unto me,
and for your money you shall be forgiven of your
sins.
33 O ye wicked and perverse and stiffnecked
people, why have ye built up churches unto your-
selves to get gain? Why have ye transfigured the
holy word of God, that ye might bring damnation
upon your souls? Behold, look ye unto the revela-
tions of God; for behold, the time cometh at that
day when all these things must be fulfilled.
36 And I know that ye do walk in the pride of
your hearts; and there are none save a few only
who do not lift themselves up in the pride of their
hearts, unto the wearing of very fine apparel, unto
envying, and strifes, and malice, and persecutions,
and all manner of iniquities; and your churches,
yea, even every one, have become polluted be-
cause of the pride of your hearts.
37 For behold, ye do love money, and your sub-
stance, and your fine apparel, and the adorning
of your churches, more than ye love the poor and
the needy, the sick and the afflicted.
38 O ye pollutions, ye hypocrites, ye teachers,
who sell yourselves for that which will canker, why
have ye polluted the holy church of God? Why are
ye ashamed to take upon you the name of Christ?
Why do ye not think that greater is the value of
an endless happiness than that misery which never
dies—because of the praise of the world?
39 Why do ye adorn yourselves with that which
hath no life, and yet suffer the hungry, and the
needy, and the naked, and the sick and the af-
flicted to pass by you, and notice them not?
40 Yea, why do ye build up your secret abom-
inations to get gain, and cause that widows
should mourn before the Lord, and also orphans
to mourn before the Lord, and also the blood of
their fathers and their husbands to cry unto the
Lord from the ground, for vengeance upon your
heads?
41 Behold, the sword of vengeance hangeth over
you; and the time soon cometh that he avengeth
the blood of the saints upon you, for he will not
suffer their cries any longer.

How did Moroni describe the last days? What examples of the events and attitudes he described do you see in the world today? Mormon condemned pride, envying, the love of money, and many other sins. What changes can you make in your life to follow his counsel?

MORONI WARNS UNBELIEVERS OF THE REALITY OF CHRIST AND HIS JUDGMENT

Moroni continued to speak to people in the latter days.

MORMON 9:1–8

And now, I speak also concerning those
who do not believe in Christ.
2 Behold, will ye believe in the day of your
visitation—behold, when the Lord shall come,
yea, even that great day when the earth shall be
rolled together as a scroll, and the elements shall
melt with fervent heat, yea, in that great day when
ye shall be brought to stand before the Lamb of
God—then will ye say that there is no God?
3 Then will ye longer deny the Christ, or can ye
behold the Lamb of God? Do ye suppose that ye
shall dwell with him under a consciousness of
your guilt? Do ye suppose that ye could be happy
to dwell with that holy Being, when your souls are
racked with a consciousness of guilt that ye have
ever abused his laws?
4 Behold, I say unto you that ye would be more
miserable to dwell with a holy and just God, under
a consciousness of your filthiness before him, than
ye would to dwell with the damned souls in hell.
5 For behold, when ye shall be brought to see
your nakedness before God, and also the glory of
God, and the holiness of Jesus Christ, it will kin-
dle a flame of unquenchable fire upon you.
6 O then ye unbelieving, turn ye unto the Lord;
cry mightily unto the Father in the name of Jesus,
that perhaps ye may be found spotless, pure, fair,
and white, having been cleansed by the blood of
the Lamb, at that great and last day.
7 And again I speak unto you who deny the rev-
elations of God, and say that they are done away,
that there are no revelations, nor prophecies, nor
gifts, nor healing, nor speaking with tongues, and
the interpretation of tongues;
8 Behold I say unto you, he that denieth these
things knoweth not the gospel of Christ; yea, he
has not read the scriptures; if so, he does not un-
derstand them.

According to Moroni, why would it be miserable to dwell with God if you were not cleansed of sin? How can you help those "who do not believe in Christ" begin to understand and believe the plan of salvation?

MORONI SPEAKS OF THE GOD OF MIRACLES AND DESCRIBES THE PLAN OF SALVATION

Moroni continued speaking to people in the latter days and directed his remarks to those who deny Christ and His gospel.

MORMON 9:10–21

And now, if ye have imagined up unto yourselves a god who doth vary, and in whom there is shadow of changing, then have ye imagined up unto yourselves a god who is not a God of miracles.

11 But behold, I will show unto you a God of miracles, even the God of Abraham, and the God of Isaac, and the God of Jacob; and it is that same God who created the heavens and the earth, and all things that in them are.

12 Behold, he created Adam, and by Adam came the fall of man. And because of the fall of man came Jesus Christ, even the Father and the Son; and because of Jesus Christ came the redemption of man.

13 And because of the redemption of man, which came by Jesus Christ, they are brought back into the presence of the Lord; yea, this is wherein all men are redeemed, because the death of Christ bringeth to pass the resurrection, which bringeth to pass a redemption from an endless sleep, from which sleep all men shall be awakened by the power of God when the trump shall sound; and they shall come forth, both small and great, and all shall stand before his bar, being redeemed and loosed from this eternal band of death, which death is a temporal death.

14 And then cometh the judgment of the Holy One upon them; and then cometh the time that he that is filthy shall be filthy still; and he that is righteous shall be righteous still; he that is happy shall be happy still; and he that is unhappy shall be unhappy still.

15 And now, O all ye that have imagined up unto yourselves a god who can do no miracles, I would ask of you, have all these things passed, of which I have spoken? Has the end come yet? Behold I say unto you, Nay; and God has not ceased to be a God of miracles.

16 Behold, are not the things that God hath wrought marvelous in our eyes? Yea, and who can comprehend the marvelous works of God?

17 Who shall say that it was not a miracle that by his word the heaven and the earth should be; and by the power of his word man was created of the dust of the earth; and by the power of his word have miracles been wrought?

18 And who shall say that Jesus Christ did not do many mighty miracles? And there were many mighty miracles wrought by the hands of the apostles.

19 And if there were miracles wrought then, why has God ceased to be a God of miracles and yet be an unchangeable Being? And behold, I say unto you he changeth not; if so he would cease to be God; and he ceaseth not to be God, and is a God of miracles.

20 And the reason why he ceaseth to do miracles among the children of men is because that they dwindle in unbelief, and depart from the right way, and know not the God in whom they should trust.

21 Behold, I say unto you that whoso believeth in Christ, doubting nothing, whatsoever he shall ask the Father in the name of Christ it shall be granted him; and this promise is unto all, even unto the ends of the earth.

What did Moroni say God created? What reason did Moroni give for an absence of miracles among the children of men? What miracles has God performed in your life?

MORONI WARNS THOSE IN THE LATTER DAYS WHO DESPISE THE WORKS OF GOD

Moroni concluded his counsel to people of the latter days.

MORMON 9:22–30, 35–37

For behold, thus said Jesus Christ, the Son of God, unto his disciples who should tarry, yea, and also to all his disciples, in the hearing of the multitude: Go ye into all the world, and preach the gospel to every creature;

23 And he that believeth and is baptized shall be saved, but he that believeth not shall be damned;

24 And these signs shall follow them that believe—in my name shall they cast out devils; they shall speak with new tongues; they shall take up serpents; and if they drink any deadly thing it shall not hurt them; they shall lay hands on the sick and they shall recover;

25 And whosoever shall believe in my name, doubting nothing, unto him will I confirm all my words, even unto the ends of the earth.

26 And now, behold, who can stand against the works of the Lord? Who can deny his sayings? Who will rise up against the almighty power of the Lord? Who will despise the works of the Lord? Who will despise the children of Christ? Behold, all ye who are despisers of the works of the Lord, for ye shall wonder and perish.

27 O then despise not, and wonder not, but hearken unto the words of the Lord, and ask the Father in the name of Jesus for what things soever ye shall stand in need. Doubt not, but be believing, and begin as in times of old, and come unto the Lord with all your heart, and work out your own salvation with fear and trembling before him.

28 Be wise in the days of your probation; strip yourselves of all uncleanness; ask not, that ye may consume it on your lusts, but ask with a firmness unshaken, that ye will yield to no temptation, but that ye will serve the true and living God.

29 See that ye are not baptized unworthily; see that ye partake not of the sacrament of Christ unworthily; but see that ye do all things in worthiness, and do it in the name of Jesus Christ, the Son of the living God; and if ye do this, and endure to the end, ye will in nowise be cast out.

30 Behold, I speak unto you as though I spake from the dead; for I know that ye shall have my words.

35 And these things are written that we may rid our garments of the blood of our brethren, who have dwindled in unbelief.

36 And behold, these things which we have desired concerning our brethren, yea, even their restoration to the knowledge of Christ, are according to the prayers of all the saints who have dwelt in the land.

37 And may the Lord Jesus Christ grant that their prayers may be answered according to their faith; and may God the Father remember the covenant which he hath made with the house of Israel; and may he bless them forever, through faith on the name of Jesus Christ. Amen.

According to Moroni, who will be saved? What do you think it means to "work out your own salvation with fear and trembling" before God? What other counsel does Moroni give to help you do this?

The Book of Ether

THE BROTHER OF JARED RECEIVES THE LORD'S COMPASSION AND DIRECTION THROUGH CONSISTENT PRAYER

About 1,700 years before Lehi and his family arrived in the promised land, a people known as the Jaredites were similarly led by the Lord to the same land, where they built a mighty civilization. After two thousand years, the Jaredites grew wicked, waged war with each other, and eventually became extinct. A record of the Jaredites was written by the prophet Ether. Ether's record was discovered by the people of Limhi during the reign of King Mosiah. Later, Moroni was given possession of Ether's record and made an abridgment of it. The Jaredites originally came from Babel, where wicked people were trying to build a great tower to heaven. As punishment, the Lord began to alter the people's language and scatter them throughout the world. Jared, the first of the Jaredite people, asked his brother to request that the Lord not confound the language of their families.

ETHER 1:34–43

And the brother of Jared being a large and mighty man, and a man highly favored of the Lord, Jared, his brother, said unto him: Cry unto the Lord, that he will not confound us that we may not understand our words.

35 And it came to pass that the brother of Jared did cry unto the Lord, and the Lord had compassion upon Jared; therefore he did not confound the language of Jared; and Jared and his brother were not confounded.

36 Then Jared said unto his brother: Cry again unto the Lord, and it may be that he will turn away his anger from them who are our friends, that he confound not their language.

37 And it came to pass that the brother of Jared did cry unto the Lord, and the Lord had compassion upon their friends and their families also, that they were not confounded.

38 And it came to pass that Jared spake again unto his brother, saying: Go and inquire of the Lord whether he will drive us out of the land, and if he will drive us out of the land, cry unto him whither we shall go. And who knoweth but the Lord will carry us forth into a land which is choice above all the earth? And if it so be, let us be faithful unto the Lord, that we may receive it for our inheritance.

39 And it came to pass that the brother of Jared did cry unto the Lord according to that which had been spoken by the mouth of Jared.

40 And it came to pass that the Lord did hear the brother of Jared, and had compassion upon him, and said unto him:

41 Go to and gather together thy flocks, both male and female, of every kind; and also of the seed of the earth of every kind; and thy families; and also Jared thy brother and his family; and also thy friends and their families, and the friends of Jared and their families.

42 And when thou hast done this thou shalt go at the head of them down into the valley which is northward. And there will I meet thee, and I will go before thee into a land which is choice above all the lands of the earth.

43 And there will I bless thee and thy seed, and raise up unto me of thy seed, and of the seed of thy brother, and they who shall go with thee, a great nation. And there shall be none greater than the nation which I will raise up unto me of thy seed, upon all the face of the earth. And thus I will do unto thee because this long time ye have cried unto me.

What led to the Lord having compassion on the family of Jared? What blessings did the Lord promise to the brother of Jared and his family? What knowledge or blessings have you received as a result of consistent prayer?

THE LORD PRESERVES THE PROMISED LAND FOR A RIGHTEOUS PEOPLE

The Lord had promised to lead the brother of Jared's families and friends to the promised land. Preparations were made for their journey, and they departed the land of Babel.

ETHER 2:4–11, 14–15

And it came to pass that when they had come down into the valley of Nimrod the Lord came down and talked with the brother of Jared; and he was in a cloud, and the brother of Jared saw him not.

5 And it came to pass that the Lord commanded them that they should go forth into the wilderness, yea, into that quarter where there never had man been. And it came to pass that the Lord did go before them, and did talk with them as he stood in a cloud, and gave directions whither they should travel.

6 And it came to pass that they did travel in the wilderness, and did build barges, in which they did cross many waters, being directed continually by the hand of the Lord.

7 And the Lord would not suffer that they should stop beyond the sea in the wilderness, but he would that they should come forth even unto the land of promise, which was choice above all other lands, which the Lord God had preserved for a righteous people.

8 And he had sworn in his wrath unto the brother of Jared, that whoso should possess this land of promise, from that time henceforth and forever, should serve him, the true and only God, or they should be swept off when the fulness of his wrath should come upon them.

9 And now, we can behold the decrees of God concerning this land, that it is a land of promise; and whatsoever nation shall possess it shall serve God, or they shall be swept off when the fulness of his wrath shall come upon them. And the fulness of his wrath cometh upon them when they are ripened in iniquity.

10 For behold, this is a land which is choice above all other lands; wherefore he that doth possess it shall serve God or shall be swept off; for it is the everlasting decree of God. And it is not until the fulness of iniquity among the children of the land, that they are swept off.

11 And this cometh unto you, O ye Gentiles, that ye may know the decrees of God—that ye may repent, and not continue in your iniquities until the fulness come, that ye may not bring down the fulness of the wrath of God upon you as the inhabitants of the land have hitherto done.

14 And it came to pass at the end of four years that the Lord came again unto the brother of Jared, and stood in a cloud and talked with him. And for the space of three hours did the Lord talk with the brother of Jared, and chastened him because he remembered not to call upon the name of the Lord.

15 And the brother of Jared repented of the evil which he had done, and did call upon the name of the Lord for his brethren who were with him. And the Lord said unto him: I will forgive thee and thy brethren of their sins; but thou shalt not sin any more, for ye shall remember that my Spirit will not always strive with man; wherefore, if ye will sin until ye are fully ripe ye shall be cut off from the presence of the Lord. And these are my thoughts upon the land which I shall give you for your inheritance; for it shall be a land choice above all other lands.

What did the Lord require of those who wanted to live in the promised land? What blessings and punishments did the Lord promise to those who would serve God and those who would not? How can you serve God?

THE LORD INVITES THE BROTHER OF JARED TO PROPOSE A SOLUTION FOR LIGHT AS THEY CROSS THE SEA IN BARGES

The brother of Jared and his people continued their journey out of the land of Babel.

ETHER 2:16–25

And the Lord said: Go to work and build, after the manner of barges which ye have hitherto built. And it came to pass that the brother of Jared did go to work, and also his brethren, and built barges after the manner which they had built, according to the instructions of the Lord. And they were small, and they were light upon the water, even like unto the lightness of a fowl upon the water.

17 And they were built after a manner that they were exceedingly tight, even that they would hold water like unto a dish; and the bottom thereof was tight like unto a dish; and the sides thereof were tight like unto a dish; and the ends thereof were peaked; and the top thereof was tight like unto a dish; and the length thereof was the length of a tree; and the door thereof, when it was shut, was tight like unto a dish.

18 And it came to pass that the brother of Jared cried unto the Lord, saying: O Lord, I have performed the work which thou hast commanded me, and I have made the barges according as thou hast directed me.

19 And behold, O Lord, in them there is no light; whither shall we steer? And also we shall perish, for in them we cannot breathe, save it is the air which is in them; therefore we shall perish.

20 And the Lord said unto the brother of Jared: Behold, thou shalt make a hole in the top, and also in the bottom; and when thou shalt suffer for air thou shalt unstop the hole and receive air. And if it be so that the water come in upon thee, behold, ye shall stop the hole, that ye may not perish in the flood.

21 And it came to pass that the brother of Jared did so, according as the Lord had commanded.

22 And he cried again unto the Lord saying: O Lord, behold I have done even as thou hast commanded me; and I have prepared the vessels for my people, and behold there is no light in them. Behold, O Lord, wilt thou suffer that we shall cross this great water in darkness?

23 And the Lord said unto the brother of Jared: What will ye that I should do that ye may have light in your vessels? For behold, ye cannot have windows, for they will be dashed in pieces; neither shall ye take fire with you, for ye shall not go by the light of fire.

24 For behold, ye shall be as a whale in the midst of the sea; for the mountain waves shall dash upon you. Nevertheless, I will bring you up again out of the depths of the sea; for the winds have gone forth out of my mouth, and also the rains and the floods have I sent forth.

25 And behold, I prepare you against these things; for ye cannot cross this great deep save I prepare you against the waves of the sea, and the winds which have gone forth, and the floods which shall come. Therefore what will ye that I should prepare for you that ye may have light when ye are swallowed up in the depths of the sea?

The Lord often provided immediate solutions to the brother of Jared, and at other times He invited the brother of Jared to propose his own solutions. In what ways has the Lord taken each of those approaches with you? What decisions and challenges are you expected to propose solutions and answers for?

THE BROTHER OF JARED SEES THE FINGER OF THE LORD

After being invited by the Lord to offer a solution for lighting the barges as they crossed the sea, the brother of Jared went to work.

ETHER 3:1–13

And it came to pass that the brother of Jared, (now the number of the vessels which had been prepared was eight) went forth unto the mount, which they called the mount Shelem, because of its exceeding height, and did molten out of a rock sixteen small stones; and they were white and clear, even as transparent glass; and he did carry them in his hands upon the top of the mount, and cried again unto the Lord, saying:

2 O Lord, thou hast said that we must be encompassed about by the floods. Now behold, O Lord, and do not be angry with thy servant because of his weakness before thee; for we know that thou art holy and dwellest in the heavens, and that we are unworthy before thee; because of the fall our natures have become evil continually; nevertheless, O Lord, thou hast given us a commandment that we must call upon thee, that from thee we may receive according to our desires.

3 Behold, O Lord, thou hast smitten us because of our iniquity, and hast driven us forth, and for these many years we have been in the wilderness; nevertheless, thou hast been merciful unto us. O Lord, look upon me in pity, and turn away thine anger from this thy people, and suffer not that they shall go forth across this raging deep in darkness; but behold these things which I have molten out of the rock.

4 And I know, O Lord, that thou hast all power, and can do whatsoever thou wilt for the benefit of man; therefore touch these stones, O Lord, with thy finger, and prepare them that they may shine forth in darkness; and they shall shine forth unto us in the vessels which we have prepared, that we may have light while we shall cross the sea.

5 Behold, O Lord, thou canst do this. We know that thou art able to show forth great power, which looks small unto the understanding of men.

6 And it came to pass that when the brother of Jared had said these words, behold, the Lord stretched forth his hand and touched the stones one by one with his finger. And the veil was taken from off the eyes of the brother of Jared, and he saw the finger of the Lord; and it was as the finger of a man, like unto flesh and blood; and the brother of Jared fell down before the Lord, for he was struck with fear.

7 And the Lord saw that the brother of Jared had fallen to the earth; and the Lord said unto him: Arise, why hast thou fallen?

8 And he saith unto the Lord: I saw the finger of the Lord, and I feared lest he should smite me; for I knew not that the Lord had flesh and blood.

9 And the Lord said unto him: Because of thy faith thou hast seen that I shall take upon me flesh and blood; and never has man come before me with such exceeding faith as thou hast; for were it not so ye could not have seen my finger. Sawest thou more than this?

10 And he answered: Nay; Lord, show thyself unto me.

11 And the Lord said unto him: Believest thou the words which I shall speak?

12 And he answered: Yea, Lord, I know that thou speakest the truth, for thou art a God of truth, and canst not lie.

13 And when he had said these words, behold, the Lord showed himself unto him, and said: Because thou knowest these things ye are redeemed from the fall; therefore ye are brought back into my presence; therefore I show myself unto you.

How did the brother of Jared show his faith in Jesus Christ? How was he blessed in return? How can you show faith in Jesus Christ? What blessings do you hope to receive as a result?

THE LORD TEACHES THE BROTHER OF JARED OF HIS IDENTITY AND PHYSICAL ATTRIBUTES

After the brother of Jared had seen the finger of the Lord, the Lord spoke approvingly of the brother of Jared's faith, revealed Himself in full, and spoke of His identity and physical attributes.

ETHER 3:14–21, 25–27

Behold, I am he who was prepared from the foundation of the world to redeem my people. Behold, I am Jesus Christ. I am the Father and the Son. In me shall all mankind have life, and that eternally, even they who shall believe on my name; and they shall become my sons and my daughters.

15 And never have I showed myself unto man whom I have created, for never has man believed in me as thou hast. Seest thou that ye are created after mine own image? Yea, even all men were created in the beginning after mine own image.

16 Behold, this body, which ye now behold, is the body of my spirit; and man have I created after the body of my spirit; and even as I appear unto thee to be in the spirit will I appear unto my people in the flesh.

17 And now, as I, Moroni, said I could not make a full account of these things which are written, therefore it sufficeth me to say that Jesus showed himself unto this man in the spirit, even after the manner and in the likeness of the same body even as he showed himself unto the Nephites.

18 And he ministered unto him even as he ministered unto the Nephites; and all this, that this man might know that he was God, because of the many great works which the Lord had showed unto him.

19 And because of the knowledge of this man he could not be kept from beholding within the veil; and he saw the finger of Jesus, which, when he saw, he fell with fear; for he knew that it was the finger of the Lord; and he had faith no longer, for he knew, nothing doubting.

20 Wherefore, having this perfect knowledge of God, he could not be kept from within the veil; therefore he saw Jesus; and he did minister unto him.

21 And it came to pass that the Lord said unto the brother of Jared: Behold, thou shalt not suffer these things which ye have seen and heard to go forth unto the world, until the time cometh that I shall glorify my name in the flesh; wherefore, ye shall treasure up the things which ye have seen and heard, and show it to no man.

25 And when the Lord had said these words, he showed unto the brother of Jared all the inhabitants of the earth which had been, and also all that would be; and he withheld them not from his sight, even unto the ends of the earth.

26 For he had said unto him in times before, that if he would believe in him that he could show unto him all things—it should be shown unto him; therefore the Lord could not withhold anything from him, for he knew that the Lord could show him all things.

27 And the Lord said unto him: Write these things and seal them up; and I will show them in mine own due time unto the children of men.

What titles did Jesus Christ use as He identified himself to the brother of Jared? What do you think is the significance of each of those titles? What did the Lord teach the brother of Jared about the Creation of man?

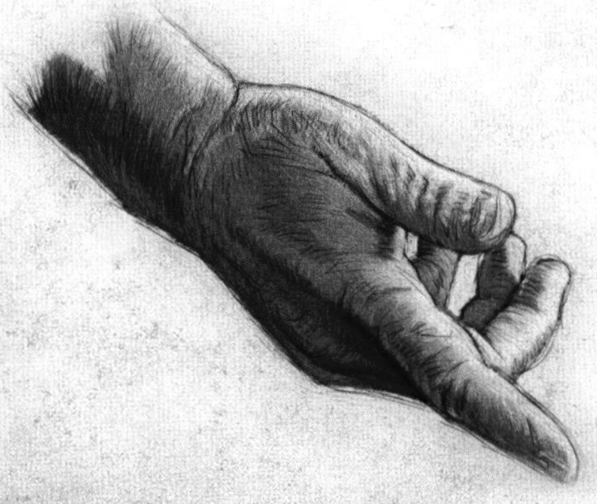

JESUS CHRIST PROMISES ALL KNOWLEDGE AND BLESSINGS TO THOSE WHO BELIEVE IN HIM

After the Lord revealed to the brother of Jared all His past and future works, the brother of Jared recorded what he had seen. Nearly 3,000 years later, Moroni included the brother of Jared's words in his record.

ETHER 4:4, 6–8, 11–15, 18–19

Behold, I have written upon these plates
the very things which the brother of
Jared saw; and there never were greater things
made manifest than those which were made man-
ifest unto the brother of Jared.
6 For the Lord said unto me: They shall not go
forth unto the Gentiles until the day that they
shall repent of their iniquity, and become clean
before the Lord.
7 And in that day that they shall exercise faith in
me, saith the Lord, even as the brother of Jared
did, that they may become sanctified in me, then
will I manifest unto them the things which the
brother of Jared saw, even to the unfolding unto
them all my revelations, saith Jesus Christ, the
Son of God, the Father of the heavens and of the
earth, and all things that in them are.
8 And he that will contend against the word of
the Lord, let him be accursed; and he that shall
deny these things, let him be accursed; for unto
them will I show no greater things, saith Jesus
Christ; for I am he who speaketh.
11 But he that believeth these things which I
have spoken, him will I visit with the manifesta-
tions of my Spirit, and he shall know and bear re-
cord. For because of my Spirit he shall know that
these things are true; for it persuadeth men to do
good.
12 And whatsoever thing persuadeth men to
do good is of me; for good cometh of none save
it be of me. I am the same that leadeth men to
all good; he that will not believe my words will
not believe me—that I am; and he that will not
believe me will not believe the Father who sent
me. For behold, I am the Father, I am the light,
and the life, and the truth of the world.
13 Come unto me, O ye Gentiles, and I will
show unto you the greater things, the knowledge
which is hid up because of unbelief.
14 Come unto me, O ye house of Israel, and it
shall be made manifest unto you how great things
the Father hath laid up for you, from the founda-
tion of the world; and it hath not come unto you,
because of unbelief.
15 Behold, when ye shall rend that veil of un-
belief which doth cause you to remain in your
awful state of wickedness, and hardness of heart,
and blindness of mind, then shall the great and
marvelous things which have been hid up from
the foundation of the world from you—yea, when
ye shall call upon the Father in my name, with a
broken heart and a contrite spirit, then shall ye
know that the Father hath remembered the cove-
nant which he made unto your fathers, O house
of Israel.
18 Therefore, repent all ye ends of the earth, and
come unto me, and believe in my gospel, and be
baptized in my name; for he that believeth and is
baptized shall be saved; but he that believeth not
shall be damned; and signs shall follow them that
believe in my name.
19 And blessed is he that is found faithful unto
my name at the last day, for he shall be lifted up
to dwell in the kingdom prepared for him from
the foundation of the world. And behold it is I
that hath spoken it. Amen.

What rewards did the Lord promise to those who believe in His words and show faith like the brother of Jared? The Lord said to Moroni that "whatsoever thing persuadeth men to do good is of me." What are some things in the world that encourage you to do good? Discuss the thirteenth article of faith and what you learn from it about "good things."

MORONI PROPHESIES OF THREE LATTER-DAY WITNESSES OF THE BOOK OF MORMON

After recording the revelation shown to the brother of Jared, Moroni wrote specific instructions to those who would assist in translating and publishing the Book of Mormon in the latter days.

ETHER 5:1–6

And now I, Moroni, have written the
words which were commanded me, ac-
cording to my memory; and I have told you the
things which I have sealed up; therefore touch
them not in order that ye may translate; for that
thing is forbidden you, except by and by it shall
be wisdom in God.
2 And behold, ye may be privileged that ye may
show the plates unto those who shall assist to
bring forth this work;
3 And unto three shall they be shown by the
power of God; wherefore they shall know of a
surety that these things are true.
4 And in the mouth of three witnesses shall these
things be established; and the testimony of three,
and this work, in the which shall be shown forth
the power of God and also his word, of which the
Father, and the Son, and the Holy Ghost bear
record—and all this shall stand as a testimony
against the world at the last day.
5 And if it so be that they repent and come unto
the Father in the name of Jesus, they shall be re-
ceived into the kingdom of God.
6 And now, if I have no authority for these
things, judge ye; for ye shall know that I have au-
thority when ye shall see me, and we shall stand
before God at the last day. Amen.

In 1830, Oliver Cowdery, David Whitmer, and Martin Harris fulfilled Moroni's prophecy. Their written testimony was included in the first printing of the Book of Mormon. They testified that 1) an angel showed them the plates from which the Book of Mormon record was translated, 2) God's voice spoke to them, declaring that the record was translated by God's power, and 3) the Lord commanded them to testify of what they had seen and heard. The "Testimony of Three Witnesses" is found in the Book of Mormon, after the title page and introduction. Consider reading and discussing it as part of this section's study.

MORONI WARNS OF SECRET COMBINATIONS PRESENT IN THE LATTER DAYS

The Lord touched the stones prepared by the brother of Jared, and the stones gave forth light in the darkness. Two stones were placed in each barge, and the people boarded the barges with their animals and supplies. The Lord caused a furious wind to blow, driving the barges across the sea. After 344 days, the people arrived in the promised land, gave thanks to God, began tilling the earth, and raised up families. As Jared and his brother began to be old, the people requested that a king be anointed to rule over them. A king was chosen, Jared and his brother passed away, and over the course of many generations the people descended into cycles of contention, revenge, murders, and rival kingdoms.

ETHER 8:18–26

And it came to pass that they formed a
secret combination, even as they of
old; which combination is most abominable and
wicked above all, in the sight of God;
19 For the Lord worketh not in secret combina-
tions, neither doth he will that man should shed
blood, but in all things hath forbidden it, from
the beginning of man.
20 And now I, Moroni, do not write the manner
of their oaths and combinations, for it hath been
made known unto me that they are had among all
people, and they are had among the Lamanites.
21 And they have caused the destruction of this
people of whom I am now speaking, and also the
destruction of the people of Nephi.
22 And whatsoever nation shall uphold such se-
cret combinations, to get power and gain, until
they shall spread over the nation, behold, they shall
be destroyed; for the Lord will not suffer that the
blood of his saints, which shall be shed by them,
shall always cry unto him from the ground for
vengeance upon them and yet he avenge them not.
23 Wherefore, O ye Gentiles, it is wisdom in
God that these things should be shown unto you,
that thereby ye may repent of your sins, and suf-
fer not that these murderous combinations shall
get above you, which are built up to get power
and gain—and the work, yea, even the work of
destruction come upon you, yea, even the sword
of the justice of the Eternal God shall fall upon
you, to your overthrow and destruction if ye shall
suffer these things to be.
24 Wherefore, the Lord commandeth you, when
ye shall see these things come among you that
ye shall awake to a sense of your awful situation,
because of this secret combination which shall
be among you; or wo be unto it, because of the
blood of them who have been slain; for they cry
from the dust for vengeance upon it, and also
upon those who built it up.
25 For it cometh to pass that whoso buildeth it
up seeketh to overthrow the freedom of all lands,
nations, and countries; and it bringeth to pass the
destruction of all people, for it is built up by the
devil, who is the father of all lies; even that same
liar who beguiled our first parents, yea, even that
same liar who hath caused man to commit mur-
der from the beginning; who hath hardened the
hearts of men that they have murdered the proph-
ets, and stoned them, and cast them out from the
beginning.
26 Wherefore, I, Moroni, am commanded to
write these things that evil may be done away, and
that the time may come that Satan may have no
power upon the hearts of the children of men, but
that they may be persuaded to do good continu-
ally, that they may come unto the fountain of all
righteousness and be saved.

What modern-day groups or philosophies can you think of that try to "overthrow the freedom" of nations? How can you defend freedom and protect yourself, your family, and your community from the influence of Satan?

ETHER AND MORONI SPEAK OF THE POWER AND BLESSINGS OF FAITH IN THINGS NOT SEEN

Over the course of many generations, the descendants of Jared and his brother continued to pursue wickedness, murder, and secret combinations. Brief periods of peace and righteousness were enjoyed, followed by the people descending again into wickedness and war as the land was cursed with famine and poisonous serpents. Prophets warned that their nation would be destroyed if they did not repent, but the people rejected their words and killed many prophets.

ETHER 12:2–9

And Ether was a prophet of the Lord; wherefore Ether came forth in the days of Coriantumr, and began to prophesy unto the people, for he could not be restrained because of the Spirit of the Lord which was in him.
3 For he did cry from the morning, even until the going down of the sun, exhorting the people to believe in God unto repentance lest they should be destroyed, saying unto them that by faith all things are fulfilled—
4 Wherefore, whoso believeth in God might with surety hope for a better world, yea, even a place at the right hand of God, which hope cometh of faith, maketh an anchor to the souls of men, which would make them sure and steadfast, always abounding in good works, being led to glorify God.
5 And it came to pass that Ether did prophesy great and marvelous things unto the people, which they did not believe, because they saw them not.
6 And now, I, Moroni, would speak somewhat concerning these things; I would show unto the world that faith is things which are hoped for and not seen; wherefore, dispute not because ye see not, for ye receive no witness until after the trial of your faith.
7 For it was by faith that Christ showed himself unto our fathers, after he had risen from the dead; and he showed not himself unto them until after they had faith in him; wherefore, it must needs be that some had faith in him, for he showed himself not unto the world.
8 But because of the faith of men he has shown himself unto the world, and glorified the name of the Father, and prepared a way that thereby others might be partakers of the heavenly gift, that they might hope for those things which they have not seen.
9 Wherefore, ye may also have hope, and be partakers of the gift, if ye will but have faith.

How did Moroni define faith? What things do you have faith in even though you cannot see them? Moroni taught that we "receive no witness until after the trial of [our] faith." Can you share a witness you have received after a trial of faith?

MORONI IDENTIFIES EXAMPLES OF MIRACULOUS FAITH THROUGHOUT HISTORY

Inspired by Ether's ancient prophecies among the Jaredites, Moroni continued to speak to modern-day readers on the subject of faith.

ETHER 12:10–21

Behold it was by faith that they of old
were called after the holy order of God.
11 Wherefore, by faith was the law of Moses
given. But in the gift of his Son hath God pre-
pared a more excellent way; and it is by faith that
it hath been fulfilled.
12 For if there be no faith among the children of
men God can do no miracle among them; where-
fore, he showed not himself until after their faith.
13 Behold, it was the faith of Alma and Amulek
that caused the prison to tumble to the earth.
14 Behold, it was the faith of Nephi and Lehi
that wrought the change upon the Lamanites,
that they were baptized with fire and with the
Holy Ghost.
15 Behold, it was the faith of Ammon and his
brethren which wrought so great a miracle among
the Lamanites.
16 Yea, and even all they who wrought miracles
wrought them by faith, even those who were be-
fore Christ and also those who were after.
17 And it was by faith that the three disciples
obtained a promise that they should not taste of
death; and they obtained not the promise until
after their faith.
18 And neither at any time hath any wrought
miracles until after their faith; wherefore they first
believed in the Son of God.
19 And there were many whose faith was so ex-
ceedingly strong, even before Christ came, who
could not be kept from within the veil, but truly
saw with their eyes the things which they had be-
held with an eye of faith, and they were glad.
20 And behold, we have seen in this record that
one of these was the brother of Jared; for so great
was his faith in God, that when God put forth
his finger he could not hide it from the sight of
the brother of Jared, because of his word which
he had spoken unto him, which word he had ob-
tained by faith.
21 And after the brother of Jared had beheld the
finger of the Lord, because of the promise which
the brother of Jared had obtained by faith, the
Lord could not withhold anything from his sight;
wherefore he showed him all things, for he could
no longer be kept without the veil.

What are some of the examples Moroni gave of miracles brought about by faith? In your own life and the lives of your family and ancestors, what miracles have come as a result of faith?

MORONI TEACHES THAT FAITH AND HUMILITY ALLOW MEN'S WEAKNESSES TO BECOME STRONG

As Moroni continued to speak to modern-day readers, he shared a conversation he had with the Lord about his fear that the Book of Mormon would be mocked by people in the latter days.

ETHER 12:22–29

And it is by faith that my fathers have
obtained the promise that these things
should come unto their brethren through the
Gentiles; therefore the Lord hath commanded
me, yea, even Jesus Christ.
23 And I said unto him: Lord, the Gentiles will
mock at these things, because of our weakness in
writing; for Lord thou hast made us mighty in
word by faith, but thou hast not made us mighty
in writing; for thou hast made all this people
that they could speak much, because of the Holy
Ghost which thou hast given them;
24 And thou hast made us that we could write
but little, because of the awkwardness of our
hands. Behold, thou hast not made us mighty in
writing like unto the brother of Jared, for thou
madest him that the things which he wrote were
mighty even as thou art, unto the overpowering of
man to read them.
25 Thou hast also made our words powerful and
great, even that we cannot write them; where-
fore, when we write we behold our weakness, and
stumble because of the placing of our words; and
I fear lest the Gentiles shall mock at our words.
26 And when I had said this, the Lord spake unto
me, saying: Fools mock, but they shall mourn;
and my grace is sufficient for the meek, that they
shall take no advantage of your weakness;
27 And if men come unto me I will show unto
them their weakness. I give unto men weakness
that they may be humble; and my grace is suffi-
cient for all men that humble themselves before
me; for if they humble themselves before me, and
have faith in me, then will I make weak things
become strong unto them.
28 Behold, I will show unto the Gentiles their
weakness, and I will show unto them that faith,
hope and charity bringeth unto me—the fountain
of all righteousness.
29 And I, Moroni, having heard these words, was
comforted, and said: O Lord, thy righteous will
be done, for I know that thou workest unto the
children of men according to their faith;

Why did Moroni fear his writing would be mocked? What did the Lord teach Moroni about the purpose of personal weaknesses? Consider a weakness you would like to overcome. How can you show faith and humility in overcoming that weakness? Can you share an example of someone you know who turned a weakness into a strength?

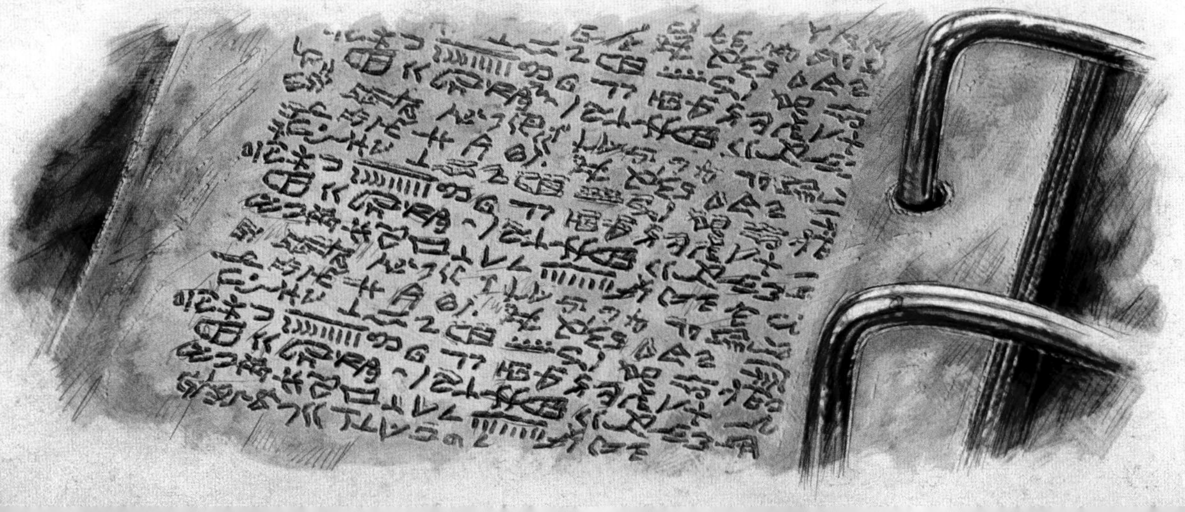

MORONI TEACHES OF FAITH AND CHARITY AND INVITES ALL MEN TO SEEK JESUS CHRIST

Moroni continued to speak to latter-day readers of the Book of Mormon as he shared a personal conversation he had with Jesus Christ, with whom he spoke face to face.

ETHER 12:30–41

For the brother of Jared said unto the mountain Zerin, Remove—and it was removed. And if he had not had faith it would not have moved; wherefore thou workest after men have faith.
31 For thus didst thou manifest thyself unto thy disciples; for after they had faith, and did speak in thy name, thou didst show thyself unto them in great power.
32 And I also remember that thou hast said that thou hast prepared a house for man, yea, even among the mansions of thy Father, in which man might have a more excellent hope; wherefore man must hope, or he cannot receive an inheritance in the place which thou hast prepared.
33 And again, I remember that thou hast said that thou hast loved the world, even unto the laying down of thy life for the world, that thou mightest take it again to prepare a place for the children of men.
34 And now I know that this love which thou hast had for the children of men is charity; wherefore, except men shall have charity they cannot inherit that place which thou hast prepared in the mansions of thy Father.
35 Wherefore, I know by this thing which thou hast said, that if the Gentiles have not charity, because of our weakness, that thou wilt prove them, and take away their talent, yea, even that which they have received, and give unto them who shall have more abundantly.
36 And it came to pass that I prayed unto the Lord that he would give unto the Gentiles grace, that they might have charity.
37 And it came to pass that the Lord said unto me: If they have not charity it mattereth not unto thee, thou hast been faithful; wherefore, thy garments shall be made clean. And because thou hast seen thy weakness thou shalt be made strong, even unto the sitting down in the place which I have prepared in the mansions of my Father.
38 And now I, Moroni, bid farewell unto the Gentiles, yea, and also unto my brethren whom I love, until we shall meet before the judgment-seat of Christ, where all men shall know that my garments are not spotted with your blood.
39 And then shall ye know that I have seen Jesus, and that he hath talked with me face to face, and that he told me in plain humility, even as a man telleth another in mine own language, concerning these things;
40 And only a few have I written, because of my weakness in writing.
41 And now, I would commend you to seek this Jesus of whom the prophets and apostles have written, that the grace of God the Father, and also the Lord Jesus Christ, and the Holy Ghost, which beareth record of them, may be and abide in you forever. Amen.

According to Moroni, what attribute must people have to inherit God's kingdom? Speaking to people in the last days, Moroni said, "I would commend you to seek this Jesus of whom the prophets and apostles have written." Discuss what you think it means to "seek" Jesus. How can you seek Him daily?

MORONI REFUSES TO DENY CHRIST AND TEACHES THE MODE OF PRIESTHOOD ORDINANCES

Moroni concluded his abridgment of Ether's record by recounting the war, murder, and secret combinations that continued among the Jaredites. The Spirit of God ceased to strive with the people, and Satan had full power over their hearts. Ether attempted to preach repentance but was forced into hiding. After approximately 1,900 years of existence, the Jaredite nation was reduced from millions of people to 59 rival warriors who engaged in a final battle that left a man named Coriantumr as the sole survivor. Coriantumr later lived among the Mulekites as they arrived from Jerusalem and settled the land of Zarahemla in about 575 BC. It was now about AD 400. Moroni, the last remaining Nephite, recorded additional events and counsel in his own book.

MORONI 1:1–4, 2:1–3, 3:1–4

Now I, Moroni, after having made an end of abridging the account of the people of Jared, I had supposed not to have written more, but I have not as yet perished; and I make not myself known to the Lamanites lest they should destroy me.
2 For behold, their wars are exceedingly fierce among themselves; and because of their hatred they put to death every Nephite that will not deny the Christ.
3 And I, Moroni, will not deny the Christ; wherefore, I wander whithersoever I can for the safety of mine own life.
4 Wherefore, I write a few more things, contrary to that which I had supposed; for I had supposed not to have written any more; but I write a few more things, that perhaps they may be of worth unto my brethren, the Lamanites, in some future day, according to the will of the Lord.

MORONI 2

1 The words of Christ, which he spake unto his disciples, the twelve whom he had chosen, as he laid his hands upon them—
2 And he called them by name, saying: Ye shall call on the Father in my name, in mighty prayer; and after ye have done this ye shall have power that to him upon whom ye shall lay your hands, ye shall give the Holy Ghost; and in my name shall ye give it, for thus do mine apostles.
3 Now Christ spake these words unto them at the time of his first appearing; and the multitude heard it not, but the disciples heard it; and on as many as they laid their hands, fell the Holy Ghost.

MORONI 3

1 The manner which the disciples, who were called the elders of the church, ordained priests and teachers—
2 After they had prayed unto the Father in the name of Christ, they laid their hands upon them, and said:
3 In the name of Jesus Christ I ordain you to be a priest (or if he be a teacher, I ordain you to be a teacher) to preach repentance and remission of sins through Jesus Christ, by the endurance of faith on his name to the end. Amen.
4 And after this manner did they ordain priests and teachers, according to the gifts and callings of God unto men; and they ordained them by the power of the Holy Ghost, which was in them.

What does it mean to be "ordained" to the priesthood? How is the mode of priesthood ordination the same today as it was in Moroni's day?

MORONI RECORDS THE WORDS OF THE SACRAMENT PRAYERS

After teaching how men are ordained to the priesthood, Moroni spoke of the proper way to administer the sacrament.

MORONI 4:1–3, 5:1–2

The manner of their elders and priests administering the flesh and blood of Christ unto the church; and they administered it according to the commandments of Christ; wherefore we know the manner to be true; and the elder or priest did minister it—
2 And they did kneel down with the church, and pray to the Father in the name of Christ, saying:
3 O God, the Eternal Father, we ask thee in the name of thy Son, Jesus Christ, to bless and sanctify this bread to the souls of all those who partake of it; that they may eat in remembrance of the body of thy Son, and witness unto thee, O God, the Eternal Father, that they are willing to take upon them the name of thy Son, and always remember him, and keep his commandments which he hath given them, that they may always have his Spirit to be with them. Amen.

MORONI 5

1 The manner of administering the wine—Behold, they took the cup, and said:
2 O God, the Eternal Father, we ask thee, in the name of thy Son, Jesus Christ, to bless and sanctify this wine to the souls of all those who drink of it, that they may do it in remembrance of the blood of thy Son, which was shed for them; that they may witness unto thee, O God, the Eternal Father, that they do always remember him, that they may have his Spirit to be with them. Amen.

What promises are made between you and Heavenly Father when you take the sacrament bread and water? Consider that Moroni and countless other members of Christ's Church heard the same sacrament prayers and made the same commitments to Christ that you now do. How does that make you feel? What could it inspire you to do?

MORONI SPEAKS OF CHURCH MEMBERS' DUTIES TO GOD AND TO ONE ANOTHER

Moroni spoke of the way members of Christ's Church interacted with each other in their pursuit of righteousness.

MORONI 6:1–9

And now I speak concerning baptism. Behold, elders, priests, and teachers were baptized; and they were not baptized save they brought forth fruit meet that they were worthy of it.
2 Neither did they receive any unto baptism save they came forth with a broken heart and a contrite spirit, and witnessed unto the church that they truly repented of all their sins.
3 And none were received unto baptism save they took upon them the name of Christ, having a determination to serve him to the end.
4 And after they had been received unto baptism, and were wrought upon and cleansed by the power of the Holy Ghost, they were numbered among the people of the church of Christ; and their names were taken, that they might be remembered and nourished by the good word of God, to keep them in the right way, to keep them continually watchful unto prayer, relying alone upon the merits of Christ, who was the author and the finisher of their faith.
5 And the church did meet together oft, to fast and to pray, and to speak one with another concerning the welfare of their souls.
6 And they did meet together oft to partake of bread and wine, in remembrance of the Lord Jesus.
7 And they were strict to observe that there should be no iniquity among them; and whoso was found to commit iniquity, and three witnesses of the church did condemn them before the elders, and if they repented not, and confessed not, their names were blotted out, and they were not numbered among the people of Christ.
8 But as oft as they repented and sought forgiveness, with real intent, they were forgiven.
9 And their meetings were conducted by the church after the manner of the workings of the Spirit, and by the power of the Holy Ghost; for as the power of the Holy Ghost led them whether to preach, or to exhort, or to pray, or to supplicate, or to sing, even so it was done.

What did members of the Church in Moroni's time do to help each other live righteously? What modern-day examples have you seen of Church members encouraging righteousness in one another? How are we strengthened when we worship together in groups?

MORMON TEACHES THAT A GOOD PERSON IS IDENTIFIED BY GOOD WORKS

After speaking of the way Nephite Church members had supported each other, Moroni recorded teachings that his father Mormon had given to the people.

Moroni 7:3–11

Wherefore, I would speak unto you that are
of the church, that are the peaceable fol-
lowers of Christ, and that have obtained a suffi-
cient hope by which ye can enter into the rest of
the Lord, from this time henceforth until ye shall
rest with him in heaven.
4 And now my brethren, I judge these things of
you because of your peaceable walk with the chil-
dren of men.
5 For I remember the word of God which saith
by their works ye shall know them; for if their
works be good, then they are good also.
6 For behold, God hath said a man being evil
cannot do that which is good; for if he offereth
a gift, or prayeth unto God, except he shall do it
with real intent it profiteth him nothing.
7 For behold, it is not counted unto him for righ-
teousness.
8 For behold, if a man being evil giveth a gift, he
doeth it grudgingly; wherefore it is counted unto
him the same as if he had retained the gift; where-
fore he is counted evil before God.
9 And likewise also is it counted evil unto a man,
if he shall pray and not with real intent of heart;
yea, and it profiteth him nothing, for God re-
ceiveth none such.
10 Wherefore, a man being evil cannot do that
which is good; neither will he give a good gift.
11 For behold, a bitter fountain cannot bring
forth good water; neither can a good fountain
bring forth bitter water; wherefore, a man being
a servant of the devil cannot follow Christ; and
if he follow Christ he cannot be a servant of the
devil.

What do you think it means to have a "peaceable walk with the children of men"? What are some good works you can do to show Heavenly Father the good intents of your heart?

MORMON INVITES MEN TO SEARCH DILIGENTLY AND EMBRACE ALL GOOD THINGS FROM GOD

Moroni continued to quote his father's teachings given previously to the members of Christ's Church.

Moroni 7:12–19

Wherefore, all things which are good com-
eth of God; and that which is evil cometh
of the devil; for the devil is an enemy unto God,
and fighteth against him continually, and inviteth
and enticeth to sin, and to do that which is evil
continually.
13 But behold, that which is of God inviteth and
enticeth to do good continually; wherefore, every
thing which inviteth and enticeth to do good, and
to love God, and to serve him, is inspired of God.
14 Wherefore, take heed, my beloved brethren,
that ye do not judge that which is evil to be of
God, or that which is good and of God to be of
the devil.
15 For behold, my brethren, it is given unto you
to judge, that ye may know good from evil; and
the way to judge is as plain, that ye may know
with a perfect knowledge, as the daylight is from
the dark night.
16 For behold, the Spirit of Christ is given to
every man, that he may know good from evil;
wherefore, I show unto you the way to judge; for
every thing which inviteth to do good, and to
persuade to believe in Christ, is sent forth by the
power and gift of Christ; wherefore ye may know
with a perfect knowledge it is of God.
17 But whatsoever thing persuadeth men to do
evil, and believe not in Christ, and deny him, and
serve not God, then ye may know with a perfect
knowledge it is of the devil; for after this manner
doth the devil work, for he persuadeth no man
to do good, no, not one; neither do his angels;
neither do they who subject themselves unto him.
18 And now, my brethren, seeing that ye know
the light by which ye may judge, which light
is the light of Christ, see that ye do not judge
wrongfully; for with that same judgment which
ye judge ye shall also be judged.
19 Wherefore, I beseech of you, brethren, that ye
should search diligently in the light of Christ that
ye may know good from evil; and if ye will lay
hold upon every good thing, and condemn it not,
ye certainly will be a child of Christ.

What instructions did Moroni give for knowing whether something is good or evil? Moroni invited all people to "lay hold upon every good thing." What good things do you currently give time and attention to? How are you blessed by doing so? What other good things would you like to pursue?

MORMON EXPLAINS HOW FAITH BRINGS MEN TO CHRIST

Moroni continued to quote his father's teachings to Church members.

MORONI 7:21–29

And now I come to that faith, of which
I said I would speak; and I will tell you
the way whereby ye may lay hold on every good
thing.
22 For behold, God knowing all things, being
from everlasting to everlasting, behold, he sent
angels to minister unto the children of men, to
make manifest concerning the coming of Christ;
and in Christ there should come every good
thing.
23 And God also declared unto prophets, by his
own mouth, that Christ should come.
24 And behold, there were divers ways that he
did manifest things unto the children of men,
which were good; and all things which are good
cometh of Christ; otherwise men were fallen, and
there could no good thing come unto them.
25 Wherefore, by the ministering of angels, and
by every word which proceeded forth out of the
mouth of God, men began to exercise faith in
Christ; and thus by faith, they did lay hold upon
every good thing; and thus it was until the com-
ing of Christ.
26 And after that he came men also were saved
by faith in his name; and by faith, they become
the sons of God. And as surely as Christ liveth
he spake these words unto our fathers, saying:
Whatsoever thing ye shall ask the Father in my
name, which is good, in faith believing that ye
shall receive, behold, it shall be done unto you.
27 Wherefore, my beloved brethren, have mir-
acles ceased because Christ hath ascended into
heaven, and hath sat down on the right hand of
God, to claim of the Father his rights of mercy
which he hath upon the children of men?
28 For he hath answered the ends of the law, and
he claimeth all those who have faith in him; and
they who have faith in him will cleave unto every
good thing; wherefore he advocateth the cause of
the children of men; and he dwelleth eternally in
the heavens.
29 And because he hath done this, my beloved
brethren, have miracles ceased? Behold I say unto
you, Nay; neither have angels ceased to minister
unto the children of men.

Mormon spoke of the saving power of faith in Jesus Christ. What do you think the difference is between faith in general and faith specifically in Jesus Christ? What do you have faith that Jesus Christ has done and will do? What promise does Mormon make about asking the Father in faith?

MORMON TEACHES OF THE REALITY AND PURPOSE OF ANGELS

Moroni continued to quote his father, teaching of the existence of angels and their divine purpose.

Moroni 7:30–37

For behold, they are subject unto him, to minister according to the word of his command, showing themselves unto them of strong faith and a firm mind in every form of godliness.
31 And the office of their ministry is to call men unto repentance, and to fulfil and to do the work of the covenants of the Father, which he hath made unto the children of men, to prepare the way among the children of men, by declaring the word of Christ unto the chosen vessels of the Lord, that they may bear testimony of him.
32 And by so doing, the Lord God prepareth the way that the residue of men may have faith in Christ, that the Holy Ghost may have place in their hearts, according to the power thereof; and after this manner bringeth to pass the Father, the covenants which he hath made unto the children of men.
33 And Christ hath said: If ye will have faith in me ye shall have power to do whatsoever thing is expedient in me.
34 And he hath said: Repent all ye ends of the earth, and come unto me, and be baptized in my name, and have faith in me, that ye may be saved.
35 And now, my beloved brethren, if this be the case that these things are true which I have spoken unto you, and God will show unto you, with power and great glory at the last day, that they are true, and if they are true has the day of miracles ceased?
36 Or have angels ceased to appear unto the children of men? Or has he withheld the power of the Holy Ghost from them? Or will he, so long as time shall last, or the earth shall stand, or there shall be one man upon the face thereof to be saved?
37 Behold I say unto you, Nay; for it is by faith that miracles are wrought; and it is by faith that angels appear and minister unto men; wherefore, if these things have ceased wo be unto the children of men, for it is because of unbelief, and all is vain.

According to Mormon, what is the purpose of angels? What examples are there of angels appearing and ministering to people in the latter days?

MORMON DEFINES CHARITY AND TEACHES THAT WITHOUT IT MEN ARE NOTHING

Moroni continued to quote his father's teachings.

MORONI 7:38–48

For no man can be saved, according to
the words of Christ, save they shall have
faith in his name; wherefore, if these things have
ceased, then has faith ceased also; and awful is
the state of man, for they are as though there had
been no redemption made.
39 But behold, my beloved brethren, I judge bet-
ter things of you, for I judge that ye have faith in
Christ because of your meekness; for if ye have
not faith in him then ye are not fit to be num-
bered among the people of his church.
40 And again, my beloved brethren, I would
speak unto you concerning hope. How is it that
ye can attain unto faith, save ye shall have hope?
41 And what is it that ye shall hope for? Behold
I say unto you that ye shall have hope through
the atonement of Christ and the power of his res-
urrection, to be raised unto life eternal, and this
because of your faith in him according to the
promise.
42 Wherefore, if a man have faith he must needs
have hope; for without faith there cannot be any
hope.
43 And again, behold I say unto you that he can-
not have faith and hope, save he shall be meek,
and lowly of heart.
44 If so, his faith and hope is vain, for none is
acceptable before God, save the meek and lowly
in heart; and if a man be meek and lowly in heart,
and confesses by the power of the Holy Ghost
that Jesus is the Christ, he must needs have char-
ity; for if he have not charity he is nothing; where-
fore he must needs have charity.
45 And charity suffereth long, and is kind, and
envieth not, and is not puffed up, seeketh not her
own, is not easily provoked, thinketh no evil, and
rejoiceth not in iniquity but rejoiceth in the truth,
beareth all things, believeth all things, hopeth all
things, endureth all things.
46 Wherefore, my beloved brethren, if ye have
not charity, ye are nothing, for charity never
faileth. Wherefore, cleave unto charity, which is
the greatest of all, for all things must fail—
47 But charity is the pure love of Christ, and it
endureth forever; and whoso is found possessed of
it at the last day, it shall be well with him.
48 Wherefore, my beloved brethren, pray unto
the Father with all the energy of heart, that ye
may be filled with this love, which he hath be-
stowed upon all who are true followers of his Son,
Jesus Christ; that ye may become the sons of God;
that when he shall appear we shall be like him, for
we shall see him as he is; that we may have this
hope; that we may be purified even as he is pure.
Amen.

How did Mormon define charity? How did he say charity is obtained? How do you think charity is different from kindness and love? Discuss the meanings of the different qualities of charity Mormon shared in verse 45. How can you develop each of these qualities more fully?

MORMON REFUTES THE INCORRECT TEACHING THAT LITTLE CHILDREN MUST BE BAPTIZED TO BE SAVED

After quoting his father's teachings on faith, miracles, and angels, Moroni recorded a letter he had previously received from his father. Mormon had learned that there were disagreements among the Nephites about whether little children needed to be baptized.

Moroni 8:7–12, 19–20, 22, 25–26

For immediately after I had learned these things of you I inquired of the Lord concerning the matter. And the word of the Lord came to me by the power of the Holy Ghost, saying:

8 Listen to the words of Christ, your Redeemer, your Lord and your God. Behold, I came into the world not to call the righteous but sinners to repentance; the whole need no physician, but they that are sick; wherefore, little children are whole, for they are not capable of committing sin; wherefore the curse of Adam is taken from them in me, that it hath no power over them; and the law of circumcision is done away in me.

9 And after this manner did the Holy Ghost manifest the word of God unto me; wherefore, my beloved son, I know that it is solemn mockery before God, that ye should baptize little children.

10 Behold I say unto you that this thing shall ye teach—repentance and baptism unto those who are accountable and capable of committing sin; yea, teach parents that they must repent and be baptized, and humble themselves as their little children, and they shall all be saved with their little children.

11 And their little children need no repentance, neither baptism. Behold, baptism is unto repentance to the fulfilling the commandments unto the remission of sins.

12 But little children are alive in Christ, even from the foundation of the world; if not so, God is a partial God, and also a changeable God, and a respecter to persons; for how many little children have died without baptism!

19 Little children cannot repent; wherefore, it is awful wickedness to deny the pure mercies of God unto them, for they are all alive in him because of his mercy.

20 And he that saith that little children need baptism denieth the mercies of Christ, and setteth at naught the atonement of him and the power of his redemption.

22 For behold that all little children are alive in Christ, and also all they that are without the law. For the power of redemption cometh on all them that have no law; wherefore, he that is not condemned, or he that is under no condemnation, cannot repent; and unto such baptism availeth nothing—

25 And the first fruits of repentance is baptism; and baptism cometh by faith unto the fulfilling the commandments; and the fulfilling the commandments bringeth remission of sins;

26 And the remission of sins bringeth meekness, and lowliness of heart; and because of meekness and lowliness of heart cometh the visitation of the Holy Ghost, which Comforter filleth with hope and perfect love, which love endureth by diligence unto prayer, until the end shall come, when all the saints shall dwell with God.

According to Mormon, why do little children not need to be baptized? How does this help you understand other scriptures that have commanded us to become like little children?

MORONI INVITES READERS OF THE BOOK OF MORMON TO ASK GOD FOR A WITNESS OF ITS TRUTH

After recording teachings and letters from his father—and prior to sealing up the Book of Mormon record—Moroni wrote to the people of the latter days.

Moroni 10:1–5

Now I, Moroni, write somewhat as seemeth me good; and I write unto my brethren, the Lamanites; and I would that they should know that more than four hundred and twenty years have passed away since the sign was given of the coming of Christ.
2 And I seal up these records, after I have spoken
a few words by way of exhortation unto you.
3 Behold, I would exhort you that when ye shall
read these things, if it be wisdom in God that ye should read them, that ye would remember how merciful the Lord hath been unto the children of men, from the creation of Adam even down until the time that ye shall receive these things, and ponder it in your hearts.
4 And when ye shall receive these things, I would
exhort you that ye would ask God, the Eternal Father, in the name of Christ, if these things are not true; and if ye shall ask with a sincere heart, with real intent, having faith in Christ, he will manifest the truth of it unto you, by the power of the Holy Ghost.
5 And by the power of the Holy Ghost ye may
know the truth of all things.

This passage of scripture is often called "Moroni's Promise." What does he promise? Share any experiences you have had in praying to know if something is true. What does it mean to know that the Book of Mormon is "true"?

MORONI IDENTIFIES THE GIFTS OF GOD

After inviting people to pray to know the truthfulness of the Book of Mormon, Moroni spoke of the gifts of God. As you read of these gifts, consider which ones you or others have been blessed with.

MORONI 10:6–19

And whatsoever thing is good is just and
true; wherefore, nothing that is good
denieth the Christ, but acknowledgeth that he is.
7 And ye may know that he is, by the power of
the Holy Ghost; wherefore I would exhort you
that ye deny not the power of God; for he wor-
keth by power, according to the faith of the chil-
dren of men, the same today and tomorrow, and
forever.
8 And again, I exhort you, my brethren, that ye
deny not the gifts of God, for they are many; and
they come from the same God. And there are dif-
ferent ways that these gifts are administered; but
it is the same God who worketh all in all; and
they are given by the manifestations of the Spirit
of God unto men, to profit them.
9 For behold, to one is given by the Spirit of
God, that he may teach the word of wisdom;
10 And to another, that he may teach the word of
knowledge by the same Spirit;
11 And to another, exceedingly great faith; and
to another, the gifts of healing by the same Spirit;
12 And again, to another, that he may work
mighty miracles;
13 And again, to another, that he may prophesy
concerning all things;
14 And again, to another, the beholding of angels
and ministering spirits;
15 And again, to another, all kinds of tongues;
16 And again, to another, the interpretation of
languages and of divers kinds of tongues.
17 And all these gifts come by the Spirit of
Christ; and they come unto every man severally,
according as he will.
18 And I would exhort you, my beloved breth-
ren, that ye remember that every good gift com-
eth of Christ.
19 And I would exhort you, my beloved breth-
ren, that ye remember that he is the same yester-
day, today, and forever, and that all these gifts of
which I have spoken, which are spiritual, never
will be done away, even as long as the world shall
stand, only according to the unbelief of the chil-
dren of men.

Moroni identified many of God's gifts. Review his list and discuss examples of those gifts blessing people today. What do you think is the purpose of these gifts from God?

MORONI COMMANDS ALL PEOPLE TO COME UNTO CHRIST AND BE PERFECTED IN HIM

As he concluded the record that would become the Book of Mormon, Moroni invited all men to receive the grace and perfection available through Jesus Christ.

MORONI 10:20–21, 27–34

Wherefore, there must be faith; and if there
must be faith there must also be hope; and
if there must be hope there must also be charity.
21 And except ye have charity ye can in nowise
be saved in the kingdom of God; neither can ye
be saved in the kingdom of God if ye have not
faith; neither can ye if ye have no hope.
27 And I exhort you to remember these things;
for the time speedily cometh that ye shall know
that I lie not, for ye shall see me at the bar of
God; and the Lord God will say unto you: Did I
not declare my words unto you, which were writ-
ten by this man, like as one crying from the dead,
yea, even as one speaking out of the dust?
28 I declare these things unto the fulfilling of
the prophecies. And behold, they shall proceed
forth out of the mouth of the everlasting God;
and his word shall hiss forth from generation to
generation.
29 And God shall show unto you, that that
which I have written is true.
30 And again I would exhort you that ye would
come unto Christ, and lay hold upon every good
gift, and touch not the evil gift, nor the unclean
thing.
31 And awake, and arise from the dust, O
Jerusalem; yea, and put on thy beautiful garments,
O daughter of Zion; and strengthen thy stakes
and enlarge thy borders forever, that thou mayest
no more be confounded, that the covenants of the
Eternal Father which he hath made unto thee, O
house of Israel, may be fulfilled.
32 Yea, come unto Christ, and be perfected in
him, and deny yourselves of all ungodliness; and
if ye shall deny yourselves of all ungodliness, and
love God with all your might, mind and strength,
then is his grace sufficient for you, that by his
grace ye may be perfect in Christ; and if by the
grace of God ye are perfect in Christ, ye can in
nowise deny the power of God.
33 And again, if ye by the grace of God are per-
fect in Christ, and deny not his power, then are ye
sanctified in Christ by the grace of God, through
the shedding of the blood of Christ, which is in
the covenant of the Father unto the remission of
your sins, that ye become holy, without spot.
34 And now I bid unto all, farewell. I soon go to
rest in the paradise of God, until my spirit and
body shall again reunite, and I am brought forth
triumphant through the air, to meet you before
the pleasing bar of the great Jehovah, the Eternal
Judge of both quick and dead. Amen.

Considering that this was Moroni's last writing, what principles of the gospel do you think were most important to him? What would you say is his central message? Moroni said that his words were true and spoke of a future day when he would meet you at the judgment of Christ. As you consider that day, what would you tell Moroni you have learned from the Book of Mormon?

About the Editor

Tyler McKellar was born and raised in Teton Valley, Idaho, where he now lives with his wife, Stephanie, and their six children. He served a mission for The Church of Jesus Christ of Latter-day Saints in South Korea and graduated from Brigham Young University with a degree in advertising. He worked for several years as a copywriter at advertising agencies in Salt Lake City, San Francisco, and Portland, Oregon. Most recently he has worked as a freelance writer and screenwriter. He likes college football, golf, milkshakes, and mountain biking.

About the Illustrator

Dan Burr, an award-winning illustrator, earned a bachelor of fine arts degree from Utah State University and a master's degree in illustration from Syracuse University. He and his wife, Patti, are the parents of two children and live in Tetonia, Idaho. Dan has illustrated many children's books, including *One Little Match, The Miracle of the Wooden Shoes, I Heard the Bells on Christmas Day,* and *The Christmas Train.*